T0305499

Revenge Capitalism

Revenge Capitalism

The Ghosts of Empire, the Demons of Capital, and the Settling of Unpayable Debts

Max Haiven

First published 2020 by Pluto Press
345 Archway Road, London N6 5AA

www.plutobooks.com

British Library Cataloguing in Publication Data
A catalogue record for this book is available from the British Library

ISBN 978 0 7453 4055 5 Hardback
ISBN 978 0 7453 4056 2 Paperback
ISBN 978 1 7868 0616 1 PDF eBook
ISBN 978 1 7868 0618 5 Kindle eBook
ISBN 978 1 7868 0617 8 EPUB eBook

Typeset by Swales & Willis, Exeter

Printed and bound by CPI Group (UK) Ltd, Croydon, CR0 4YY

Contents

Figures

Acknowledgments

This book is dedicated to all those who, daily, tame revenge in the name of a greater avenging, all those who endure oppression and indignity and, rather than unleashing their justified but apocalyptic fury, bide their time, build solidarity, and organize for a world where the source of their agony is abolished, not only for themselves and their kin, but for everyone. Every one of us only exists because of the wisdom of our ancestors, who chose the longer work of realizing a transformative avenging imaginary over the momentary satisfaction of fulfilling a revenge fantasy. We must carry on their work.

My thanks to: Phanuel Antwi, Richard Appignanesi, Franco Berardi, Francesca Coin, Mark Featherstone, Nick Fox-Gieg, Marc Garrett, Inte Gloerich, Hugh Goldring, Judy Haiven, Larry Haiven, Omri Haiven, Oliver Lerone Schultz, Charles Levkoe, Siddhartha Lokanandi, Geert Lovink, Frances Negrón-Muntaner, Georgios Papadopoulos, David Peerla, Amanda Priebe, Jerome Roos, CS Soong, Rob Stewart, Magdelena Taube, Rachel Warburton, Meagan Williams, and Krystian Woznicki. Thanks too to all the participants in the ReImagining Value Action Lab's Summer 2019 retreat who offered feedback, as well as to all those whose names I do not know who offered critiques and suggestions at various academic conferences and public presentations where these ideas were presented over the past few years. Candida Hadley, Aris Komporozos-Athanasiou, Leigh Claire La Berge, Eli Meyerhoff, Christian Nagler, Scott Stoneman, Cassie Thornton, and Ezra Winton were kind enough to read parts of this manuscript and offer incisive feedback, which I mostly failed to heed. Many thanks to David Shulman and all at Pluto for their faith in and work on this book. I would like to also thank the Canadian people for their continued support of the Canada Research Chairs program of which I am the beneficiary, and my colleagues at Lakehead University for this opportunity. My greatest thanks go to Cassie Thornton, avenger.

Parts of Chapter 2 originally appeared in "The Art of Unpayable Debts" In *The Sociology of Debt*, edited by Mark Featherstone (London: Policy, 2019). Part of Chapter 3 originally appeared in "Currencies of the Undercommons: The Hidden Ledger of Proletarian Money Sabotage" in *State Machines: Reflections and Actions at the Edge of Digital Citizenship, Finance, and Art*, edited by Yiannis Colakides, Marc Garrett, and Inte

Gloerich (Amsterdam: Institute for Network Cultures, 2019). Part of Chapter 4 originally appeared in "Our Opium Wars: The Ghosts of Empire in the Prescription Opioid Nightmare" in *Third Text* 32 (2018).

Preface

The genesis of this book is a story my father told me when I was still quite young about his own father, who died before I was born and after whom I am named. It's about the first real fight they had.

My grandfather was a survivor of Auschwitz and the Nazi Holocaust. Like many of his generation he rarely spoke of it to his children. For such survivors, struggling to thrive in a new country, dark things were better left behind.

Still, my father knew some stories of the camps. These were stories not so much of the monumental, almost clinical horror of industrialized murder, but of the sadistic and vindictive acts of individual guards, their swaggering impunity, the sick joy of power, the mockery, the humiliation: small stories of injustice and indignity that seem almost quaint in contrast to the scale of the atrocity.

As the Red Army approached the death camp in January of 1945, my Grandfather was among the 60,000 inmates evacuated by the Nazis and forced on a brutal march towards Germany. He recalled to my father the horrors he witnessed on that march and in the wake of war: the once-great city of Dresden reduced to something like the surface of the moon; the starving German women and children in tattered clothing; and, after the Red Army liberated the inmates, the vindictive brutality of the Russians toward any Nazi they found, soldier or civilian. How, my father asked, could you feel sorry for these people after what they did to you? His father would shrug.

I think this preternatural sympathy for the Germans was, in a deep but complex way, formative for my father, and he passed on to me a complex set of feelings about revenge. I'm fascinated by revenge, but don't have the heart for it. I'm too quick to forgive and to empathetically justify the disappointing or hurtful actions of others, even if they probably don't deserve it. As a child, my father was confused, angry even, at his own father's lack of apparent vengefulness. His father, a baker, worked with a German woman who had migrated to Canada after the war and steadfastly denied she or her compatriots knew anything of the camps, a (false) claim that my grandfather greeted with steadfast courtesy. It was a different time, he explained to my father.

George Orwell toured continental Europe immediately after the war and reported a story from South Germany.[1] There, he visited a hangar that had been transformed into a detention camp and was led to a special holding area, little more than a concrete floor, for suspected SS officers, likely those in charge of the concentration and death camps. Orwell's guide, a young Jewish man whose whole family had been killed in the camps, delighted in showing his guests the debased Nazis, once so powerful, now a pathetic mass of filthy, sick waste. "I wondered whether the Jew was getting any real kick out of this new-found power that he was exercising" writes Orwell.

> I concluded that he wasn't really enjoying it, and that he was merely – like a man in a brothel, or a boy smoking his first cigar, or a tourist traipsing 'round a picture gallery – telling himself that he was enjoying it, and behaving as he had planned to behave in the days he was helpless.

Orwell continues, "there is no such thing as revenge. Revenge is an act which you want to commit when you are powerless and because you are powerless: as soon as the sense of impotence is removed, the desire evaporates also."

But Orwell, for all his insight, missed something.

The break came in June of 1967, around dinner time. My father was returning home from his classes at the University of Toronto where he was dutifully studying to be a doctor to fulfill his working-class immigrant family's dream. He found his father gleefully cheering on Israeli tanks and planes as they pursued fleeing Egyptian soldiers in what would come to be known as the Six-Day War, which would result in the (still ongoing) occupation of Jerusalem, the West Bank and Gaza. My grandfather, to that point, had generally had little time for Zionism, whose adherents he mocked as zealots, nor any particular attachment to the fortunes of the State of Israel. Yet in that moment my father saw in his father a terrifying vindictiveness, a passion for retribution.

What did these Arabs ever do to you to make you delight in their suffering?, he demanded. The two fought. My father, in his own clumsy way (he was only 19) accused his father, rightly I think, of projecting his hatred of the Nazis and of what was done to him onto what he perceived as a less honorable or more contemptable Other. They didn't speak for some weeks. Something shifted permanently in their relationship.

This story has always haunted me, and not only for the puzzle about morality, memory, and justice it represents but because it has, I think, profoundly shaped who my father is and who I became as well. This incident caused my father to question much of what he had been taught and much of what was expected of him. Soon he would drop out of the medical track and turn his studies toward the theater. He became a Marxist and a trade union organizer. Along with my mother, he became a life-long outspoken advocate of Palestinian human rights.

There are other impetuses for this book as well. Some of them are personal. I have witnessed campaigns of vengeance cloaked in the language of justice. I have persecuted them in petty ways, and I have been persecuted by them, almost to death. Of course, we live in an age when revenge politics is on the march. I make my home and benefit from citizenship in a country, Canada, that was established through the vindictive policies and procedures of a settler colony, which framed Indigenous people as pathologically vengeful "savages," thus justifying their murder, incarceration, abandonment, and dehumanization.

It is in the context of my life and activism in Thunder Bay, a city which in so many ways emblematizes this systemic revenge,[2] that this book emerges, in part as a reflection on those circumstances. It also emerges, in part, through my own clumsy exposure to Anishinaabe practices of grassroots radical theorizing in the course of my work with my friends building a group called Wiindo Debwe Mosewin (Walking Together in Truth), a feminist platform for community care and grassroots safety that actively experiments with "two eyed seeing," merging Anishinaabe and non-Indigenous methods of theory and practice to seek to overcome settler colonialism.

The group was formed in a context of extreme racist violence and abandonment, including at the hands of police,[3] and organizes regular street patrols that offer help to those in need. We practice what Ivory Tuesday calls "Indigenous sous-veillance" to monitor police abuses.[4] As Leanne Betasamosake Simpson shows, Anishinaabe theorizing is inseparable from doing/making and from the practice of story that creates connections between generations and resonates with a resurgent, Indigenous anti-colonial ethos.[5] I have been inspired by the example of many elders, thinkers, and activists in my community who use story as a means to awaken and sharpen what I have come to think of as the radical imagination.[6] As Thomas King argues, Indigenous storytelling on Turtle Island ("North America") almost never ends in a moral nor offers a neat conclusion, inviting the listener to use their intelligence to take the lessons they need.[7] Reflecting back on my approach to this book, I have come to recognize that my desire has been to tell stories about how our world came to be as it is that do not offer a neat or easy "take away," but that, rather, aim to inspire the radical imagination.

Artwork by Amanda Priebe

Introduction

We want revenge

The cruelties of property and privilege are always more ferocious than the revenges of poverty and oppression. For the one aims at perpetuating resented injustice, the other is merely a momentary passion soon appeased … When history is written as it ought to be written, it is the moderation and long patience of the masses at which men will wonder, not their ferocity.

C. L. R. James[1]

To the (purported)(would-be) hero, revenge is monstrous, heard but not seen, insatiable, blind with desire, the Cyclops robbed of her eye. To the self-designated hero, revenge hails a spectre of something best forgotten, a ghost from a criminal past. To the monster, revenge is oxygen.

Eve Tuck and C. Ree[2]

When you live in someone else's utopia, all you have is revenge. We live in capitalism's utopia, a world almost completely reconfigured to suit the needs of accumulation. And the world's alight, and ours is an age of vengeance. It is vengeance, sadly, that is usually directed at those who least deserve it and which leaves those whose actions led to the current state of affairs, or who benefit from it, free or even more empowered.

Ten years after the global financial meltdown of 2008 the world is haunted by revanchist politics: far-right, reactionary and neofascist formations that seem to be based not on any glorious vision of a better future but on taking revenge for what they think of as a stolen past. Revenge on whom? Revenge for what? The specifics are vague; the sentiment is razor-sharp. Everywhere, it seems, whole polities pivot toward agendas that promise to do little to alleviate their social suffering but, rather, offer a vehicle for antipathy. These revenge politics are not only the province of the far-right. My argument is that vengefulness can be observed in some form across the sorry ruins of the political spectrum: a certain cynical, nihilistic vindictiveness that emerges part and parcel of an equally cynical, nihilistic, and vindictive form of capitalism.

But don't mistake me for adding to the chorus who feign surprise at the rise of what they dismiss as "anger" or "resentment" or "populism." By revenge I mean not only a passing sentiment but a logic of retribution, what Francis Bacon called a "wild justice," a ruptural claiming of unpayable debts. My goal is deeper than describing the political mood of our moment. I want to explore the notion that capitalism itself is a *revenge economy*: a system that appears to be taking needless, warrantless, and ultimately self-defeating (but, none the less, profitable for some) vengeance on the world. Revenge capitalism breeds *revenge politics* among the populations that reel from its impacts and lash back, though usually, tragically, at the wrong targets. I think it is long overdue for us to imagine what it would mean to *avenge* what it has done to us and to the planet. The line between revenge and avenging is subtle, both linguistically and conceptually. But whereas revenge fantasies fixate on retribution in the coin in which the original injury was dealt, and thereby risk perpetuating that economy, an *avenging imaginary* dreams of the abolition of the systemic source of that injury and the creation of new economies of peace and justice.

Such a reckoning is justified. Reliable estimates confirm that millions of largely innocent people will die and billions will suffer and be displaced by the effects (floods, droughts, volatility) of climate change, due predominantly to the carbon emissions of industrial and consumer capitalism.[3] Even though major players in key industries and positions of power knew of these realities decades ago, they purposefully buried the information to ensure profitability and competitiveness.[4] It is hard to think of a more monumental crime against humanity, but not a single person has been brought to justice, nor will they be under the current global order. We have heard a great deal recently about climate grief – the melancholia of being made to bear witness to the terrors of ecological calamity – but nothing of climate revenge.[5] Why?

Much the same could be said for the executives of the corporations whose products introduce toxins into the world and our bodies, who hire ruthless paramilitaries to defend their mines and plantations, or who otherwise externalize the costs of their profiteering onto populations made vulnerable by decades or centuries of exploitation or colonialism. The politicians who beat the drums of war, or whose policies have led to the grim neoliberal abandonment of millions of people, will never, under this system, be made to pay. One cannot read about the agonizing premature death suffered by the predominantly poor, racialized inhabitants of Grenfell Tower in the 2017 fire, made susceptible to tragedy by systemic oppression, crass profiteering and government neglect, without seeing red.[6] One cannot recall the similarly patterned abandonment of Black neighborhoods to Hurricane Katrina, or the wanton annihilation unleashed in the Middle East by the War on Terror, or the impunity of the far-right death squads of Latin America, without tasting blood. In the shadow of the vindictive borders, beloved bodies drown or waste away to assuage the fear and protect the comforts of the privileged. The world is saturated with heart-wracking injustices that, even more grotesquely, are not even framed as injustices in the worldview of the powerful, just a regrettable necessity or a hiccup of progress.

SYSTEMIC VENGEANCE

So I am also interested in what it might mean to face our fear of revenge head-on, and to ask: what would it mean, today, in the face of the rise of reactionary revenge fantasies, to cultivate an *avenging imaginary* as a revolutionary force. From one perspective, revenge could be seen as merely the slander the powerful use to defame and castigate the claims to justice of the oppressed, whereas their own daily economic and juridical terrorism – what I am thinking of as *systemic vengeance* – simply names itself law or necessity. Such systemic vengeance is enabled by, and helps to enable, an economy of oppression. Through the phrase "economy of oppression" I intend to name a broad range of interconnected systems in which the value of life is (mis)accounted: from the material economy to the economy of justice overseen by courts and laws to the economies of representation superintended by the media or formal educational institutions. In the face of these economies of oppression, I propose that an avenging imaginary can be cultivated, within which some collective "we" comes to recognize its shared fate and elevates its vengefulness into a transformative force. Rather than simply reclaiming a debt, seeking reparations, or answering a harm within the same economy of oppression, an avenging imaginary yearns for the negation of the negation and the abolition of that economy in the name of collective liberation.

In the absence of avenging imaginaries, the world is plagued by self-perpetuating cycles of revenge politics. The ongoing War on Terror offers a profound example: for decades during and since the Cold War American imperialism acted vengefully in the Middle East to ensure "political stability" and extract resources; blowback came in the form of isolated terrorist attacks against civilians, notably those of September 11, 2001; a massive theater of war was unleashed that destroyed multiple countries, killing, impoverishing, and traumatizing millions of people, to say nothing of, back home, gutting what remained of the welfare state and dooming so many Americans to debt, poverty, and abandonment; new revenge politics arise in the ashes, most dramatically so-called ISIS; meanwhile, the weaponized and traumatized American soldiers returned from war not only trained and armed for modern combat, but suffused with white-supremacist ideology to wreak their political revenge on the home front, in many cases targeting those (feminists, queer folk, Muslims, Jews, Black people, etc. etc.) whom they mistakenly believe stole the American dream.[7] Who, ultimately, profits? In spite of the massive human and economic cost of these wars, on balance the major corporations listed on the DOW, NASDAQ, and other indexes have been the beneficiaries.

WHAT IS REVENGE?

But do not mistake me for rehearsing the worn-out trope that "en eye for an eye makes the whole world blind," and that revenge is an endless, merciless cycle.[8] In many cases, this cheap moralism hides the actuality of power relations and does a grave injustice to the vastly disproportionate costs by substituting a sentimental "both-sidesism" for a substantial analysis. Every life is precious, indeed; if we actually believe it, we owe ourselves the kind of honesty that would allow us to understand and hopefully abolish the kinds of imperialism, white supremacy, colonialism, capitalist exploitation, patriarchy, and other modes of oppression that create systems and structures of revenge.

We have been led to believe, and perhaps it's true, that revenge is an eternal human passion, the terrible but captivating way the violence and cruelty of which humans seem uniquely capable is wedded to the sublime cunning of our singular species.[9] The revenger's plot is sickly fascinating. We have been told, by no less than the greatest poets and philosophers of many civilizations, that revenge only begets revenge, opening a chasm to hell which rips apart people, families and whole societies. Meanwhile, quests (often tragic) to avenge a wrong or an injustice represent some of our oldest and most celebrated stories. Likewise, many of the world's major religions provide wise words about the virtues of forgiveness, or offer supernatural assurances that, even if we cannot avenge the wrongs done to us and those we love in this material realm, the scales will be balanced in God's judgment or the cosmic accounting of karma.[10]

Let us set aside these timeless questions here and now. Echoing Sarah Ahmed's approach to the cultural politics and political economy of happiness, my question here is not what revenge *is*, but what, as a cultural and economic factor, revenge *does*.[11] In this book, when I speak of revenge, and of avenging, I have a historical and materialist argument in mind: I want to know about it in the here and now and the role it plays in the first truly worldwide human system of (global neoliberal racial) capitalism. One of the core arguments of this book is that revenge is a useful adjective to attach to capitalism because it helps explain the seemingly irrational, certainly bloodcurdling violence of that system, which reduces so many of us to utter worthlessness and disposability. Calling up the term revenge also helps us better understand this system's foundations in the cruelties of empire, colonialism and the racial ordering of humanity. These cruelties that continue to this day as humans are, completely unnecessarily, warehoused in prisons, left to die in slums, worked to death in mines, abandoned to the border, or denied the care they require.[12] This vengeance emerges as capitalism responds, directly and indirectly, to constant resistance to its rule. This resistance is, ultimately, the source of the contradictions and crises that drive its innovations and its excesses.[13]

FOUR PRELIMINARY THESES

This book is a hybrid work of revolutionary storytelling with scholarly characteristics. I am not aiming to offer a comprehensive theory of revenge or of capitalism but, rather, to explore the generative tensions that come from holding revenge and capitalism together in uncomfortable proximity. Let me begin with four theses on revenge capitalism that will recur throughout this book.

Revenge is inherent to capitalism

Liberal and neoliberal philosophers have insisted that capitalist democracy is the climax of human political achievement, the culmination of centuries of human social evolution that has seen the knights of reason and the law banish the dragon of revenge to the borderlands, but revenge is with us still.[14] Indeed, a kind of vengeance is at the core of capitalism, though a revenge largely executed without any single human intending it, operating through the everyday and allegedly inevitable banalities of the economy.

In the first case, this is the necessary vengeance of maintaining the expanding capitalist power, undertaken on the frontiers for capitalist accumulation such as colonies or on the front lines of class struggle.[15] As I will argue, this violence typically masquerades as justice and claims that it is its victims who are pathologically vengeful. But I am more interested in how capitalism develops, within it, structures and patterns that are themselves perhaps best described as vindictive, where a seemingly counter-productive cruelty and logic of (usually unwarranted) retribution appear to characterize the motion of the system as a whole. My argument here is that, while there are indeed many individuals and institutions that bear much of the blame for these patterns, they, and we all, exist in a system that sustains itself and its cruelties by seeking to transform each and every one of us into a replaceable competitive agent of its reproduction. I am arguing that, under capitalism, a system driven by contradiction and competition rather than by coherence and conspiracy, systemic revenge emerges without any single agent intending it. That's the tragedy, curse, and challenge of our moment.

Revenge capitalism generates revenge politics

Revenge capitalism, as its crises deepen and its violences become obscene, awakens revenge politics. By revenge politics I mean primarily but not exclusively the global reactionary turn that is often misleadingly labeled as "populism." On the one hand, as numerous authors have made clear, as the actual systemic sources of misery, precariousness, alienation, and fear are obscured, those who experience these terrors are all too easily turned by unscrupulous political agents toward convenient hatreds, often hatreds of race sewn into the fabric of society by the histories of empire.[16] On the other hand, revenge politics speaks to the ascendency of a fascistic politics that has long been plotting vengeance against all those "minority" groups whose victories over the past century or more have unsettled the rule of the powerful: women, queer folk, ethnic and religious "minorities," unions, intellectuals and artists, and the like. But revenge politics is at work on the so-called "Left" as well, though with nowhere near the same implications or consequences. Here, at the proverbial "end of history," when "capitalist realism" has all but strangled the radical imagination and our ability to manifest a compelling vision of what a better society might look like, we easily fall to a reactive kind of revenge politics.[17] In the absence of a revolutionary vision or strategy, radical tactics can become obsessive and vindictive, narrowly targeting individuals, corporations, or policies in ways that inhibit, rather than contribute to, collective liberation.

The staggering reality of actually existing revenge politics today is gender-based violence, the vast majority of it perpetuated by cis-gendered men. The vast majority of this vengeance is exacted against female intimate partners or family members whom the perpetrator deems to be guilty of betrayal, dishonor or disobedience.[18] There is also, worldwide, a huge amount of other lethal violence, vastly disproportionately enacted by men, against queer, trans or non-binary people, violence that often seeks to take revenge for failure to obey conservative norms of gender and sexuality.[19] While patriarchy long predates capitalism, numerous thinkers have illustrated their integration.[20] We can, for instance, observe the link between patriarchal vengeance and three angles of revenge capitalism that I will consistently return to throughout this book: unpayable debts, the surplussing of populations and what I term hyperenclosure: Veronica Gago, Silvia Ferderici and Sayak Valencia all theorize the connection between the rule of unpayable debt and the rise of gendered violence.[21] It is also exhaustively documented that the forms of displacement, dispossession and vulnerability experienced by the "surplussed" populations, including migrants, refugees, incarcerated and formerly incarcerated people, and those who are ghettoized, give rise to dramatically increased gendered violence.[22] And contrary to dreams that an interconnected world would lead to a decline in gendered violence, the globally extensive and dramatically intensive reach of an indifferent, exploitative, alienating, and ultimately nihilistic form of capitalism into every aspect of life in part contributed to the growth of misogynistic reactionary political tendencies and movements that seek to restore meaning, authenticity, and community through the rigid and often violent policing of gender and sexuality.[23]

Capitalism shapes our understanding of revenge

Capitalism, like all systems of power, is reproduced not simply through brute force (though that is certainly part of it) but also through a whole contradictory moral order where its violences and inequalities are normalized, and in which those who refuse or rebel are framed as bestial, stupid, and doomed. It is within liberal capitalism's dominant moral economy that we have come to even understand revenge. It may well be an eternal human drama, but our interpretation of that drama, our notion of what revenge is, is a discursive formation shaped by the moral order of the historically unique system in which we are steeped and to whose reproduction we are compelled to contribute. How we imagine revenge is shaped by a system of revenge. Thus capitalism appears, in its preferred cosmology, as not only the natural expression of basic and inexorable human impulses to compete, accumulate, and barter, but as the triumph of order, peace and plenty.[24] Capitalism has (in a sense) benefited from the (justified) timeless opprobrium for revenge, framed only as an individual drive, to mask its own systematically vengeful nature and to castigate its enemies as heinously, nihilistically vengeful.

It is common enough to hear reactionary pundits and politicians sneer at popular demands for economic redistribution and justice with accusations that they are driven by envy and vindictiveness against the hard-working rich.[25] Throughout capitalism's history, anti-colonialism and working class rebellions have been narrated by the powerful as vengeful spasms of inchoate rage from uneducated and morally deficient mobs, taken as evidence, ironically enough, that the very conditions of (vengeful) subjugation and punishment that led to the uprisings were necessary in the first place.

For this reason, in this book revenge represents, in part, the name the powerful give to claims to justice, to settlement, or to closure "from below," from those imagined not to be entitled to them. Those who seek to step outside the moral and legal regulations of the current order – to balance the scales, to call on an unpaid debt, or to answer a harm – are slandered as vengeful threats to the common good, which is really simply the good of the wealthy and powerful. Our fear of revenge, then, is not simply the patrimony of thousands of years of literature and moral thought. It is also something instilled in us by the system in which we live to tame the radical imagination.

What would it mean to avenge the crimes of capitalism?

For those of us who continue to survive these injustices, for those of us who can barely live in a world of such injustices, for those of us who know there are great debts of history to be repaid (for slavery, for colonialism, for the exploitation of our ancestors, for the terrors of inequality), what promise does revenge hold? How might we move from volatile and unreliable *revenge fantasies*, which seem to increasingly define politics today, to an *avenging imaginary* capable of inspiring and holding together the kind of revolutionary assemblage of the exploited? How could avenging be a dream that moves us beyond vindictive violence and toward the horizons of cooperation and care that are the stuff of the new world we must build?

This book is not an apologia for revolutionary violence, but nor is it a condemnation of it. It seems to me less and less deniable that our choice now as a species is between revolution or slow annihilation, and that any revolution against so violent a system is likely to have violent elements. Perhaps this revolution is already underway. And perhaps so too is the even more bloody counter-revolution.

Rather, this book asks the question: if we were to take revenge seriously, what would it tell us about the times in which we live and, more importantly, how to change them?

ECONOMIES OF REVENGE

In this book, revenge will appear in a number of forms to help us triangulate the operations and impacts of capitalism today: sometimes it names a political affect or "structure of feeling" generated within capitalism and which helps in some way reproduce the system.

Other times revenge appears as a metaphor for the particularly horrific, self-justifying and destructive operations of capital in a moment of crisis. Still other times revenge describes a characteristic of the overarching structure of capitalism's accumulation. If, as I have argued, how we talk about revenge is a matter of cultural power and political meaning-making, then this book seeks to make an intervention in that field: my gambit is that by redefining revenge as systemic, structural and inherent to capitalism, something new comes into focus.

Why add another adjective to preface to capitalism? Such a description should be taken alongside, rather than as a competitor, for recent analyses of gore capitalism, racial capitalism, carceral capitalism, surveillance capitalism, cognitive capitalism, narcocapitalism, empire, biocapitalism, financialized capitalism and neoliberal capitalism.[26] This cruel god has many faces. Revenge capitalism is a way to reflect on both an *inherent tendency* within and a *specific period* of capitalism.

Revenge is an *inherent tendency* in two ways. First, in the obvious sense that capitalist accumulation has always relied on punitive, preemptive, and vindictive violence by its beneficiaries or their agents to maintain the conditions of accumulation and put down rebellions. Why I frame this violence as vengeful, rather than simply sadistic or cruel, will become clear in the coming pages: it (often retroactively) justifies itself and operates as punishment. Second, while there is a danger in anthropomorphizing capital, my desire to identify it as a vengeful system seeks to name an inherent tendency for it to produce, on the level of the society it dominates, vengeful impacts and effects above and beyond the particular motivations and sentiments of any one capitalist agent. Revenge is the outcome, not the motivation, of capitalism.

This is especially so in our age of financialization when, in an unprecedented way, capitalism itself directly manages the global flows of goods, services, labor and wealth. Hence, as a *specific period*, revenge capitalism aims to illuminate the vindictive qualities of our present moment, nearly a half-century into the neoliberal revolution. Here, my focus in this book will return again and again to three patterns of revenge capitalism that I want to punctuate here: unpayable debts, surplussed people and hyperenclosure. Elements of these patterns have existed throughout the history of capitalism, and in systems other than capitalism. In our moment of revenge capitalism, these are three key patterns that, together, help to triangulate the reckless, vengeful global system under which we live.

UNPAYABLE DEBTS

As I discuss in Chapter 2, these are the debts that (almost) everyone recognizes cannot or will not be repaid, but which are still enforced, in spite of the often horrific humanitarian consequences. By and large, these are what I term "debts from above," which is to say debts owed by the oppressed to the powerful. On the one hand, we have the personal debts of individuals that grow under revenge capitalism, most of which were incurred as impoverished people sought to make ends meet in a hostile capitalist economy.[27] These might include the oppressive and inescapable debt incurred for medical services or for university tuition in the United States, or the huge mortgages required nearly everywhere to secure the right to housing. We live in a financialized world of proliferating and intertwined debts.[28] On the other hand, we have the massive unpayable debts of public institutions and whole nations. These debts (largely of the Global South) are typically incurred and relied upon (for many such actors need more and more access to debt year after year, often to pay interest on or refinance earlier debts) as neoliberal governments, deprived of the power to tax the wealthy elements of society, turn to borrowing. Other times, these debts were incurred thanks to coercion, corruption, or financial manipulation, and in any case typically used as a justification for more neoliberal medicine (cuts to public services and capital regulations).[29] Whether they are the debts of individuals or of whole nations, these debts act vengefully upon the borrower, not only inhibiting their ability to live and thrive but compounding a sense of moral shame and personal or collective failure.

Then we have the unpayable "debts from below": those debts which are owed to and sometimes claimed by the oppressed, but which are not honored or acknowledged by the powerful. These include demands for repatriation, reparation, and restoration of lands and artifacts stolen in the process of colonialism, imperialism, or restitution for harms or deprivations suffered.[30] I suggest that, while sometimes the claiming of these debts does manage to articulate itself in ways that can be registered and accommodated within reigning legal and economic orders, they are at the most radical when they make a demand that is practically or ontologically impossible within those orders, when they call into question the legitimacy and foundational narratives of those orders. Here, unpayability strikes at the fundamental injustice of those systems; the only true recompense is their abolition, such that the violence is impossible for anyone.

The notion of a world haunted by unpayable debts also helps explain the growing political cynicism, and the candor about that cynicism, that defines the spectrums of revenge politics today. We live in an age when the claims to fairness, opportunity, the rule of law, reason, and freedom promised by liberalism are cruelly belied and betrayed by the reality of a form of rapacious capitalism that has grown out of that imperialist liberalism and has advanced in its name.[31] If today there may appear on the world stage to be a "populist" reaction, it is in no small part due to resentment against the unpaid debts of this high-minded liberal rhetoric, which has failed to deliver much to most except new forms of exploitation, degradation, and alienation.

SURPLUSSED POPULATIONS

Revenge capitalism is marked by the diverse rise of surplussed populations. I have opted to adjust the verb here to recognize that so-called "surplus" populations are not responsible for or defined by their fate, and they do not accept (nor should we) it actively refusing their conditions both through explicit political mobilization and an infrapolitics of survival and solidarity.[32] Briefly, surplussed populations are those that, thanks to war, ecological destruction, enclosure, colonialism or "economic necessity," are stripped from lands on which they sustained themselves and made dependent on participation in the capitalist economy for survival.[33] Yet, the capitalist economy does not depend on their labor, thanks to a series of global political-economic factors including the rise of worldwide commodity-production chains, aggregate productivity gains, mechanization, and the chaos of international competition. The results are whole populations, often highly indexed to historic patterns of racial and ethnic oppression and exclusion, who are in many cases left to die. Sometimes this necropolitical economy expresses itself along the lines of citizenship, where displaced persons appear as refugees or asylum seekers; other times it expresses itself in terms of chronic unemployment or incarceration.[34]

Revenge capitalism is most clearly seen in the monstrous ways surplussed populations become the targets of both direct and systemic violence: made killable, left to drown, held in camps, warehoused in prisons, chained by extortionate debt, or made to compete for the scraps.

The reactionary revenge politics of our age are increasingly shaped by the response of various institutions and polities toward these surplussed populations.[35] The authoritarian turn of our age (though diversely articulated around different religious fundamentalist or ethnonationist myths) exploits the anxieties of populations who fear becoming surplussed. The siren song of these authoritarians is the offer to cohere a political community around a jealously-guarded in-group. In a hostile world, they promise (falsely as it usually turns out) to protect their adherents from falling into abjection. Conversely, they foment loathing for the surplussed as a means to do it.[36] Fear of the vengeance of the surplussed is mobilized as a means to justify vengeance against them: the manipulative refugee; the recidivist super-predator; the welfare cheat... What is perhaps an important distinction in our financialized age is that these narratives are frequently calibrated by the myth of society as little more than a collection of competitive entrepreneurs, bound together by shared risks and common assets. Today's fascistic revenge politics, then, take on an added dimension of capitalist reason: the surplussed pose a threat to "our" ability to compete for survival.

HYPERENCLOSURE

Capitalism has always been defined in part by processes of enclosure: the seizure and combustion of social wealth into capital. The term's origins speak to the ways in which landlords claimed as their private property the commons that English peasants customarily relied on and governed together for their collective wellbeing.[37] The dispossessed then became reliant (as noted above) on capitalist markets for sustenance and eventually became the proletariat. Similar processes occurred all over the world through colonialism, whereby populations were stripped of their lands and resources and, moreover, made dependent on an exploitative system.[38]

This process, where common lands and resources are seized, can be thought of as "enclosure 1.0." Enclosure 2.0 represents the further combustion of social wealth into capital through, for instance, the privatization of public services, or the deregulation of industry that destroys ecosystems, or the extractive politics of unpayable debt, where social wealth is funneled away. Enclosure 3.0, or hyperenclosure, represents the use of technology to seize upon the commons of the imagination, cognition, communication and creativity.[39]

Here I have in mind the way that individualized financialized forms of debt come to preoccupy the lifeworld of individuals and whole peoples toward generating wealth that is soon siphoned away; the way that a relentlessly competitive, financialized capitalist economy exhorts each of us to adopt the persona of the speculator, transfiguring nearly every aspect of our lives into material and immaterial assets to be leveraged and seeing society as a landscape of risks to be managed;[40] the means by which the wealthy and powerful leverage data and targeted advertising to dramatically influence the course of elections and politics more generally;[41] the rise of new patterns and technologies that seek to fragment and entrepreneurialize work, emblematized by the so-called "gig economy" where, under the banner of freedom from institutional boredom and in the name of creative self-actualization we each become competitive freelancers enmeshed in unforgiving and accelerating systems;[42] the relentless push of advertising, branding and marketizing into every nearly every sphere of life.[43] I have in mind the way the promise of widespread digital technology has become a massive, lawless corporate-led experiment in hacking into the human psycho-social network, transforming each of us and our relationships into a source of monetizable data or segmenting and selling our attention to the highest corporate or political bidder.[44]

The result, as we will explore in Chapter 5, is what Geert Lovink calls "platform nihilism," which stems from the deadlock between, on the one hand, constant stimulation and, on the other, utter stagnation.[45] Here we appear to be given only two choices. We can become what might be called fractal capitalists, enthusiastically embracing this brave new world of hyperenclosure and embracing the "freedom" to compete and consume it offers (vainly) hoping that by hard work, ruthlessness and luck we will rise above our fellows. Or we can join any number of forms of neofundamentalism, banding together under the shelter of some fetishized notion of "authenticity" that allegedly exists outside hyperenclosure: religious, racial, ethnonational, political, personal. These range from the seemingly harmless (for instance, crazes for yoga, mindfulness, or minimalism)[46] to apocalyptic (for instance, the revanchist sadism of white nationalism, or weaponized Christian, Muslim, or Hindu fundamentalism).[47] Both the fractal capitalist and the neofundamentalist are children of revenge capitalism and each, in their own way, is filled with easily misdirected vengeance that furnishes revenge politics with its terrible energies.

INTERLOCUTORS

There are a number of lines of critical thought which intersect my approach to revenge, if only to somewhat clarify my central concept. I am deeply influenced, for instance, by recent attempts to reread Nietzschean and Fanonian notions of resentment through an anti-colonial lens.[48] Resentment and revenge are deeply connected. I am inspired by, for instance, Glen Coulthard's argument that "resentment, unlike anger, has an in-built political component to it, given that it is often expressed in response to an alleged slight, instance of maltreatment, or injustice. Seen from this angle, resentment can be understood as a particularly virulent expression of politicized anger."[49]

On the importance of dwelling with "bad feelings" like resentment and revenge I am also deeply inspired by recent feminist scholarship on affect, notably Sarah Ahmed's critical phenomenological considerations of the importance of anger and the political blackmail that surrounds the imperative toward happiness.[50] This work is joined by a host of recent works that theorize the rise of discourses and whole capitalist industries aimed at a kind of soft enforcement of "positive" affects and optimistic thinking as false, individualized solutions to collective crises.[51] In this vein, like Coulthard, I have a high degree of skepticism toward the political imperative, and liberal theoretical turn, toward forgiveness and reconciliation. I also, along with Joshua Clover, want to dwell on the structural conditions that impinge upon today's forms of resistance and rebellion, for better and for worse.[52]

Meanwhile, another set of inspirations that inform this book is a tradition of anti-colonial thought that seeks to understand the perplexing cruelty of the powerful, the kind of normalized sadism of domination, especially as it circulates around race, including the pivotal explorations of Frantz Fanon and the more recent work of theorists like Saidya Hartman and Jasbir Puar.[53] I am also informed by recent debates around the possibility of radical social change, largely in dialog with the influential work of Ernesto Laclau and Chantal Mouffe, that stress antagonism and agonism within democratic polities.[54] Likewise, I am also inpired by the long-standing and recent attempts, in fields like anthropology, sociology, and political science, to account for the rise of reactionary ethnonationalism, revanchist (proto-)fascism, violent fundamentalisms and similar tendencies within and as part of capitalism.[55]

I also write in a kind of sideways response to more popular approaches to the rise of "populism" that seek to exceptionalize our moment as an age of anger, resentment or backlash, but which tend to limit this to the purely political realm and elide the centrality of capitalism to this process.[56] Of the form of capitalism, and the pathologies to which it gives rise, I am also deeply influenced by a number of scholars who, in contrast to a conventional Marxist approach which seeks to schematize the infernal clockwork of its logic of accumulation, try to understand this system at its pathological and illogical excesses, especially as these circulate around processes of colonialism and racialization.[57]

While this book concludes with a theoretical argument for cultivating a collective avenging imaginary, it offers no direct solutions or strategic advice for our current moment. I am here seeking to triangulate something I am calling revenge at the intersection of culture, politics, and economics. This book, while at times strident in tone, is diagnostic, not prescriptive. I will leave the implications of this framework for struggle and justice for another time. I will confess that to write this book I have dug deep into the cruelties and pathologies of the present and into my own complex feelings. I have chased the darkness, convinced that if ever we needed unflinching creative honesty it is now.

I emerge from this book anti-anti-revenge. The people who are destroying the earth and our future have names and addresses. They ought to be brought to justice. We know that, in the current system, they will not be, but also that any one of them is almost instantly replaceable, with so many already competing for places at the top. Without a revolutionary movement, their power will be undiminished and capitalism will continue to wreak its vengeance. Yet I confess myself to be too full of the milk of human kindness to have a taste for revolutionary violence. My argument throughout this book, however, is that, whether we agree with it or not, revenge is here, and all our saccharine moralizing against it just stokes its flames. The debts of history will be paid, one way or another.

1

Toward a materialist theory of revenge

This March is Shit
The Future is Shit
All I Want is Revenge

2010 London protest banner

Revenge is a human dream ... there is no way of conveying to the corpse the reasons you have made him one – you have the corpse, and you are, thereafter, at the mercy of a fact which missed the truth, which means that the corpse has you.

James Baldwin

This chapter draws on a wide archive of critical theory, on examples from popular culture, and on the rise of the revenge politics of Donald Trump to develop a *materialist* theory of revenge. By examining these intertwined histories of colonialism, patriarchy, and capitalism I want to frame revenge as, on the one hand, something that describes the (il)logic of systems of domination as well as a pervasive political sentiment to which those systems give rise. I argue that such systems project vengefulness onto those whom they oppress and exploit precisely to hide their patterns of systemic revenge. I frame revenge capitalism as a system *in extremis* which, like a mad king, appears to be taking needless, warrantless revenge on its subjects. But underneath are structural contradictions that generate pathological forms of accumulation and a dangerous reactionary political climate. To face these head-on, we will need to let go of our allergy to thinking seriously about revenge.

THE LIVES AND DEATHS OF WITCHES

A man that studieth revenge, keeps his own wounds green, which otherwise would heal, and do well. Public revenges are for the most part fortunate; as that for the death of Caesar ... But in private revenges, it is not so. Nay rather, vindictive persons live the life of witches; who, as they are mischievous, so end they infortunate.[1]

So concludes Francis Bacon's 1625 treatise *On Revenge*, which in many ways presents, in germinal form, the conventional proto-bourgeois modern political theory of revenge. It is notable that Bacon wrote these words while gravely in debt, having some years earlier, thanks to a conspiracy of his rivals, been stripped of the title of Chancellor to James I for corruption and sedition, barely escaping with his head. This came after years of public service in which Bacon had helped plan and facilitate England's nascent settler colonial adventures into Virginia and Newfoundland, and had presided over the Tudor enclosure of the commons and the dispossession of peasants to help enrich the Crown.[2] As Carolyn Merchant observes, much of Bacon's thought, and the metaphors of the torture and interrogation of nature which would become so influential to the development of the Scientific Method which he is credited to have fathered, emerged in the context of James I's enthusiasm for witch-hunting.[3] While there is a vigorous historical debate about Bacon's own involvement in and opinion of witch trials, the dire warning at the close of his essay *On Revenge* resonates with the hegemonic view of his day.

Silvia Federici and Maria Mies have both drawn key connections between colonialism, enclosure, and the witch trials as central to the birth and rise of capitalism. Witch hunts were characterized by public spectacles of vengeful vitriol that helped misdirect proto-proletarian anger at growing social insecurity and discord along gendered lines, setting the stage for the imbrications of capitalism and patriarchy to come.[4] Bacon was a key figure in this shift, as well as in the development of a prototypical modern theory of science that feminist thinkers have shown was based in the violent and sexualized subjugation of a passive and exploitable notion of nature, which is at the root of today's violent forms of instrumental and scientistic rationality, and also the pseudoscience of bourgeois political economy.[5]

It is, I think, no accident that Bacon would also give us a prototypical theory of revenge, which is later echoed in the work of Thomas Hobbes, John Locke and Adam Smith.[6] Here, revenge is seen as a base, animal instinct dangerous to the social order. It is presented as ultimately self-destructive, an urge that consumes the subject and does not allow psychic and social wounds to heal. Revenge appears as something supernatural and untimely, a suspension of the holy order. Its suppression is the basis of the legitimacy of the state: by nominating a leviathan to adjudicate disputes and mete out punishment, man raises himself above an animalistic nature.

As such, for Bacon "public revenges," those undertaken by or for the sovereign or which, in retrospect can be said to be justified in the name of the commonwealth (as narrated by its victors), are legitimate, especially as they target those "witches," those unruly, uncanny, un-godly subjects who refuse to abandon their right to revenge outside of the state's vengeful law.

MERGERS AND ACQUISITIONS

In the late 1980s a lower middle class Virginian man in his early 30s quit his job as special assistant to the chief of naval operations at the Pentagon to attend Harvard Business School. Bright and ambitious but older, poorer, and lacking the cultural and social capital of most of his colleagues, his chances were dim. One night he was a wallflower at a Goldman Sachs recruitment party and got into a conversation with two equally awkward men about baseball. They turned out to be two of the company's executives; he was hired shortly afterward and, thanks to his maturity, cunning, ruthlessness, and yen for the grueling hours, he quickly rose to become one of the firm's vice-presidents (not as high and mighty a position as it sounds) in the burgeoning mergers and acquisitions department.

Thanks to Reagan-era deregulation, mergers and acquisitions had become one of the bank's key profit generators, facilitating the merciless takeover of smaller, local firms by large monopolies in sectors including retail, manufacturing, communications, infrastructure, and banking itself. The resulting financial boom has given us the film- and tell-all memoir-inspired stereotypes of the coked-up, oversexed financier so desperate to make his commission he'll sell his own grandmother to his fellow wolves of Wall Street. But this stereotype individualizes a systemic and structural problem: financialization, driven by the crisis-prompted acceleration of capitalist competition for profit, was actively destroying the bedrock of the Keynesian capitalist economy on which it preyed, gutting jobs and benefits, specifically targeting for destruction firms with strong unions and low profit margins (see Chapter 5). Our financier, to whom we shall return, for now we know him well, was among those who aided and abetted a system of economic vengeance on American proletarians.

THE RULE OF HISTORICAL RETRIBUTION

Marx's relationship to revenge is ambiguous, perhaps because he unhappily inherits a Western tradition that understands revenge as a retrograde, atavistic, dark force unworthy of a humanist let alone a materialist. For a man who sought, in Harry Cleaver's words, to put intellectual weapons in the hands of the oppressed, exploited and brutalized working class, it is somewhat surprising he rarely mentions vengeance.[7]

Writing in *The Condition of the Working Class in England* in 1845, Engels, with whom Marx surely agrees on this point, assures bourgeois readers that

> it does not occur to any Communist to wish to revenge himself upon individuals, or to believe that, in general, the single bourgeois can act otherwise, under existing circumstances, than he does act ... Communism, rests directly upon the irresponsibility of the individual. Thus the more ... workers absorb communistic ideas, the more superfluous becomes their present bitterness, which, should it continue so violent as at present, could accomplish nothing; and the more their action against the bourgeoisie will lose its savage cruelty.[8]

So a mature political approach is one that renounces or transcends individual acts of violence. According to what Engels would later identify as dialectical materialism, history itself will avenge the wrongs of capital. Elsewhere, Engels associates vengefulness with the immature socialism with the followers of Auguste Blanqui, the towering professional revolutionary of the nineteenth century whose writings are full of trenchant fury and vengeful promises for the bourgeois oppressors, but contain little systematic analysis of their power.[9] For Engels, mature communism is the antidote to vengeance, in part because it foresees a world without systemic injustice, in part because, as a political movement, it sublimates vengeance into political organization and aims for a horizon of transformation, rather than retribution. Indeed, it sees this as necessary because to a very real extent, it is predicated on the irresponsibility of the individual, both the bourgeois and the proletarian: both, historically speaking, are motivated by systemic forces that mean their actions are not entirely their own. The final goal of the proletariat is not to decapitate this or that capitalist but to abolish all classes, both bourgeoisie and proletariat.

Yet, importantly, the other place revenge appears is as a condemnation of sanctimonious and false bourgeois appeals to justice and necessity. For instance, the term appears in Marx's excoriating analysis of the bourgeois response to the Paris Commune of 1871: the murder of tens of thousands of communards in the streets, the show-trials and exile of tens of thousands more.[10] Likewise, Marx comments with horror on the racist, revanchist vitriol whipped up in the bourgeois press for the punishment of what the British Empire called the "Sepoy Mutiny" of

1857 (in actuality it was a much wider anti-colonial revolt), which led to the mobilizing of an British Army of Retribution that unleashed sickening public executions and torture, mass rapes and looting, with a death toll of up to 10 million people.[11] Marx, who publicly decried the fake news propounded by the English press about the sexual crimes of Indians against white women and girls that justified the revanchist expedition,[12] sagely offered the following:

> However infamous the conduct of the Sepoys, it is only the reflex, in a concentrated form, of England's own conduct in India, not only during the epoch of the foundation of her Eastern Empire, but even during the last ten years of a long-settled rule. To characterize that rule, it suffices to say that torture formed an organic institution of its financial policy. There is something in human history like retribution: and it is a rule of historical retribution that its instrument be forged not by the offended, but by the offender himself.[13]

I think Marx means two things here. The first is that revenge and retribution enacted by the oppressed and exploited are forged in the normalized torture of the oppressor and exploiter's extortionate economy, something thinkers like C.L.R. James and Aimé Césaire echoed and expanded in their treatment of Caribbean anti-colonial revolts.[14] Second and related, the primary act of vengeance is always that of the oppressor against the oppressed, but this vengeance is presented by the oppressor as the legitimate, legal, and even benevolent, in this case the business of the East India Company.[15] Even more profoundly, this vengeance is endemic to the system itself, so normalized and routine that it becomes invisible, at least to the abusers. The economy of revenge only becomes visible when its typically one-way flows are reversed. That "torture formed an organic institution of its financial policy" implies that, when it comes to systemic vengeance, *the punishment always already comes before the crime.*

Marx corroborates this approach in an 1849 article on English bourgeois power in the *Neue Rheinische Zeitung*:

> In England's workhouses – those public institutions where the redundant labor population is allowed to vegetate at the expense of bourgeois society – charity is cunningly combined with the revenge which the bourgeoisie wreaks on the wretches who are compelled to appeal to its charity … These unfortunate people have committed the crime of having ceased to be an object of exploitation yielding a profit to the bourgeoisie – as is the case in

ordinary life – and having become instead an object of expenditure for those born to derive benefit from them.[16]

Here we see the glimmer of a theory of systemic vengeance to which we shall shortly return: the notion that, far from the obsequious theories of establishmentarian philosophers like Bacon or Hobbes, vengeance is not banished with the witches at the borders of the State, but, rather, is inherent, integral, and immanent to the workings of power. Indeed, power works to conceal its fundamental reliance on unwarranted, preemptive, banalized revenge precisely by defaming its antagonists and rebels as consumed by the demonic, base, and animalistic passion of revenge. Beyond the sanctimony of the law, which claims to save us from the endless cycles of primordial vengeance, there is the mystified vengefulness of the system itself, in this case cunningly disguised as charity.

THE VENGEANCE OF RACE

For all that defamation, proletarians and other oppressed and exploited people have consistently drawn on the thematic of revenge as a key means to mobilize themselves.

Consider the famous lines of Toussaint L'Ouverture, the visionary military and political leader of the Haitian Revolution, the first modern movement to establish truly equal rights and abolish slavery.

> Brothers and friends: I am Toussaint L'Ouverture; perhaps my name is known to you. I am undertaking the vengeance of my race. I want liberty and equality to reign in Saint Domingue. I am working to make that happen. Unite, brothers, and fight with us for the same cause. Uproot with me the tree of slavery.

It is difficult to know where to begin with these incisive, explosive lines that catalyzed the imagination of tens of thousands of enslaved people with the conviction to liberate themselves and completely reinvent their reality. Here perhaps their first and most important act of vengeance was not the bloody reprisals against slaveowners and their functionaries but the act of hailing themselves as friends and as brothers, and the speaking aloud of the open secret: revenge was owed them. As C. L. R. James makes clear in his landmark study of the Haitian revolution, the violence unleashed was neither (as the slavers claimed) an atavistic and animalistic bloodlust, nor simply a bloody negation of slavery's own vengeful cruelties.[17] It was a calculated and necessary set of procedures to nullify and petrify the slave system in the colony and in the metropole. And it was a process by which those who were enslaved collectively gave themselves value, not as property but as agents of their own history, as the proper subjects of the reign of liberty and equality on their own terms.

It almost goes without saying that vengeance was pivotal to the reproduction of chattel slavery such as that practiced in pre-Revolutionary Haiti: with near-absolute power over life and death, slavers and their functionaries reprised the slightest hint of disobedience or infraction with unspeakable brutality and often naked sadism. Typically, this vengeance was justified in the name of using terror to suppress enslaved people's allegedly inherent, bestial vengefulness that was held to always be simmering beneath the surface. Yet even for the most fortunate and gently treated of enslaved people, the system was itself vengeful: a kind of unearned punishment for a never committed crime driven not by the particular vindictive cruelty of any one slaver but by the pressures of anonymous economic necessity and a system of normalized domination.

After the revolution it is noteworthy that, in an unusually coordinated act of vengeance, the French, American, British and Spanish governments, unable each in turn to bring Haiti back under the rule of slavery, opted to impose upon the nascent nation a massive unpayable debt. Partly in order to ensure the continued export of cheapened sugar, partly to quicken the social discord of poverty, the self-emancipating Haitian people were made to compensate their own-time French owners for the latter's loss of property.[18]

This imposition of a ruinous and colonial debt through gunboat diplomacy was extremely common in the nineteenth century.[19] This fate befell many of the rulers of the principalities that would come under the suzerainty of the British East India Company and, eventually, the British Raj on the Indian subcontinent.[20] The cancerous drip-feed of debt was the means by which the French and English pried open Egypt and took command of the vitally strategic Suez canal.[21] The imposition of extortionate debt as compensation for treaty violations (as determined by Europeans) was a key means by which China was held in the thrall of European opium exporters.[22] And in in North America Indigenous people and nations' non-payment of poisonous or extortionist loans was frequently used as justification for the seizure of their lands.[23]

In all these cases, the logic of colonialism dictates that the colonized are always already in debt for the gift of civilization, religion and the rule of law. Deemed morally, intellectually and culturally deficient from the outset by virtue of race, the colonized are made to honor a vengeful debt that can never be repaid for their own dispossession and degradation.[24]

IF BLOOD BE THE PRICE OF YOUR AWFUL WEALTH ...

Consider this text from a bilingual English/German poster produced in the wake of Chicago's 1886 Haymarket massacre, which exhorts workers:

> To arms! Your masters sent their bloodhounds – the police – to kill six of your brothers ... because they, like you, had the courage to disobey the supreme will of your bosses ... and to show you ... that you must be satisfied and contented with whatever your bosses condescend to allow you ... if you are men, if you are the sons of your grand sires, who have shed blood to free you, then you will rise in your might, Hercules, and destroy the hideous monster that seeks to destroy you.[25]

The gendered language here indicates, perhaps, the ways in which the largely migrant workers of Chicago's industrial boom felt emasculated by the racist and xenophobic system under which they labored, which licensed itself to murder them and their families not only on the picket-line but daily in the factory or through the grinding cruelties of poverty. There was no recourse for them to the fabled "rule of law" when a child died of malnutrition or was crushed in the industrial machines. We might productively take up this language to note the way that it creates a narrative of intergenerational strength and rebellion, and also in a roundabout way centers the right to social reproduction over the dignity of productive labor: rebellion here is framed as a debt to the past, and a debt to the future as well.

Consider too, the Industrial Workers of the World (IWW) song *We have Fed you all for a Thousand Years*. The song was a wry parody of Kipling's imperialist paean to the British Navy *The Song of the Dead*, which justified England's empire with recourse to the price paid for it in the blood of its stalwart mariners. Repurposed for more radical proletarian service, the IWW hymn insists:

> We have fed you all for a thousand years and you hail us still unfed,
> Though there's never a dollar of all your wealth
>   but marks the workers' dead.
> We have yielded our best to give you rest and you lie on crimson wool.
> Then if blood be the price of all your wealth,
>   Good God! We have paid it in full!
> There is never a mine blown skyward now
>   but we're buried alive for you.

There's never a wreck drifts shoreward now
  but we are its ghastly crew.
Go reckon our dead by the forges red
  and the factories where we spin.
If blood be the price of your cursed wealth,
  good God! We have paid it in!
We have fed you all a thousand years
  for that was our doom, you know,
From the days when you chained us in your fields
  to the strike a week ago.
You have taken our lives, and our babies and wives
  and we're told it's your legal share,
But if blood be the price of your lawful wealth,
  good God! We bought it fair![26]

At stake in these dangerous expressions of proletarian vengeance is an implicit rebuttal to the bourgeois condemnation of vengeance as an infantile, individualistic, and emotive reaction. Rather, revenge becomes a call to a collective action, indeed, an action that creates a new revolutionary collectivity. This collectivity binds together workers in the present, but it also binds them to a lost or subjugated history. It makes them the collectors of a historical or ancestral debt and the redeemers of past generations of struggle.

And yet, terrifyingly, it is also more than evident that all too often the vengefulness of the oppressed, however justified, can be mobilized by their enemies against misidentified foes. Indeed, it is often the case that this dark collective passion is marshaled by reactionary forces who, rather than promising a revolutionary overturning of the conditions of oppression, rather offer a spasmodic surge of vengeful rage, all too frequently directed not at the authors of oppression but at those even more oppressed. The pogrom, the lynch mob, the witch hunt all testify to the way that the powerful are able to mobilize, deputize, and franchise out revenge politics as an outlet for the social agonies they themselves have created.

I, TITUS

Revenge defines not only politics but also our culture today. It has been a key weapon in the arsenal of Hollywood and, more broadly, the corporate- and profit-driven media since the birth of capitalism. Revenge today is perhaps the most economically productive genre of popular culture. Consider the incredible success of the HBO serial *Game of Thrones*, which to date has swelled the profits of its parent company,

Time Warner, largely thanks to a (absurdly anachronistic) narrative that is driven almost exclusively by violent, sexualized revenge. One estimate suggests that each episode of the show cost $6 million to produce and netted at least $60 million in revenue: a 10:1 ratio.[27] Revenge is also the key thematic of the incredibly popular films of Quentin Tarantino, and also a driving force behind the lucrative horror movie industry. I am not arguing that these spectacles and genres directly generate or reinforce revenge politics, although perhaps that is partly true. In all of these cases, the forms and narratives of revenge are complex and open to multiple readings and interpretations. Rather, I am suggesting that their incredible popularity today indexes something shifting deeper in the political-economic tectonics of our age. I am interested in what their popularity, rather than their scripts, can tell us about revenge today.

The fascination with revenge is, of course, nothing new. One of Shakespeare's most popular plays during his lifetime was by far his worst: *Titus Andronicus*, an excruciatingly long racist bloodbath of a play that includes no less than "14 killings, 9 of them on stage, 6 severed members… 3 rapes, 1 live burial, 1 case of insanity and 1 of cannibalism – an average of 5.2 atrocities per act, or one for every 97 lines."[28] T. S. Eliot called it "one of the stupidest and most uninspired plays ever written."[29] It follows the vengeance and counter-vengeance of its eponymous tragic hero, a noble Roman general returned from war against the Goth barbarians to find himself and his whole family embroiled in the backstabbing, conniving capital of the empire. Francis Bacon almost certainly saw the play, probably several times, and also dozens and dozens more like it: revenge was one of the most popular genres in early modern England as well.[30]

Without wishing to venture to a comprehensive hypothesis, I would suggest that one parallel between Shakespeare's age and ours is this: in moments when the powerful operate vengefully upon the oppressed with impunity, and when that impunity is disguised as necessary, unavoidable, natural, and just, the revenge denied to the oppressed manifests in popular fantasy, and occasionally as "terrorism."

Let us return to the figure of our Wall Street man with whom I began, who, in the early 1990s, was sent by Goldman Sachs to Los Angeles to oversee the booming market in mergers and acquisitions in the entertainment industry. New analog and later digital technologies were ensuring that back catalogs of films and secondary rights to distribution of theatrical releases were big business, and our financier soon took his expertise to spin off his own boutique financial firm specializing in speculating on popular culture content. Eventually, our financier retired from finance to become an executive producer and producer of

Hollywood films. Wall Street had made him wealthy, yes, but also bitter: in spite of his success he had never truly been included in the ranks of the elites and was disgusted by the crony-capitalism of the establishment that had so enriched him.

In 1999, he teamed up with Julie Taynor, maker of the bestselling Broadway musical of Disney's *The Lion King* (itself a transformation of Shakespeare's *Hamlet* from a beautifully enigmatic revenge tragedy to a twee melodrama with racist, imperialist and homophobic characteristics: white lion, aided by ambiguously white-ethnic herbivore sidekicks and simianized African mentor, takes vengeance on gay English uncle and his hyena henchmen voiced by Black women[31]). Together, they produced the film *Titus*, a bombastic and maudlin adaptation of the Shakespeare tragedy that in many ways predicted the hypermasculine martial atavism of later blockbusters *300* or *Sparta*. These latter films are, today, cited by the militarist-cum-financier-cum-filmmaker in question as among his favorites, and the favorites of the legions of reactionaries to whom he caters, depicting as they do the heroic triumphs of unapologetic supermen undaunted by conventional morality or the craven cowardice of their would-be countrymen, banding together to defend the integrity of their embattled tribe against the invading barbarian hordes.[32]

In contrast, the 1999 film *Titus* retains its tragic mode, depicting a noble Roman general, played by Anthony Hopkins, caught up in cycles of gory revenge with, on the one hand, his country's barbaric foreign enemies (the Goths), and, far worse, with the "elites" of his own nation who have betrayed Titus and his (also elite) family. Importantly, one of the key antagonists in the play is the figure of Aaron the Moor, a racialized foreigner figure who is possessed of an irrational and dehumanizing lust for sexualized vengeance. It is strongly hinted that his corrupting presence within Rome is in part to blame for triggering the endless cycles of revenge that give the play its motive force. Though Titus and his kin are almost all maimed or slaughtered by the end of the film, *Titus* depicts and arguably celebrates a man willing to bring about a violent revanchist apocalypse to cleanse the world of corruption.

The producer and financier's name is Steven Bannon, former campaign tsar and advisor to Donald Trump and, today, dean of worldwide extreme right revenge politics.[33]

DESCENT

It should of course be pointed out that the narrative of Bannon's *Titus* is very close indeed to the myth of German innocence and integrity propounded by the Nazis and their conservative allies in the 1920s and 1930s, which suggested that Germany had lost the war and been ripped off at Versailles thanks to corrupt, cosmopolitan, and treasonous forces within the government, notably Jews.[34] Then and now it makes for a narcotic metanarrative. It is also a metanarrative at the core of his transformation of the Trump campaign from a dumpster-fire of amusing narcissism into a precise smart-bomb of cultural politics.

Whatever else might be said about his victory, and much indeed might be said, I would hazard that, above all, what Bannon and Trump promised white voters was revenge. Revenge against the media, against the shadowy "elites," against an out-of-touch left, indeed against the nihilism of life itself under neoliberal austerity. Writing in *Jacobin* days after Trump's election, Dan O'Sullivan glosses the affect:

> "Vengeance is mine." So thought a lot of people last Tuesday [following Trump's electoral victory], consciously or not – a posture which poses an implied question that is never answered: Vengeance for what? Maybe they didn't entirely know themselves; just a vague, painful throbbing at the base of their necks, a pregnant, silent anger, an inability to look at the mirror.[35]

While always a reactionary, Bannon's life was fundamentally altered by the 9/11 attacks and the resulting War on Terror. While certainly not against the war, Bannon had a deep-seated contempt for the corrupt, self-serving neoconservatism of the Bush dynasty which used the War on Terror as a means to accelerate and entrench neoliberal globalization. For Bannon, such "establishment" conservatives were the worst of all traitors, continuing to sell out America to transnational finance and corporations and engage in muscular imperialism rather than focus on building a strong national economy and long-term white American global hegemony. Bannon's famed economic nationalism is heavy on isolationism, both political and economic. But it is also, fundamentally, based on revenge.

The vehicle for his revenge politics came in the form of Breitbart News, named after its founder who died prematurely just as the site was about to launch in 2012. In the intervening decade, Bannon leveraged his skills as a film producer, and his wealth, into creating far-right documentaries. Some purported to uncover vast conspiracies of liberal politicians to grease their pockets while stiffing white working class Americans. Others paid homage to reactionary politicians like Sarah Palin and Ronald Reagan, or movements like the Tea Party. Revenge here, figured as a means to bind an imagined community around the myth of loss, the fabled "America" which was once great, and which could be made great again.

At Breitbart and in his documentaries Bannon channeled the spirit of *Titus*: America and normative-white, heartland Americans are presented as imperfect but noble, trusting and honorable at their core. Like Titus, such simple, battlefield virtues find themselves out of place in the decadent, cosmopolitan, effeminate and backstabbing world of career politicos and hangers-on. Noble American Titus is drawn into a cycle of endless, mutually destructive vengeance because of his loyalty to his country and family. And while he commits heinous acts, somehow they do not besmirch his honor. As Donald Trump so aptly put it following revelations about his misogynistic antics and long history of abuse, (to paraphrase): I never said I was perfect. But together, we're going to Make America Great Again. Or, as his and Bannon's key funder, the free market libertarian hedge-fund billionaire Robert Mercer and his far-right activist daughter Rebekah Mercer put it in their defense of their courageous embattled general:

> We are completely indifferent to Mr. Trump's locker room braggadocio ... America is finally fed up and disgusted with its political elite. Trump is channeling this disgust and those among the political elite who quake before the boombox of media blather do not appreciate the apocalyptic choice America faces on November 8th. We have a country to save and there is only one person who can save it. We, and Americans across the country and around the world, stand steadfastly behind Donald J Trump.[36]

THE PORNOGRAPHICS OF REVENGE

Trump's victory was built in no small part on white-supremacism, a theme to which we shall shortly turn. It was also, evidently, built on misogyny. Breitbart has been among the chief vehicles for a fulsome pornographic banquet of neopatriarchal tropes inherited from and reinforcing a virulent online culture of anti-feminist backlash.

Rather than parsing the history of #Gamergate and other festivals of revanchist masculinity,[37] I would recall our earlier discussions of Francis Bacon, the developer of one of the first theories legitimating the revenge of the powerful. Bacon's denigration of vengefulness from below, his distinction of legitimate "public revenge" in the name of the sovereign or social order from "private revenges," hinges upon the figure of the witch, whose "mischievous" life, he threatens, will end with "infortune." As noted above, Bacon was a key legislator and advisor to James I at a time when the monarch vigorously expanded the persecution of perceived witches. The witch hunts, as Federici and Mies note, unleashed wave after wave of warrantless, socially transformative vengeance against women. This most public of revenges, as Federici points out, was not only overseen by agents of the state, it was also a profitable spectacle.[38] It facilitated the imposition of a new form of patriarchy at the level of institutions (with, for instance, doctors replacing midwives and priests replacing wise-women), at the level of the economy (with the often women-led reciprocity of commoners giving way to male-dominated waged labor), at the level of politics (with women leaders routed and burned) and at the level of culture (with women and femininity in general becoming bearers of abjection and suspicion), and consigned to the private sphere.

Indeed, Federici makes clear that the European early modern witch trials were a modality of class warfare. It was not only that women were key organizers within their communities in whose absence social solidarity and resistance to enclosure and exploitation suffered. It was also women's political fury that had to be contained and destroyed. We may presume that this was entangled with the emerging ideologies of gender binarism, in which vengefulness (beyond petty vindictiveness) was recoded as masculine, thus women possessing it were evidently unnatural.

This redirection of social antagonisms and vengefulness away from (male) elites and toward (non-elite) women is a pattern we have seen repeated time and time again, and was indeed propounded as a method of colonialism. As Chandra Talpade Mohanty and other anti-imperialist feminists have shown, the reconfiguration of the gender system was key to the colonial methodologies of divide and conquer. Mohanty, for one, has illustrated how an imperialism dedicated to "saving" racialized women from racialized men both draws on and reproduces a long history of colonial patriarchy and also invites new forms of (allegedly) anti-imperialist patriarchy and misogyny as well.[39] Fanon notes the way that women of colonized populations become the target of colonizing and colonized men's fantasies and rage.[40] Andrea Smith has cataloged the numerous ways in which vengeful sexual violence against Indigenous women has been a key method of settler colonialism to destroy the resistance of Indigenous communities, historically and in the present.[41] Ann Stoler has fruitfully unpacked the fear of the "revenge of the repressed" as a key discourse for interpreting colonial relations, with the repressed desires and crimes of colonists displaced onto a mythological colonial other whose fabled carnal vengefulness becomes a justification for violent domination in the first place.[42]

As Lisa Nakamura explains, these entanglements of race, gender and capital persist and are reproduced in new ways in the realm of digital and social media around both text and image, often accelerated and legitimated by a hyperbolic and revanchist fear of white, male persecution, oppression, impotence, or irrelevance.[43] The recent epidemic of revenge pornography, where (archetypically) men horde images of women who have shared intimacy with them as a means to blackmail or humiliate their one-time lovers, is only the latest manifestation of a long trend and tendency. Male vengefulness is assumed to be natural and, if not rational, at least logical in its own right.

Meanwhile, female vengefulness is pathologized or romanticized. Through there is a generative debate around, for instance, the feminist sense that can be made of the rape-revenge film one is still hard-pressed not to at least in part agree with Carol Clover's early analysis of the genre as an arena for masculine fantasy, where a (typically conventionally attractive) female body becomes the object of gruesome sexualized violence and an agent of titillating retribution.[44] The reality is that only a tiny handful of women who survive sexual assault report it, that even fewer press charges, that an even tinier fraction of these charges lead to convictions, and that even fewer women still take the law into their own hands and avenge the wrong done to them.[45]

"Men's rights" activists and other organized misogynists, such as those who made up a strong phalanx of Trump and Bannon's conquering army, feel that men have been stripped of agency by a vindictive if nebulous feminist conspiracy. These perspectives are often fueled by some notion that modern men have been "cuckolded" by obedience to conventional norms of civility and morality, and that this is leading both to men's suffering and the breakdown of a naturally patriarchal society.[46] The antidote is an iconoclastic individualism marked by purposefully offensive speech and action, even by men who don't fit the conventional "alpha male" stereotype.

But as Leigh Claire La Berge notes, this dream of a renegade, self-made masculinity that operates outside the laws and conventions of society because of a kind of meta-knowingness is the product of political-economic shifts, notably toward financialization, and has been lionized in films and literature that celebrate ruthless, violent financiers such as Martin Scorsese's *Wolf of Wall Street*, or, indeed, *The Art of the Deal* by Donald Trump.[47]

The reactionary male hysteria that imagines that feminists control nearly every social institution and are coordinating the elimination of "traditional" masculinity is the direct descendant of the witch hunts of

Bacon's time. Like those horrific events, "women" are endowed with secret supernatural powers to cause dangerous effects well beyond the limits of their individual words or bodies, are presumed to be meeting and conspiring, and are ultimately blamed for social and economic conditions that are, in fact, authored by capitalism and social elites, almost all of them men. As with the witch hunts, the spectacle of a "public revenge" is legitimated in the name of avenging all the "private" revenges women have allegedly taken on men. As with the witch hunts, this spectacle takes place in the open, today on social media or in YouTube comments, or through doxxing (the making-public of private or personal information), or through revenge porn and the like.

These personal attacks on particular women are these pornographics of patriarchal revenge, whether they contain "erotic" images or not. They are merely iterations of a kind of sadistic genre of media that, in another form, is manifested in the dog-whistle, click-bait sensationalism of the right-wing outrage machine.[48] Bannon perfected this genre during his time as editor of Breitbart and which he brought to Trump's run for the White House. In what is surely the height of irony, one of the favorite themes of such stories is the so-called witch hunts allegedly orchestrated by feminists against courageous men who dare overcome "censorship" and exercise their "free speech" about gender or race relations.

All this in a context when, as we have already observed, the undeniable reality of actually existing lethal revenge around the world is the preponderance of women killed by intimate partners or family members for alleged betrayal, dishonor or disobedience.[49]

THE RADICAL SPIRITS OF HATRED AND SACRIFICE

Trump and Bannon's victory can be attributed to many factors. For the moment, I rather want to focus on the way that liberal forces, in their pathological moderation, ceded vital ground. Here, as ever, Walter Benjamin's fateful *Theses on the Philosophy of History*, his last major work before his tragic death, is instructive. Writing of the tragic reversals of the Weimar Period, which began with Germany on the brink of a Communist revolution (led by the Sparticists Rosa Luxemburg and Karl Liebnicht, who were assassinated on the orders of the more moderate Social Democrats) and ended with the ascendency of the Nazis, Benjamin observed that:

> In Marx the proletariat appears as the last enslaved class, as the avenger that completes the task of liberation in the name of generations of the downtrodden. This conviction, which had a brief

resurgence in the Spartacist group, has always been objectionable to Social Democrats. Within three decades they managed virtually to erase the name of Blanqui, though it had been the rallying sound that had reverberated through the preceding century. Social Democracy thought it fit to assign to the working class the role of the redeemer of future generations, in this way cutting the sinews of its greatest strength. This training made the working class forget both its hatred and its spirit of sacrifice, for both are nourished by the image of enslaved ancestors rather than that of liberated grandchildren.[50]

Benjamin here aims at a properly materialist theory of revenge: for Marx, a transformative revenge is the task of the industrial proletariat who have the historically unique possibility of avenging not only the crimes enacted upon them, but the crimes of capitalist history leading up to the present. Their capacity to elevate revenge from isolated acts of violence to a transformative, truly revolutionary *movement* stems from their unique structural and systemic position as, we might say, the necessary targets of truly *capitalist* vengeance, which is to say that the violence they endured was endemic (rather than incidental) to the economic logic of the system itself. Thus, the "sinews of their greatest strength" are not only strategy, organization and ideology, they are also hatred and a spirit of sacrifice, which stem from taking up the task of avenging their "enslaved" ancestors.

When, instead, Social Democrats insist the proletariat are solely the redeemers of *future* generations, they actually prepare them to adopt fascism. As Benjamin writes, elsewhere, the problem with the Social Democratic concept of progress was that it

> bypasses the question of how [the] products [of proletarian labour] might benefit the workers while still not being at their disposal. It recognizes only the progress in the mastery of nature, not the retrogression of society; [as such] it already displays the technocratic features later encountered in Fascism.

Here, the Social Democratic focus on a boundless, universal, technocratic future, unfolding with the gradual, peaceful and harmonious evolution of society into socialism. This tragically but predictably handed fascism its torch. The fascist claim was two-fold: first that they, rather than the Social Democrats or communists, could bring about the real culmination of progress through racial purification; second, that they could do so by purging the body politic of racial and ideological burdens that were posed as the real cause of proletarian oppression.

It might be argued that, for Benjamin, fascist revanchism thrived where socialism capitulated to bourgeois morality and, in their fashion, eschewed and defamed vengeance. The German Social Democrats had, in abolishing the legacy of Blanqui and literally ordering the murders of the Spartacist leadership, monopolized the discursive field and championed a notion of a peaceful, orderly and formal-democratic transition to socialism, banishing the specter of vengeance to the margins where fascists found it, befriended it, and claimed its power.

To offer an oversimplified formulation: capitalism, like all systems of domination, is held together through a kind of normalized vengefulness, which is mystified as law, tradition, economic necessity, or justice. Within this order, the dreams and demands of the oppressed brew, but are denied full articulation or expression except when they are publicly decried as heinous, vengeful fantasies and as evidence that the powerful must exercise vigilance and vengeance to keep them in check. As this moral and economic cracks in the heat of its own inherent contradictions and crises, those dreams of a kind of unimaginable justice seep to the surface. Yet those dreams are much more easily harnessed, mobilized and preyed upon by reactionary forces that would ultimately entrench oppression by offering the oppressed vengeful expression and release against disposable targets, rather than by revolutionaries who would truly overturn the ruling order.

Echoing Benjamin, Franco "Bifo" Berardi has written of our present moment of Trump, Brexit and the rise of revanchist fundamentalisms around the world, that, in the past:

> The workers' movement defended the existing composition and occupation of labour, so that technology appeared as an enemy of the workers. Capital took hold of technology in order to increase exploitation and to submit the wellbeing of society to a now-useless labour. All the world's governments preached the need to work more, precisely when the moment was ripe to organise the break out of the regime of waged labour [and] transfer human time from the sphere of rendering service to the sphere of care for the self. The effect was an enormous stress overload, and an impoverishment of society. With workers no longer needed, labour was cheapened. It cost ever less, and became ever more precarious and wretched. Workers tried, by way of democracy, to stop the liberal laissez-faire offensive. But they only got a measure of the impotence of democracy... Ultimately the workers became enraged. The result was that the impotence took revenge, and is today overturning the liberal order. This is the revenge of those whom neo-liberalism has denied the joy of life. Of

those who are compelled to work ever more and to earn ever less, deprived of the time to enjoy life and to know of the tenderness of other human beings in a non-competitive condition, deprived of access to knowledge, compelled to turn to the media agencies that propagate ignorance, and finally, convinced through ignorance that their enemy is the people who are even more impotent than they.[51]

While the language of impotence here recalls the discussion of gender above, it also signals a broader crisis of power in general. If to some extent modern colonial forms of government elevate the state to the former role of God, the monopolist of the legitimate exercise of vengeance, what do we make of a moment when transnational capital seizes this power directly and submits the state itself, as well as workers and other people, to its needless, warrantless vengeance?

FINANCIALIZED REVANCHISM

Bifo, like Benjamin, provides an acute Marxian cultural and political analysis for how fascism seizes on and produces a revenge politics to sustain capitalist exploitation, even if it means the most heinous atrocities, even if it means the suspension or recalibration of capitalism away from free markets, globalization, and competition and toward corporatism, ultra-nationalism, and monopoly. Even, indeed, if it means the material nihilism of war, genocide and ecological catastrophe.

But how could a theory of revenge become truly materialist, which is to say, see revenge as both the product of, and at the same time necessary to, the contradictory structural economics of capitalism?

Marxist geographer Neil Smith has recuperated the notion of revanchism to describe the way:

> The 1990s witnessed the emergence of what we can think of as the revanchist city ... Severe economic crisis and governmental retraction were emulsified by a visceral reaction in the public discourse against the liberalism of the post-1960s period and an all-out attack on the social policy structure that emanated from the New Deal and the immediate postwar era ... Revenge against minorities, the working class, women, environmental legislation, gays and lesbians, immigrants became the increasingly common denominator of public discourse.[52]

Importantly, for Smith, revanchism names not only a vindictive political *affect*, but also a structural *economic process*:

By the 1970s gentrification was clearly becoming an integral residential thread in a much larger urban restructuring. As many urban economies in the advanced capitalist world experienced the dramatic loss of manufacturing jobs and a parallel increase in producer services, professional employment and the expansion of so-called "FIRE" employment (Finance, Insurance, Real Estate) their whole urban geography underwent a concomitant restructuring.

It is a by-now familiar story: as profits dwindled in the post-war period due to the appeal of speculation in the finance, insurance and real estate sectors soared. In that period, the unique culture of the city, which was forged at the intersections of racialized, migrant, queer, and working class struggle, was appropriated and transformed by capital into a noxious tourist-oriented gimmick and a wide variety of legal and quasi-legal techniques were mobilized to accelerate a process of "urban renewal," lately known as gentrification.[53] Vast increases in the budget for punitive policing were justified through recourse to racialized invective that posed the "law-abiding" (read: white) citizens as victims of their own generosity and tolerance toward misbehaving if not racialized others.[54] This legitimated urban enclosures on a massive scale, aimed at feeding a speculative real estate bubble that still has not really burst. Lest we forget, it was from this toxic mess of smash-and-grab capitalism and white-supremacist fear and loathing that Donald Trump's fortune and persona emerged.[55]

So, for Smith, revanchism in a sense names both the spirit of reactionary urban planning and also the logic of what we can call financialized, neoliberal racial capital. In terms of that logic, we might say, drawing on the frames provided by Smith's colleague David Harvey, a new combination of the beginning and the end of capital's accumulation cycle: raw accumulation by dispossession on one end, crisis-ridden financial speculation on the other.[56] In the first place, cities built – literally and figuratively, materially and culturally – by the collaborative, cooperative labors of citizens are expropriated from those citizens thanks to increased housing costs; on the other, this stripping is facilitated by, and helps reproduce, finance capital. Revanchism can describe a particular character or tenor of capitalist accumulation at the zenith of an accumulation cycle, a moment that Giovanni Arrighi has identified with "late capitalism," when, as Fredric Jameson makes clear, culture is integrated and implicated directly in the reproduction of capitalism not merely as superstructure but as a central element.[57]

According to Costas Lapavitsas, financialization names the process and period when the capitalist economy encounters accelerating paroxysms of crisis as the gap grows and grows between the production of actual surplus value (represented in the formula M-C-M') and the much more rapid growth of financial wealth (represented in the formula M-M').[58] Harvey, elucidating Marx as well as Rosa Luxemburg, illustrates that various facets of capital desperately seek to close this gap, a gap I have elsewhere insisted is at least in part a gap in the imagination itself:[59] employers squeeze more from workers; resource-extractive corporations scour the earth for more wealth; non- or semi-capitalist communities are torn apart or thrown into the market; retailers seek to accelerate consumerism (often by expanding consumer debt); financiers seek to offload bad debts onto one another, dupes or the state; states themselves compete to see who will be made to pay.[60] These and renewed tendencies toward imperialism, war, authoritarianism, and untold human cruelty, might be framed as *the structurally necessary forms of revenge* wreaked by a stricken capital shot through with speculative adrenaline and merciless contradictions.

CRYPT

It is vital now to highlight how central race and racism are to the politics of revenge and the economics of revanchism. Smith is unequivocally clear that this tendency, as it was expressed in New York City and throughout the United States, both drew on and reinforced racist tropes and structures for its lifeblood. Urban revanchism was squarely aimed at racialized populations who were accused of exploiting and abusing white benevolence and ruining the city with lawlessness, laziness, and barbarism. The financiers who drove this process forward were almost exclusively white, as were the politicians and judicial officials who superintended it. Thus, a new chapter of the long dark saga of the dispossession of people of color under American capitalism was added, with its victims once again cast as villains.[61]

Yet this chapter echoed its predecessors. James Baldwin, among others, has pointed out that fantasies of Black vengeance have long defined the stunted political imagination of white America,[62] blossoming into an appetite for revanchist anti-Black violence, whether enacted by police or lynch-mobs. Angela Davis, Ruth Gilmore and Michele Alexander have all traced the way the American system of mass incarceration – like the firearms industry, municipal police forces and white-supremacist organizations – was built in the wake of the Civil War and Emancipation in part to assuage the paranoia of whites regarding Black vengeance.[63] Indeed, as Saidiya Hartman argues and illustrates, the white fantasy of Black vengeance necessitated the creation of a sadistic regime of legal and extrajudicial terror which, not coincidentally, served as the means to discipline and further exploit Black labor as well, what we might term a kind of preemptive revanchism.[64]

As Gilmore and Davis argue, the purpose of mass incarceration was also the continued devaluation of Black lives and Black labor necessary for the perpetuation of American capitalist accumulation and the management of surplussed populations. Others, including David Roediger and Theodore Allen, have understood these institutions as central to the psychic and material wages of whiteness that have conscripted white proletarians to a fidelity to white capital.[65] It's not simply that the current regime of mass incarceration fails to produce rehabilitation or reduce crime: it was never intended to do so. Beyond offering a politically expedient spectacle of retributive justice the American prison continues to be a vehicle for capitalist accumulation through the jobs it provides, the privatization or semi-privatization of services, and the cheapening of labor within and beyond its walls. Once again, preemptive racialized revenge is the bedrock on which the economy is built.

For this reason, Loïc Wacquant has drawn on Smith's notion of revanchism to frame what he calls hyper-incarceration, preferring the term for its ability to pinpoint that system's specific targeting of poor Black ghettoized men and for its ability to name a system that encompasses not only prisons but also the policing and court system, the parole and bond system, and the massive prison-labor and para-punishment industries, all of which he argues have been absolutely central to the financialized, neoliberal movement of capitalist accumulation in the post-Civil Rights era.[66] For Wacquant, we might say, revanchism here names a political affect *and* an economic structure: on the one hand it animates the racist antipathy that justifies the ruinous expansion of what he calls the penal-state, the self-destructive form of extreme neoliberalism that answers the crisis of care and social welfare it has created itself by spending more and more on prisons; on the other, revanchism speaks to this seemingly irrational, punitive, and ultimately self-destructive urge within the logic of capitalist accumulation.

The prison here is the grim crypt of white-supremacist capitalism. It is a means of encrypting speculative capital in the carceral institution.[67] As the prison becomes a (perhaps *the*) central institution of racial capitalism, it also encrypts, at the center of that system, a zone of endless revenge.[68] In prisons, absent the heroic solidarity of inmates, we are led to imagine that the monetary or moral economy is replaced by an economy of revenge wherein one's status and ability to avoid premature death as a captive becomes dependent on one's ability to threaten vengeance against potential abusers (guards and other inmates). The hyper-exploitation of the image of the prison and prisoner in popular culture relies precisely on projecting a racialized spectacle of vengeance that mirrors, in extreme form, the hidden broader economy of revenge capitalism. These dungeons of endless racialized, financialized vengeance, which obviously have nothing to do with public safety or rehabilitation, are the sacrificial altars of American revenge capitalism and they burn bright in the public imagination, to some as warnings, to some as beacons.

ENDLESS ENDGAME

And now vengeance has come calling with the absolute and systematic dismantling of seemingly any and all social welfare provisions of the nation-state, with a near-complete deregulation of capital except for those regulations that serve the purposes of a radical economic nationalism and that punish and avenge themselves against already-oppressed people: the explosion of private prisons, the paramilitarization of policing against Black and racialized communities, mass deportations, internments of death en route, attacks on reproductive rights, the list goes on and on.

As Aimé Césaire pointed out decades ago now, the rise of fascism in Europe ought rightly to be seen as the visitation on the white metropoles of the kinds of cruelty and degradation once reserved solely for the racialized colonies.[69] Colonialism, he argued, rotted out the very soul of Europe such that something like fascism could grow. Today too we are witnessing the revenge of the repressed, the fascistic riptide of history where the forms of systemic revenge (debt, incarceration, disposability) once shrugged off as the regrettable but necessary cost of the advance of liberal global capitalism are now emerging everywhere. The particular sadistic *jouissance* of the fascist imaginary is with us too. The popular notion that those who suffer "get what's coming to them" – for failing to obey the border, for enacting criminalized activities to survive, for taking drugs to numb the pain – should alert us to the way revanchism has always been a means to at once conscript and dehumanize, just as it was for poor American whites grinning at a lynching, or the men who jeered at the witch on the pyre, or the buffoonish guards at Abu Ghraib.

Yet let us not lose sight of the structural dimensions here. Naomi Klein, for one, has noted that the corporate backers (and now many of the senior cabinet ministers) of the Trump administration rightly feared the growing global discontent that followed the 2008 financial crisis, as well as the growing climate justice movement.[70] While we should not downplay the deep and rancorous splits between capitalist actors today, we can also, along with Yanis Varoufakis and others, note an emerging alliance between global ultranationalists, not coincidentally brought together by Bannon.[71] Disturbingly, we are also seeing a growing tolerance for their ideas by capitalists who, in spite of perhaps preferring the older neoliberal globalization (and its more palatable debonair Davos political class), aim to turn the situation to their advantage. Other capitalists, notably those associated with Silicon Valley, see Trump and his ilk as dark angels of disruptive innovation, willing to let the boys have their fun with artificial intelligence, cybernetics, automation and geoengineering without any meaningful public oversight – or perhaps more accurately because the panoptic disciplinary power of finance has rendered itself the supreme and unrivaled form of "public" oversight.[72]

These are all the contradictions of capital come to a head. Without parsing them too deeply, I would offer the formulation that, at a certain climax in the accumulation cycle, capitalism's inherent vengefulness emerges naked and, as ever, "dripping from head to foot, from every pore, with blood and dirt."[73]

Capitalism's vengefulness here is not merely an anthropomorphic metaphor. Capitalism's whole history has been a saga of vindictive acts perpetrated against those on whom it depends for its lifeblood: proletarians, including – indeed especially – those excluded from waged work and made "surplus."[74] It has constantly and persistently awakened and harnessed the revanchist dreams and fantasies of the oppressed and exploited to turn them against one another. And it has constantly defamed notions of proletarian and anti-colonial vengeance as subhuman, animalistic and degraded as a means to silence and quell righteous fury.

Yet now, at a moment of its own massive, unassuageable crisis, capital doesn't just turn to revenge politics to save itself, it also reveals its true vengeful nature. It is not only on a metaphorical level that this undead thing, capital – this horrific manifestation of dead-labor that is ontologically dependent on the vitality of its adversary, living labor – is driven by a Nietzschean *ressentiment*.[75] It is also that late, financialized capitalism is so desperate to sustain itself through its manifold and fatal contradictions it turns to the worst forms of vindictive cruelty to support itself in its madness. Hyper-incarceration, gentrification, the debt crisis, the ecological crises: all of these are forms of capitalist vengeance that are, in fact, cancerous to and unsustainable within capital itself (see Chapter 5). Yet they accelerate thanks to the inherent momentum of the system, driven as it is by no single rational conductor, but by a million individual acts of capitalist competition. As ever, the only way for capitalism to save itself from itself in situations such as these, as Rosa Luxemburg taught us, is to entrust itself to the care of authoritarianism or the cleansing fires of inter-imperialist warfare.[76]

FANON OF THE WHITES?

For this reason right-wing (though anti-Trump) *New York Times* commentator David Brooks might well have accidentally stumbled onto something worthwhile when he posited in a post-election column that "Steve Bannon is the Frantz Fanon of the whites."[77] Such a statement goes well beyond Brooks' lackluster intent, which is to trod the well-worn ground of castigating campus intersectionalist privilege politics and bemoan a culture of exploitative victimhood. Offering Bannon as the Fanon of whites might suggest that he is their theorist of political revenge. Or more accurately, Bannon *wishes* to be the Fanon of whiteness.

Fanon, famously, provided a philosophical, moral, and political rationale for anti-colonial revolt, and for violence as a means to achieve national liberation. This is all within a context, of course, where colonial regimes' claims to legitimacy were often based on their "benevolent" gift of the so-called "rule of law" to Indigenous and colonized populations, which allegedly replaced what colonists imagined was a prehistory of endless, limitless vengeance. Not only did such an assumption erase the complex legal, juridical and diplomatic structures that predated their arrival, it also disguised and normalized the inherent, structural and extremely brutal vengefulness and impunity of individual colonists and the colonial systems as a whole.

These colonial notions operate still, even in allegedly post-colonial times, in for instance the mythscape of endless, limitless atavistic vengeance woven around the image of the racialized gang in the (highly profitable) American media. Another example is the fantasy of the "failed state" where, in the absence of Western institutions, racialized populations "regress" into an economy of limitless and self-perpetuating vengeance. Such myths serve to disguise and normalize the inherent, structural, and extremely brutal vengefulness of the police or neocolonial systems as a whole. In a sense, colonialism was and is always already the "public revenge" of whiteness for a crime or infraction never committed but endlessly fantasized about. Bannon, then, is more Bacon than Fanon.

Fanon, for similar reasons to Marx and Engels, is distrustful of revenge. He offers the following: "Racialism and hatred and resentment – a 'legitimate desire for revenge' – cannot sustain a war of liberation …

hatred alone cannot draw up a program."[78] Revenge here is legitimate, but not strategic – it is not morally wrong but rather insufficient for generating a movement of liberation that can sustain itself. For Fanon, revenge is generally presented as a base, reactionary emotion that motivates understandable but ultimately unstrategic actions. For instance, he speaks about the almost spiritual dimension of public anti-colonial violence, or about the sense of revenge germane to the sexual fantasies of race. But these alone cannot sustain a movement, and indeed imperil it.

On another level, Fanon's whole oeuvre is a theory of *avenging* in the more systemic and structural fashion I have been aiming at here. Just as Marx wrote *Capital* to put a weapon of righteous, patient, and slow *avenging* in the hands of proletarians, so too is Fanon's *Wretched of the Earth* a guide to how to avenge the brutality of a system of colonialism that has been built around racist colonial revanchism and, as such, built to withstand and indeed incorporate small and petty individual acts of revenge.

Glen Coulthard, for one, has revisited both Fanon and Marx for clues as to how to think about Indigenous resistance and resurgence in "North America" in a moment when, on the one hand, settler colonies like Canada encourage a politics of reconciliation and, on the other, the conditions of genocidal colonial usurpation persist for Indigenous people, in deadly form.[79] For Coulthard, as for many anti-colonial thinkers before him, Fanon holds the seeds for a refusal of recognition, the power to collectively reject inclusion within a system of slow death and subjugation. At stake for Coulthard is not simply a revenge fantasy but a broader, wider notion of revenge based in an autonomous Indigenous resurgence.

Here we may be coming closer to a notion of vengeance worthy of our dreams, one that would surpass the castigation of revenge as a brutish, reactionary emotion that we inherit from Francis Bacon and a long line of ruling class white philosophers, whose secret work, we have seen, has been to hide the logic of vengeance at the very heart of the system that has privileged them.

THE PROFITS OF FORGIVENESS

I want to briefly distinguish this notion of anti-capitalist and anti-colonial avenging from a politics of anti-vengeance orchestrated by the powerful using the horrifically reanimated corpses of three revolutionary leaders: Mahatma Gandhi, Martin Luther King Jr. and Nelson Mandela. I will not here go into detail regarding the way their own thinking, writing and action in life, grounded in anti-colonial traditions, contradicts the way their likenesses have today become the puppets for a spectacle of bleached reconcilophelia.

Rather, I want simply to note that these figures have been press-ganged into service as Disneyfied "profits of forgiveness," trotted out to admonish those who dare dream dangerously.[80] Each, of course, had a complex (and sometimes problematic) theory of revenge and, importantly, a *strategic* argument for forgiveness or nonviolence.[81] Yet that strategic dimension has been paved over by a parking lot of cheap moralism that, until recently, served to once again reify and reinforce the dominant castigation of the revenge of the oppressed as subhuman and to, at the same time, disguise and naturalize the constant, unrelenting vengeance of the powerful.

This compulsory ideology of forgiveness has smothered the radical imagination, insisting on a saccharine, demobilizing affect that, to draw upon Benjamin, has cut the sinews of our greatest strength. As Jacques Derrida argues, the contemporary politics forgiveness risks fortifying and legitimizing the neoliberal global order by assuming it represents a kind of "normal" or equilibrium to which we can and should return.[82] What it hides, he argues, is that this order, like all orders, is founded in and perpetuated by violence, including what I have here been calling the systemic vengeance of racial capitalism.

To return to Fanon, the signature maneuver of the oppressor has always been to blame the oppressed for the dissonance between the propounded ideology of normalcy and the actuality of constant oppressive violence, to insist that it is the oppressed who are responsible for the turmoil of their lives, and to render anti-colonial violence, rather than colonialism itself, barbaric. Perhaps it is only through a rekindling of a generative and revolutionary notion of avenging that this trap can be escaped.

In contrast to the gruesome spectacle where the corpses of the three profits of forgiveness are made to dance for the pleasure of the oppressor, what Fanon teaches us is that vengeance means more than just acts of violence; it means a rejection of the oppressors' and exploiters' thought-world and stunted, narcissistic moral universe.

DIG TWO GRAVES

I am, of course, all too worried about the way vengeance can become an all-consuming passion, one that hollows us out from the inside, leaving nothing but retaliatory momentum. The adage attributed to Confucius, that "if you set out for revenge, first dig two graves," is apt. As James

Baldwin poetically put it in a fascinating treatment of the cinematic interface of race and revenge, "revenge is a human dream." Upon its successful culmination "there is no way of conveying to the corpse the reasons you have made him one – you have the corpse, and you are, thereafter, at the mercy of a fact which missed the truth, which means that the corpse has you."[83] To live for vengeance in this way is to be already dead, to be in the hands of the dead, or to be in one's own dead hands.

Two graves, then, lie agape, their bodies missing, condemned to lead an endless, sleepless afterlife.

But as Baldwin equally makes clear, being compelled to constantly swallow one's revenge, to witness and endure the vengeance of a system upon you and those you love and be unable to answer the debt, is equally (if not more) catastrophic. It, too, rots one from the inside out. Revenge will find its expression whether we admit it or not; as the title of his meditation of the subject insists, *The Devil Finds Work*.

How then, might the Confucian adage be reinterpreted and how might a private revenge fantasy be transmuted into a common *avenging imaginary*? Perhaps one digs two graves because revenge is the "negation of the negation": and at its close both negations will be surpassed. In avenging the crimes and cruelties of a vengeful system, one aims at a form of radical transformation of both society and the subject. Are we not foretold as the system's gravediggers? Today, capital keeps both graves empty: its own because it continues to lead its parasitic undeath; ours because we are its source of horrific nutrition and reproduction, kept alive only to feed its endless hunger.

Avenging in this sense is also a politically radical self-annihilation and overcoming, and what comes after is unknown and unknowable. The avenging hero cannot imagine what we will become after they walk into the sunset, their all-consuming, seemingly hopeless quest concluded. In this sense, avenging (in contrast to revenge) is not simply some dark, pathological base desire but, rather, an act of faith in ourselves, or more accurately what we might become, together, after …

So it may be true that, as has been so often said, living well is the best revenge. But even the privileged among us cannot truly live well under capitalism, colonialism, white supremacy and patriarchy. To live well, these revenge systems must necessarily be abolished. The practices of abolition, including land and resource reclamations, including protests and poetry and so-called riots, including the forging of new relations for care and the salvaging of suppressed traditions, will be castigated by the beneficiaries of those revenge systems and their mercenary intellectuals as mere revenge politics.

Interlude: Shylock's vindication, or Venice's bonds?

Figure 1 A Venetian Ducat minted between 1400 and 1413. Image in the public domain.

I

In the climatic court scene of *The Merchant of Venice*, the villainous Jewish money-lender, Shylock, demands the honoring of his contract with the racist merchant Antonio and the pound of the latter's flesh to which he is entitled in case of non-payment. Shylock has lent Antonio the funds on the assurance of the returns on the latter's investments in colonial trading voyages so that Antonio, in turn, could give the money to his crony Bassanio, who needs it to seduce the wealthy heiress Portia. But Antonio's ships are said to be ruined at sea and he is bankrupt. While Shylock and Antonio appeared, earlier in the play, to enter into their macabre debt contract as a joke, Shylock is now adamant: he will have his bond.

In its name, Shylock appeals to the presiding Duke of Venice, reminding him that failure to enforce contracts, no matter how odious, will result in the delegitimation of his sovereignty and ruin the Venetian Duchy's international reputation as a safe harbor for honest trade. Merchants cannot operate where their contracts will not be honored and in Venice the laws of the Duke protect even foreigners, including Jews who, in spite of having been in the city for centuries and being a key reason for its international commercial success, can never become citizens.

But as the case unfolds it is revealed that Shylock's concern for the law and the good of Venice is a ruse: he has always been out for revenge against his nemesis Antonio, the leader of an elite gang of racist bullies who subjected Shylock and other Jews of Venice to relentless physical and social abuses. More recently, another member of Antonio's gang seduced and eloped with the widower Shylock's only daughter, who took with her his worldly wealth. Shylock's demanded pound of flesh, then, can be read as the settlement of unpayable debt within a reigning racist order, a kind of cruel parody of the revenge he and other Jewish people in Venice have been made to suffer by the exalted Antonio and his gang without any recourse for years, perhaps generations. The sacred contract is revealed to be the monstrous license of vengeful violence.[1]

But thus it has always been: after all, so long as Antonio and other merchants abided by the rule of the contract and didn't interfere in lawful trade, they could brutalize the Jews as much as they liked up until that day. The Jews were, after all, subordinate foreigners in all ways except their equality under contract law. Shylock's revenge seems immanent: just as the law protects commercial but not human rights, so too will that law now protect Shylock's gruesome commercial bond, and Antonio, the exalted subject of Venice, will be its human sacrifice.[2]

II

Then, as only Shakespeare can do, the world is turned upside down. As Shylock sharpens his knife to close the contract once and for all, Portia, disguised as a young lawyer, turns the case. The contract, she argues, never specified that Shylock was allowed to spill Antonio's *blood*, only to remove his *flesh*. Shylock's revenge is thwarted by a loophole in the very contract in which it was guaranteed.

Of course, the reason one has human judges in the first place is to prevent loopholes like these from sinking a case, to uphold not only the letter but also the spirit of the law. That the Duke seems to accept Portia's strange argument as legally reasonable reveals that the order of the contract, though it claims to be impartial, is always a matter of interpretation of those tasked with enforcement. For instance, while many Indigenous groups around the world signed treaties with colonial powers in good faith, or in the hopes of forestalling domination and destruction, when those powers used their military might to declare the sole right to interpret those contracts (for instance to rule on land rights in their own courts) the truth of the situation revealed itself.[3] Likewise, when colonial powers disliked the laws of the land where they were trading they ignored them and declared the enforcement of laws by local governors to be acts of aggression, necessarily to be answered by "punitive" expeditions in the name of "civilizing" the Other (see Chapter 4).

Back in Shakespeare's imagined Venice, Portia's upending of Shylock's ability to enforce his bond, to claim his debt, is followed by the accusation that the Jew, knife in hand, is an attempted murderer: a heathen foreigner who has plotted to spill the blood of a respected Christian citizen. The court now takes its vengeance on Shylock who, to the jeers and insults of his abusers, is given the choice between either death or being stripped of his wealth and converting to Christianity to become a servant of Antonio. That the court case does not simply end at the nullification of Shylock's revenge but concludes with the humiliating legal vengeance of the Venetian state is very revealing. Recall that Shylock's fantasies of revenge are spurred in the first place by the experience of what we would today call systemic and institutional racism, by a kind of unacknowledged vengefulness of the racially-privileged subjects (Venetian citizens) on the Jews. Perhaps the Venetian Christians (and Shakespeare's audience) considered this legitimate revenge based on the idea that Jews are collectively and eternally responsible for the murder of their Messiah, Jesus, 1,400 years prior.[4] Whatever the case, in the narrative arc and racist logic of the play the only revenge that is named and condemned as such is the villain Shylock's stymied scheme. The *economy* of revenge that led to this moment and the vengefulness of the state itself in his "punishment" is presented as natural and indeed celebrated: the play is, after all, a comedy, not a tragedy.

III

Shylock's (thwarted) revenge could also be seen as a kind of revolutionary threat. From the perspective of the oppressor, Shylock's attempt to use Venetian law to murder an upstanding citizen might today be seen as a reactionary warning against tolerance and multiculturalism: these savage people may smile at you on the street, lend you money, buy your wares, but secretly they are irrationally vengeful.[5] Thus the colonizer has always been the colonized, the slave-owner the slave. Paranoia about the revenge fantasies of the oppressed other come to justify their surveillance, policing, murder, and expulsion.[6] Today, the far-right in "the West" is obsessed with the idea that Muslims are infiltrating "Western" countries to take revenge for the defeat of the Ottoman Empire, the Sykes-Picot line, or the Reconquista of Al-Andulus, either through acts of terrorism or through a cultural and reproductive war culminating in the imposition of Sharia Law. Take revenge on them now, before they can take revenge.[7]

But if Shylock is a figure of the vengefulness of the untrustworthy internalized outsider (who is the victim of an unspoken but chronic vengeance) then he is also, in a strange way, a figure of something I will theorize as *avenging*, the kind of transformative power of collective liberation that aims to collect a moral debt that not only goes unpaid within the dominant order, but which actually cannot be paid within that order. Shylock is offered the money Antonio owes him many times over, more than enough to make him one of the richest men in Venice. He wants not the money, but his bond. He wants the flesh. He doesn't want a justice that will balance the Duke's scales but one that will obliterates the oppressor, Antonio. Shylock as a character is odious, petty, vain, self-centered, obsessive, and vindictive. Shylock as a revolutionary figure is glorious. There is not enough money in Venice to satisfy the debts that are owed him; after all, the wealth of Venice depended on him and other Jews acting as moneylenders, merchants, and intermediaries. They made Venice rich and he, through Venice's own laws, will bring it down, forcing the Duke to accede to the brutal murder of this favorite son of the city right in his own court. The scales will not be balanced: they were never balanced to begin with, they were always tipped in the favor of the dominators. The scales will be destroyed.

2

The work of art in an age of unpayable debts

Social reproduction, geopolitics, and settler colonialism

Debt's origins come from colonialism's origins. Those who lend us money are those who colonized us. They are the same ones who used to manage our states and economies. These are the colonizers who indebted Africa through their brothers and cousins, who were the lenders. We had no connections with this debt. Therefore we cannot pay for it … Under its current form, controlled and dominated by imperialism, debt is a skillfully managed reconquest of Africa, intended to subjugate its growth and development through foreign rules. Thus, each one of us becomes the financial slave, which is to say a true slave, of those who had been treacherous enough to put money in our countries with obligations for us to repay. We are told to repay, but it is not a moral issue. It is not about this so-called honor of repaying or not …. We cannot repay because we don't have any means to do so. We cannot pay because we are not responsible for this debt. We cannot repay but the others owe us what the greatest wealth could never repay, that is blood debt. Our blood has flowed.

Thomas Sankara [1]

This chapter provides a reading and a contextualization of three recent performative public artworks to map the way unpayable debts manifest across politics, economics, culture, and society under the global order of financialized capitalism today. By unpayable debts I have two tendencies in mind. On the one hand, debts from above: the proliferation of punitive and vindictive financial debts that cannot be repaid that characterize what I am calling revenge capitalism; on the other, debts from below: the subterranean, collective moral or political debts of history (for colonialism, slavery, and structural violence) that, though they are not honored by the institutions of revenge capitalism, can offer catalysts for the radical imagination.[2]

I. AN EMPIRE OF UNPAYABLE DEBTS

There is a long and noble history of scholarship, mostly in the field of anthropology, that links revenge to debt.[3] Indeed, according to one key strand of anthropological thought, debt (and, by extension, money) is ultimately a kind of institutionalization of revenge, emblematized in the shared etymological root of "pay" and "pacify."[4] This argument, broadly speaking, suggests that, in order to avoid succumbing to cycles of endless, socially destructive vengeance, early societies agree (formally or informally) on various forms of material and immaterial reparation for the infractions and harms of individuals, ranging from compensation in special commodities to blood sacrifices. The idea here is that, if something is taken from one party, something of equivalent value must be returned, materially or symbolically.

But as David Graeber makes clear, this anthropological commonplace theory deserves a great deal of scrutiny.[5] Like the bucolic story of the origins of money in barter (explored in Chapter 3), this tale of debt misses both the profound creativity of people and societies and also the reality of deep power imbalances. Ultimately, Graeber's overarching argument is that debt (and money) don't emerge naturally from some neutral mechanism to hold society together; they emerge from power and coercion. Rather than money being a neutral human tool that then inequitably accumulates in the pockets of some rather than others, money and debt were "invented," so to speak, in order to normalize, legitimize, and facilitate power. My argument about revenge is very similar.

We would be led to imagine that revenge is a base and almost animalistic attempt to settle scores, to deliver justice, to compensate the afflicted. Without government, order, authority, and the law, this bloody birthright arises and consumes individuals and societies as cycles of vengeance accelerate to apocalyptic proportions.[6] Thus, successful societies institute orders that take revenge out of the hands of individuals, families, and clans and, instead, produce common laws, protocols, and spiritual practices that transform vengeance into a kind of debt.

But what if we were to, instead, follow Graeber's line of thinking here (and that of a number of other scholars) and think of those laws, protocols, and spiritual practices that are said to quench the thirst for justice with the tonic of order as instead institutionalizations of power relations, as a kind of normalized, even sacralized vengeance. And what if we were to admit that, following Nietzsche, this revenge emerged and persists to reinforce inequalities, authority, and power relations?[7]

Such a universalizing thesis is best left to the anthropologists and historians. For now, I ask the reader to entertain it as a means to understand our own contemporary world order which is held together, at so many levels, by the vengeful persecution of unpayable debts. Here, I will delineate two forms of unpayable debts: in the first case, unpayable "debts from above" which are imposed by and through power and powerful institutions, intended not to compensate the powerful for some infraction against them or loss on their part, but, ultimately, to keep the debtor in a situation of subjugation. This sort of systemic or structural vengeance-through-debt is normalized, legitimated, and, ultimately, blamed on the debtor.

On the other hand, I wish to propose the radical potential of claiming of unpayable debts from below: turning of the tables on the powerful to insist that the oppressed and exploited are owed debt that, importantly, cannot be repaid in the currency, value paradigm, or legal apparatus of the powerful. This unpayability is rooted in the fact that the currency, value paradigm, or legal apparatus itself was built on and is perpetuated by the vengeful debts that subordinate and ensure the exploitability of the oppressed: it is, in a sense, their own stolen wealth that is now offered back (in bastardized form) as compensation for the theft, always somehow calculated to perpetuate or renovate the conditions of that theft.

Those who would claim unpayable debts from below are at their most radical when they seek reparation or compensation not in the coin minted for their oppression or exploitation, but when they yearn for those systems' abolition and the formation of a new financial, political, and moral economy. While it is not the subject of this chapter *per se*, when the oppressed and exploited do organize to claim the unpayable debts owed to them it is typically labeled by the powerful as extrajudicial revenge or "wild justice," not only a moral abomination but an affront to civilization itself.[8]

Because these topics strike so deeply at the fundamental pillars of our social understandings and norms, and because I intend to track this pattern across a diverse range of examples that go beyond simply monetary debt, I have selected three artworks to be our guide. I have elsewhere argued at length that critical contemporary art can be a particularly useful field to explore in terms of offering new insights into the deeper patterns of financialization: the economic, political, social, and cultural power and normalization of speculative capitalism.[9] This is not because art somehow retains some romantic autonomy from the economy, some privileged and transcendental immunity that offers a purer view of society – quite the opposite. Ever since there has been such a category of "art," as distinct from craft, sacrament, and entertainment (i.e., roughly the seventeenth century), art has been bound up with money, debt, and finance. It's not simply that the patrons of art-*qua*-art have always been financiers, or that the great art capitals of capitalism have always also been financial hubs (Florence, Amsterdam, London, Paris, New York). It's also that we come to understand "art" and define its parameters in the shadow of money or money's power. Art can only be "art" (transcendental, cerebral, virtuous, meaningful, inspiring) in part because it is *not* money (earthly, brutal, venal, banal, and encouraging of turpitude).

Hence the limited autonomy provided to art within capitalism creates the potential for a kind of critical friction. I'm deeply skeptical about art's ability to actually challenge the system in any meaningful way, indeed I have joined others in arguing that art's provocations toward the capitalist system of which it is a part is precisely why it is maintained within that system: such provocations offer that system a means of reflexivity and prompts for adaptation to changing circumstances.[10] Yet at the same time this contradiction can render art, beyond the intentions of any particular artist, a particularly useful tool for helping us understand much broader patterns and processes within capitalism, especially where they intersect "culture," belief, aesthetics and the seemingly irrational.

II. THE ART OF UNPAYABLE DEBTS

Pocket Money Loans^{TM}

North London, circa 2014: a silent war zone.

Once home to a diversity of ethnicities trying to make a living and a life in the capital of the British Empire, gentrification and rampant housing speculation in the neoliberal period have profoundly transformed the social fabric.[11] It is important to see this as one of the ways financialization acts as a mechanism through which capitalism further infiltrates and recalibrates the field of social reproduction. Whereas once capitalism seemed content to exploit the time of workers in the factory for a wage, today the mechanisms of debt, the acceleration of consumerism, the financialization of housing, and the commodification of "service" labor all conspire to make everyday life a field for the exploitation of labor and the extraction of rents, with the metropolitan "global city" as its fulcrum.[12] Nowhere is this more clearly seen than the emergence of the "metropolitan factory," and the way the social fabric of global cities are transformed into zones for speculation and the ratcheting-up of a kind of ambient capitalist discipline.[13] Perhaps the most recognizable geographic symptom of these ills are manifestations of "fringe finance" institutions: payday lenders, check-cashing outfits, pawn shops, and other businesses who prey upon the urgent needs of the poor and so-called "unbanked," who are disproportionately migrants, people of color, and members of the working class squeezed by the financialized recalibration of cities.[14]

For this reason, when a small independent art gallery in North London's rapidly gentrifying neighborhood of Stoke Newington appeared to have been replaced by a new payday loan shop in 2014, it is unlikely anyone paid much attention. Those who did were horrified. With a design palette and cutesy icons reminiscent of children's Saturday morning cartoon advertisements, the boutique offered "Payday loans 4 kids!" at a mere 5,000% annual percentage rate interest. The interior of the gallery/store featured a comically austere environment surrounded by posters encouraging children to take out loans backed by their toy cars, or for a tooth fairy offering "cash 4 teeth," or mortgages on bouncy castles, and "pro-aging cream." "We help you buy the things you can't afford!" reads a speech bubble emanating from a decal of the shop's mascot, a cartoon coin, plastered at toddler-height on the gallery's front door.

Figure 2 Darren Cullen, *Pocket Money Loans*, 2014–2017 (installation at Glastonbury Festival 2016). Image appears courtesy of the artist.

Darren Cullen's offer of "Payday Loans for Kids!" (2014–16) immediately drew harsh criticism from those who, understandably, had been so habituated by the unscrupulousness of the fringe finance industry and the ubiquity of increasingly invasive advertising targeting children that they failed to note the satire (loans to children, while entirely plausible, are illegal in the UK). The artist would receive similar backlash – which he leveraged into widespread media attention – at subsequent iterations of the installation at galleries, exhibitions (including Banksy's widely-visited Dismaland temporary theme park), and outdoor music and performing-arts festivals (including the Glastonbury Festival, the largest such event in the world).

The indebted child

The success of Cullen's projects rests on aiming the double-barreled capitalist threat of extortionate debt and hyper-consumerist marketing at the fetishized figure of the child. Even as early as the mid-nineteenth century, Marx and Engels, writing in the *Communist Manifesto*, derided the cynical way in which bourgeois morality revered the nuclear family and especially the innocence and purity of (middle class, white) children while, at the same time, supporting a capitalist system that conscripted millions of proletarian children to life (and death) in factories or poverty and consigned millions of non-European children to slavery and starvation.[15] A range of theorists of education have noted the way that formal schooling systems inscribe children into capitalism depending on social and class background and expectation.[16] Others including Jack Zipes, Henry Giroux, and bell hooks have noted the educative and indoctrinating character of popular culture in reinforcing class, race, and gender hierarchies.[17] This is to say nothing of advertising itself, which, especially since the widespread adoption of television, targets children explicitly and unrelentingly.[18] More recent theorists, notably Lee Edelman, have identified the way the child under capitalism, and particularly under neoliberal capitalism, becomes the icon of a deeply heteronormative "reproductive futurism" that is used to justify conservative and austere politics today in the name of an endlessly deferred "better tomorrow" for our children.[19] Meanwhile, Zygmunt Bauman, among others, has noted the ways that far-right and reactionary imaginations and movements congeal around real or perceived threats to the child, especially when that child is associated with ethnic, national, or religious ideals, yet ignore systemic and structural threats to children's wellbeing, including poverty.[20]

Leigh Claire La Berge, in her deeply insightful book-length study of financialization, labor, and contemporary social practice (or participatory) art, focuses on the way such artists have engaged with children in the last decades, "employing" children in roles ranging from hairdressers to financial consultants, from creators to destroyers of art.[21] La Berge's overarching argument is that, because children (in the "Global North," at least) are legally prohibited from working for a wage (thanks to generations of working class struggle), their employment by artists is a method to reveal a broader shift in the capitalist economy toward what she terms the increased decommodification of labor: the fashion in which labor which was once waged ceases to be remunerated, even though it remains subject to the discipline of capital. So, for instance, artists themselves increasingly "work for free," or for "exposure," but so too do many aspirants to what were once imagined to be "middle class" jobs: it is common and understood that an un(der)paid internship or zero-hours contract is a necessary (but by no means sure) stepping-stone to a career in journalism, finance, law, or academia, a kind of distended compulsory economic adolescence.

For La Berge, all of these are signals of a deeper shift in capitalism due to financialization, and toward neoliberalism as a policy and a cultural/ideological hegemon. In the same book, she explores the work of artists Cassie Thornton and Thomas Gokey, who have recast debt (specifically student debt) as a medium of creative expression, arguing that, in an era of the decommodification of labor, going into and managing debt becomes a work-like activity. In Cullen's "Pocket Money Loans," the two come together. The hypothetical child borrower works on two fronts, as artist and as debtor.

Innocence and experience

We can observe the play of two unpayable debts in "Pocket Money Loans." On the one hand, the fear and concern evoked by the artwork revolves around the notion that children, who have not yet developed a fully mature neoliberal economic subjectivity, will be scammed into taking out loans to support profligate purchases and enter adulthood with a massive if not unpayable debt. Yet this begs a number of questions. First, arguably the reason we, as a society, forbid children from taking out loans in the first place is because we (rightly) want to protect them from the predation of the market so they might live out their tender years in relative peace. But this high-mindedness does precious little for the 30% of children living in poverty in the UK, a number that has increased with neoliberalism and austerity.[22] Indeed, in a horrendous sort of way, a small loan, repayable in adulthood, might actually facilitate children's access to some elements of what we conventionally associate with a "decent" childhood. Nor does it address the reality that, in spite of the fact children are forbidden from borrowing money from financial institutions, their childhoods are still financialized at the level of (a) the family, where parents are exhorted to go into debt to upgrade children's human capital through expensive curricular or extra-curricular education[23] and (b) the chronically indebted state, which is increasingly encouraged to see education, pediatric public health, and child-centered civic infrastructure or programming as "investments" in the future workforce or taxbase.[24]

As ever, the innocence and protection of the child here appears precisely as a means to distract from and normalize the presumed untrustworthiness and economic abandonment of poor and indebted adults. Why should it be so unacceptable to use the latest advertising arsenal to offer predatory loans to children when we have essentially based our entire economy around doing so to adults, as the subprime loan debacle illustrated? Indeed, in a society where the fate of most adults is to spend their lives in debt, and where the first major adult economic experience many young people have is going into debt to pay for a university education, the protection of children from debt is pyrrhic at best.

Second, while many debts that children of poor and middle class families will incur when they become adults are individually payable, it is more than likely that those children to whom Cullen's projects offers predatory loans will come of age in a society that will see them indebted unto death. Certainly, if present trends continue, a larger and larger number of people in the UK will retire indebted and never repay what they owe before they die.[25] Declining real (inflation adjusted) wages for working and middle class workers, as well as rising costs for housing, transportation, fuel, food, and education, promise a future where debts pile atop one another in cascading waves.[26] Even if one is lucky enough to pay down the first, the next is not far off. This is the existential condition that awaits the majority of children and of which they are already implicitly aware, as I have argued in my study of children's financialized engagement with the popular Pokémon brand.[27]

Ultimately, this is the nature of the society "we" have created for our children. Put otherwise, this is the modality of social reproduction "we" have orchestrated, one based on and reproductive of unpayable debts. Here financial debt serves to supply, co-opt, and pervert one of the most primordial unpayable debts that has guided human evolution: the bonds that undeniably exist between past, present, and future generations. While it may be more hopeful to name these relationships as gifts, rather than debts, there is something about the notion of intergenerational bonds that speaks to the obligations and expectations of care, nurturance, and cultivation that are the *sine qua non* for any society, not only as they exist between kith and kin, but also more broadly as they are expressed by social institutions.[28] The critical impact of Cullen's work relies on revealing to us the way this fundamental set of qualitative and generative unpayable debt relationships has been commodified, financialized, and weaponized in ways that, ultimately, advantage the short-term reproduction and accumulation of capital at the expense of the field of social reproduction, part of what Nancy Fraser calls the crisis of care.[29]

What would it mean to take this debt to future generations seriously? It would likely mean the relentless struggle to abolish a system that condemns so many of them (of all of us) to a fate of unpayable debt, financial debt but also the toxic legacies we leave behind: climate debt, ecological debt, the sociological debts of a world riven by inequality, and the violence it produces.

In recent years, there have been efforts by young people to launch lawsuits against governments and corporations for their failure to act on climate change, which, the plaintiffs argue, will spell loss for them in the future.[30] As laudable and righteous as these campaigns are, in isolation from the much wider youth movements for climate justice they remain locked within the framework that is causing the ruination. The court can only hear a claim to a probable loss. In the civil suits, this loss is often figured as financial. Even in constitutional cases, which allege governments are depriving youth of their inherent rights, if the court were to order governments to take certain actions, we all know it is doubtful those governments would do so, preferring the relatively minimal costs of endless litigation to the prospect of inconveniencing the corporate authors and beneficiaries of reckless greenhouse gas emissions. Even if, against all odds, the governments being targeted were to act, their rationale for dragging their heels has an element of truth: we could reign-in industry to salve our conscience, but another country or jurisdiction will take the opportunity to then outcompete us in the globalized market.

Ultimately, then, the lawsuit's horizon of monetary compensation or legal remedy seeks repayment for an unpayable debt in the coin and kind in which the injury or harm (climate change) was wrought. A deeper vision is necessary, one that aims at the abolition of such systems or at least a profound revolution in their operations.

Payment of Greek debt to Germany with olives and art

In a large gallery, in Athens' National Museum for Contemporary Art, a stylish senior Latin American woman in designer sunglasses sits back-to-back with a middle-aged European woman in a red blazer who looks and acts unnervingly like German Chancellor Angela Merkel. They are seated in swivel-chairs in front of a shallow tank of brimming with black olives; the smell of brine saturates the space. As the performance begins, the two use their feet to pivot their stationary chairs as if in an awkward dance. Eventually (awkwardly, as if unrehearsed) the two women stand and the Merkel look-alike delivers an earnest address to the audience, the gist of which is that she has realized that Greece's ruinous debt has already been paid, thanks to the seminal contributions made by Ancient Greek civilization to the founding of the Western world. This public dream ends with the artist in the sunglasses, Argentina's celebrated pop and performance artist Marta Minujín, gifting the Merkel doppelganger a slimy handful of olives from the tank to seal the deal.

Eternal return

The work was the kick-off event for the Documenta 14 festival and its title, "Payment of Greek Debt to Germany with Olives and Art," succinctly explains the concept. At this iteration of the festival – which occurs once every five years, hitherto exclusively in Kassel, Germany – Minujín also erected a massive, skeletal replica of Athens' famous Parthenon in Friedrichsplatz, Kassel's main square, and invited the public to donate banned or censored books to cover the exterior.[31] Significant because this was the location where the Nazis burned books some seven decades earlier, Minujín's "The Parthenon of Books" (2017) was a reprise of the same piece, "El Partenón de Libros" installed in Buenos Aires in 1983, in celebration of the fall of the censorious military Junta that year.[32] "Payment of Greek Debt to Germany with Olives and Art" was also a restaging of a past work, in this case Minujín's 1985 performance "Payment of the Argentine Foreign Debt to Andy Warhol with Corn, The Latin American Gold."[33] Minujín also repeated the performance, in a way, in her 1996 "Solving the International Conflict with Art and Corn," where she presented the staple crop to a Margaret Thatcher impersonator (though why her is unclear: the Iron Lady by then had been out of power for six years).[34]

Minujín's series of performances quite explicitly encourages audiences to reimagine debts and how and if they ought to be repaid.

Many of the debts that Minujín was seeking to dissolve in her 1985 piece with Andy Warhol stemmed from the kleptocratic and militarist machinations of the (US-backed) Junta, such that when Argentina emerged as a capitalist democracy it was already on its financial back foot, a situation that would, by the 1990s, lead to massive neoliberal restructuring and, in 2001, a major economic crisis.[35] In 1985, Minujín's gesture rightly fathomed international debt as not an objective eternal criterion but something held in place by the orchestration of power, relationships, performance, and ritual. Collaborating with one of the US's most prominent (and commercially successful) contemporary artists, Minujín's work questioned if and how debts so onerous as to be unpayable might be repaid otherwise, in this case by symbolically offering corn, a traditional staple of Latin American agriculture. This work had the virtue of both revealing and reframing debt as, ultimately, a matter of the weaponized imagination, beyond the particular quantitative figures in which it might typically be denominated and legal blackmail of its enforcement.

The passion of Greece

Whatever critical dimension the piece may have had in 1985 was almost completely evacuated in its 2017 reprisal at Documenta 14, though to understand why we must first sketch its context. Documenta has never been without controversy. Tasked with, in some fashion, capturing and representing "the contemporary" in a global sense, the festival's origins stem from an attempt to grapple with and transcend the dark legacy of the Nazis, whose antipathy to cosmopolitan, "degenerate" modern art is well known, and who enjoyed widespread political and economic support from Kassel and the broader region of Hesse of which it is the capital.[36] With such a mandate and such a history to contend with, it is no surprise that the festival is one of the global art world's most significant, anticipated, and (therefore) vexed. The 2017 edition of the festival, curated by an all-star team of critical international art world luminaries, was no exception to this trend, thanks to at least two unique historical factors.

First, following criticisms of previous iterations of the festival which had tended to associate "the contemporary" with Western Europe and North America (following a tacitly white-supremacist and colonial logic), the 2017 edition dedicated itself to "Learning from the South" and opted to, for the first time, split its activities between Kassel and another city: Athens. While Greece is typically associated with the mythologies of "Western civilization," this choice came in the context of the catastrophic paroxysms of debt-driven austerity and social collapse forced on the small nation in the wake of the 2008 financial crisis, which Greek commentators from across the political spectrum have likened to a form of financial and political colonialization by the Troika: the informal name given to the European Central Bank, the European Commission and the International Monetary Fund.[37] It is far from insignificant that the first two of these institutions are widely understood to be dramatically influenced (if not controlled) by Germany, the European Union's largest economy and a major source of investment/speculation in Greek private and public debts.[38]

Documenta's appearance in Athens came three years after the historical showdown between the Troika and Greece's left-wing SYRIZA party who in 2015, following a decisive electoral victory and unsuccessful negotiations to write off the debt or reduce the austerity that was destroying the country's social fabric, called a national plebiscite to gauge if the Troika's bailout package (and dramatic austerity agenda) should be accepted.[39] Implicit though ambiguous in the referendum was the broader question of Greece's further participation in the European Union. The "OXI" or NO vote was decisive, but days later, in a shocking about-face, the SYRIZA government ended up accepting the bailout package when faced with the moralistic recalcitrance of hardliners in the Troika (notably representatives of Germany and other "Northern European" states).[40] As the then-finance minister Yanis Varoufakis (who quit SYRIZA following the referendum) illustrates, the message was clear: the social and economic life of Greece would be sacrificed in order to shore up the precarious state of the international banking sector, notably Germany's hegemonic Deutsche Bank.[41]

Everybody knows

For our purposes one of the most remarkable dimensions of this debacle was the reports issued by the IMF (one third of the Troika) even before the referendum that indicated that, in spite of so much high-minded moralism insisting Greece had to answer for its profligate borrowing in the 1990s and 2000s, further austerity was almost certain to fail in its stated aim of creating the conditions of debt repayment: without significant economic growth that could only be catalyzed through massive government stimulus spending, the Greek economy would weaken and weaken.[42] There is, of course, the very significant question of whether the debts Greece owed were even legitimate in the first place.[43] But what does it mean for the Troika to insist on the repayment of a debt that even they realize can never be repaid, a debt that, in fact, fatally undermined the debtor's ability to ever repay? At this point, the debt appears less and less like a financial obligation and more and more like a kind of vengeance.

Were it the case that, somehow, the debts of Greece could materially be shown to have led to the actual or even potential privation or sacrifice of others, there would, perhaps, have been a case to be made that this privation demands compensation. But economically speaking the "Northern European" nations who are so insistent on repayment have been the net beneficiaries of (or at least far less hard hit by) the Eurozone crisis. Even so, Greece represents a miniscule part of the Eurozone economy, so the idea that somehow Greek debt is a burden to the collective whole is absurd.

Surplus and scarcity

While various national stereotypes have been trotted out to make sense of the German and "Northern European" self-defeating hardline approach (stereotypes that, at least in Greece itself, recall the officious viciousness of the Nazi occupation of that country), a broader look at European and global political economy are more revealing.[44] Allowing Greece to default on its debts, or debt reduction, or an easement of austerity, would, from the perspective of Germany and other creditor nations, send a dangerous signal to other debt-encumbered states in Europe and around the world.[45] While Greece itself represents an almost insignificant economic player within the EU and global economy, its martyrdom was calculated to demonstrate to other nations including Spain, Portugal, Ireland, and Italy (now reclassified as the "European periphery") that they would receive no sympathy from the Troika or global markets, and that austerity was obligatory.[46] Meanwhile, beyond Europe, there may have been significant fear that, if Greece was given any quarter, it would soon be demanded by nations in the Global South who have been ensnared in neocolonial debt peonage for generations (thanks in large part to the machinations of the IMF).[47] The unpayable debts must be paid.

This is the first factor that helps explain the curatorial and artistic context of Documenta 14. The second is the so-called Refugee Crisis that "began" in the summer of 2014 as millions of people fled the ravaged war zones of Syria, Iraq, Afghanistan, Libya, as well as the economic privation and political repression of nations in northern Africa, daring extremely risky crossings over land and sea to seek asylum in Europe, particularly in wealthy "Northern European" nations.[48] Let us set aside the important question of how these "wealthy" nations derived their wealth and stability, in part, from the histories and legacies of the same imperialism and colonialism that led to the instability and poverty from which the refugees fled (a kind of debt we shall return to in the final section of this chapter). For now it is significant to note the fanfare, both within and beyond Germany, when, in 2015, Chancellor Angela Merkel declared (somewhat deceptively) that the Federal Republic would have an open-door policy toward Syrian refugees, eventually admitting nearly 1 million.[49] Never mind that Lebanon, Jordan, Turkey, and Egypt accepted many times this number. Never mind that the specification of Syrian refugees aimed to attract generally highly-skilled, well-educated, middle class asylum seekers who could make an important contribution of Germany's economy and aging workforce (in a long tradition of German exploitation of foreign "guest workers").[50] Never mind that this arrangement would eventually necessitate a deal between the EU and the notoriously punitive and authoritarian regime in Turkey to deny refugees access to Europe, and also the stranding of over 60,000 refugees in the austerity-ravaged Greece.[51]

Debt for guilt, guilt for debt

What is significant for our purposes here is the way that Merkel's move was arguably calculated to in some sense repay or amortize Germany's historic and moral debts. It is not only that this move came shortly after Germany's ugly leadership on the question of the Greek debt. It was also that, in such a monumental gesture of liberal humanism, Germany was perhaps encouraged to imagine itself as finally liberated from the profound collective guilt owing to the Nazi Holocaust (not insignificantly, German speakers use the same word for guilt, shame, and debt).[52] While Germany paid (and continues to pay) economic reparations to Jewish Holocaust survivors and their families, and to the State of Israel, for the debts of the world-historic crime of the Nazi genocide,[53] Merkel's would-be world-historic gesture was arguably in part aimed at repaying that debt on another set of levels. It should be noted that this explanation for Merkel's refugee policy was also widely propounded by Germany's far-right as part of a campaign to suggest that it was high time for the nation to let go of its ideologically stifling and (to their mind) ethno-nationally "suicidal" guilt complex,[54] suicidal because it has led to a tolerance for ethnic and religious "others" who, in the paranoid imagination, will soon be poised to demographically or culturally "replace" the German-ethnic norm.

In any case, by 2017, the success of Merkel's policy was widely questioned. By that time, the conflict in Syria had escalated and unleashed one of the most terrifying specters yet seen: the so-called "Islamic State," a monstrous manifestation of fascistic vengeance cloaked in Muslim fundamentalist garb, that imposed a grotesque legal code on the territories it controlled and coordinated and inspired freelance acts of political violence targeting civilians in "Western" nations like Germany.[55] In those nations, far-right and neofascist groups greatly profited from these attacks, using them to whip up xenophobic fear, resentment, and antipathy toward refugees.[56] Immediately following Documenta 14, Germany's far-right Alternative für Deutschland (AfD) would go on to enjoy 12.6% of the popular vote in the 2017 German Federal elections.[57] Indeed, a local Kassel AfD candidate, a lawyer, took it upon himself to launch a vengeful lawsuit against the festival, nominally due to its significant budgetary deficit (incurred, in part, because of the logistical challenges of splitting the festival between two cities).[58] The lawsuit was a key example of the kind of right-wing populist political resentment that has made the AfD and similar parties so successful: Documenta was framed (in a language eerily and intentionally reminiscent of the Nazis' popular castigation of "degenerate art") as the appropriation of hard-working Germans' tax dollars and a give-away by liberal "elites" to haughty cosmopolitan internationals for inaccessible and insulting "art."[59] In this context, Minujín's over-budget, aesthetically awkward skeletal "Parthenon of Books" in Kassel's main square was lambasted by the AfD and their allies in the right-wing German press as a particularly egregious example of the art world's conspiracy to both rob and mock the Volk.[60] This sentiment would crystalize later in a more specific far-right antagonism to a popular statue created for the festival by Nigerian-born, US-based artist Olu Oguibe titled "Das Fremdlinge und Flüchtlinge Monument" (Monument for Strangers and Refugees) which the AfD and allies succeed in having dismantled from the main square and moved to a less frequented though still public location.[61]

Bad art for bad debt

These contextual factors help explain why Minujín's re-heated performance of "Payment of Greek Debt to Germany with Olives and Art" in Athens was such an artistic and critical failure. In the first place, even if the analogy between Argentina's debt in 1985 and Greece's debt in 2017 were accurate (it's not),[62] it simply does not make sense that (a) Merkel would replace Warhol and (b) Minujín would stay in her role, as opposed to, say, a prominent Greek artist (… though perhaps no prominent Greek artist agreed). In the second place, Minujín's half-baked performance demonstrated much more about the international art world's ill-informed and condescending pity toward Greece than it did about the crisis of austerity.[63]

Space does not permit a full explication of all the dimensions of this hubris or its origins and implications, but it does help us to understand a few things about the question of unpayable debts. Minujín's obvious gambit is that she can excavate an unpayable cultural debt of Europe to Greece which "trumps" the (also unpayable) financial debt owed by contemporary Greece to "Europe" (mostly to Germany, its banks, and their global clients). In the first place, this maneuver reifies not only the contemporary financial debt (the piece declares the debt repaid, not illegitimate in the first place), but also the categories of "Greece" and "Europe" that are at the core of the financialized imaginary of nation-states that is arguably the source of the problem in the first place. There is, of course, an element of critical truth to the idea that a debt to culture, philosophy, and art ought to be more valuable than mere money, especially when that money is itself the hallucination of unanswerable financial institutions or a weapon of geopolitics. But this point is pedestrian and unactionable, except to the extent it can call together some sort of common political-economic agency or collectivity. "We" (the international art world) all get the joke, but no one wants to do anything about it, because the joke is on us: we are the beneficiaries of that same system, as represented by the (professionally ambivalent) institution of Documenta.[64]

To be clear, I do not think Documenta's value is exhausted by these complicities and contradictions: there were many other fine works at the festival, and some of them addressed the political-economic moment of unpayable debts with critical sophistication and aesthetic acuity. However, Minujín's piece, which was also the keynote opening performance of the festival's presence in Athens, reveals that even work that seeks to make some of the dimensions of an unpayable debt visible can, in the end, reinforce or re-inscribe the relationships and symbolic infrastructures that were the conditions of the unpayable debt in the first place.

"Gone Indian"

It's after midnight and a million people, many of them inebriated, ramble through downtown Toronto's financial district on a warm September night.[65] As they make their way between the charismatic art installations of the 2009 edition of the city's Nuit Blanche all-night public arts festival, some encounter a dilapidated and muddy burgundy van, a set of deer antlers affixed to its hood, its roof covered in an embroidered buckskin rug with a couple of old armchairs secured on top, as it drives slowly through the streets, blaring Indigenous pow-wow music (drumming and singing) from a large sound-system. Eventually, the van pulls up on the curb at the headquarters to the Royal Bank of Canada, one of the world's largest financial institutions whose imposing two-tower edifice is literally made of gold infused into its glistening sheet-glass siding.[66] A crowd gathers, most of them non-Indigenous, to watch "Gone Indian," a performance by Rebecca Belmore, perhaps Canada's best-known and most celebrated Indigenous performance artist.[67] The title is a sly pun: the Indian is gone from these lands, eliminated to make room for the bustling financial district and larger city; but "going Indian" was also a phrase used to describe European settlers who developed what were perceived to be unhealthy attachments to the place and its people, being adopted into Indigenous communities or otherwise abandoning what the British called "civility" for "savage" ways.[68]

Belmore's performance was layered and complex, blending Anishinaabe, Cree, and settler[69] symbolism. Near the outset, Belmore, barefoot and wearing feather-adorned army-green coveralls and a black toque, placed several red cloth bags full of Canadian pennies at the

Figure 3 Rebecca Belmore, *Gone Indian* (2009), performance in NIGHTSENSE, Nuit Blanche, Toronto. Photo: Paul Litherland, courtesy of the artist and DisplayCult.

periphery of the performance space and later cut them open with a knife, spilling the coins onto the sidewalk before tying the torn red fabrics to her ankle (red fabric is customarily used to wrap sacred objects). Meanwhile, celebrated Cree actor and dancer Michael Greyeyes, dressed in full pow-wow[70] regalia, performed a series of choreographed modern dance routines, first to an Indigenous hip hop track, next to a recording of pow-wow drumming and singing. While Greyeyes' movements referenced pow-wow dancing, they were original contemporary compositions, often exhibiting jerky, halting motions as if his body were at times possessed and/or constrained by unseen, unfriendly forces. The whole performance was quietly overseen and occasionally photographed by a silent Indigenous man conspicuously wearing dress pants, a white collared shirt, a black tie, a black fringed buckskin jacket, and sunglasses (despite it being nighttime), appearing as a not-so-secret state or corporate agent. As the performance unfolded, Belmore, on her knees, used what appeared to be a heavy traditional stone mortar and pestle to attempt to grind the pennies as one might corn or medicines to produce an edible or healing substance. The performance ended with Greyeyes drifting, as if in slow-motion, through the space and Belmore giving up on her impossible task. The pennies remained scattered on the ground and the company drove away in the van.

Haunting finance

This piece was intentionally ambiguous in part because, to my mind, it attempted to haunt the colonial imagination precisely at the fraught intersection where, drawing on the work of Sherene Razack, space meets place in a colonial settler state:[71] in this case the site where Indigenous land has been turned into a zone of financial speculation. This choice of location is by no means coincidental. As I have elaborated elsewhere, the theft of lands from Indigenous people, and the elimination of Indigenous presence on those lands, has always been a financialized affair.[72] All three key dimensions of the so-called FIRE sector (finance, insurance, and real estate) were essentially born in the crucible of European imperialism and (settler-)colonialism: Both stock markets and the joint-stock, limited liability corporation had their origins in Amsterdam and London in the financing of colonial ventures, settler colonies and the slave trade.[73] Authors including Ian Baucom, Anita Rupprecht, and Zenia Kish and Justin Leroy have demonstrated that the origins of modern insurance laws and practices cannot be separated from the transformation of enslaved African human beings into speculative property.[74] And Brenna Bhandar, Rachel O'Reilly, and

K-Sue Park have all argued that the notion that land could become "real estate" to be speculated upon and exchanged had its roots in the colonial transformation of territory into private property.[75]

In Belmore's few public comments about "Gone Indian" she has stressed that, in transporting a pow-wow into the financial district, she was attempting to create a spectacle not so much of remembrance of the past but a haunting image for the attendees, the vast majority of whom are urban settlers.[76] Before this space was a financialized place (the headquarters of Canada's largest bank) it was something, or somewhere, else. But the performance Belmore choreographed does not afford the viewer the satisfaction of the anthropological gaze so germane to settler colonies where, as Patrick Wolfe notes, the state attempts to continue its genocidal elimination of Indigenous presence on the land precisely by adopting, accommodating, and appropriating its chosen versions of Indigenous "culture."[77] "We," the audience, arrive expecting to be entertained; we leave haunted by ghosts that were always already hidden in plain sight.[78]

The finance of settler colonialism

The choice of the RBC headquarters is quite specific. As Canada's largest bank inherits the legacies of financialized settler colonialism, which for instance financed the fur trade on which the nation was built, or the expansion of the railway across the nation which led to the mass displacement of multiple Indigenous peoples. RBC is also a key participant in the continued colonization of the land today: the bulk of the savings and investments it manages are routed through firms on Canada's nearby TSX stock exchange, where, by some estimates, 60% of global extractive industry venture financing is generated.[79] Indeed, Canada has repeatedly named the extractive industry, both at home and abroad, as one of its key strategic economic interests.[80] This in spite of the fact that numerous international non-governmental organizations have condemned Canadian-funded mining corporations for environmental and human rights abuses both within Canada and around the world, especially as they have affected (and, indeed, targeted) Indigenous people and Indigenous lands.[81]

Meanwhile, in Canada, settler colonialism itself has taken on a financialized dimension. Since the nineteenth century, the Canadian government has imposed on Indigenous communities a form of limited "self-governance," mandated through the Indian Act, a set of laws for the governance of Indigenous life that, at one time, included restrictions on Indigenous people's right to leave reservations without a pass authorized by a (white) Indian Agent, their right to hunt and fish, their right to practice Indigenous spirituality and ceremonies, their right to organize politically, their right to hire lawyers, their right to use modern farming implements, and their right to speak their languages.[82] This Act also permitted the abduction of Indigenous children from their families to be placed in Church-run Residential Schools, where they were severely punished for any behaviors deemed "savage" (e.g., speaking their language) and where they were subject to the horrific predations and abuses of the clergy and staff. All of this is a matter of public record and discussion thanks to a landmark legal case by survivors that resulted in a national Truth and Reconciliation Commission that was ongoing during Belmore's 2009 performance and released its final report in 2015.[83]

Today, the administration of settler colonialism in Canada stresses Indigenous self-governance, but the top-down colonial framework still persists: as Shiri Pasternak has demonstrated, the Canadian government exerts profound and corrosive disciplinary pressure on Indigenous governments through financialized means.[84] In the first place, the Canadian government holds the purse-strings for funds that support nearly all services on Indigenous reservations and uses a series of laborious and disciplinary accounting and reporting mechanisms to constrain and delimit Indigenous communities' spending. Meanwhile, it holds out the threat of auditing and forced third-party management to dissuade those governments from taking actions that might jeopardize the colonial settler state's interests, notably blocking or intervening in attempts to locate extractive industries (e.g., mines) or infrastructure (e.g., pipelines) on Indigenous lands.[85] Meanwhile, the same neoliberal governments have sought to fix the "Indian Problem" through financialized means. Responsibility for the endemic poverty and horrendous health and social indicators that characterize life on reservations is transferred from the Canadian government's inaction and caustic paternalism toward the failure of markets in those spaces.[86] Numerous governments have sought to dissolve Indigenous collective title to lands and transform them into individual fee-simple holdings, the hope being that the introduction of private property will inspire entrepreneurialism, allow Indigenous people on reservations to borrow against their holdings, relocate to take advantage of labor markets elsewhere, and, ultimately, lead them to become proper capitalist subjects.[87] Needless to say, this agenda has been strenuously rejected by many Indigenous nations who insist that their communal, non-commodified relationship to a land-base is at the heart of their existence as a people. For this reason, Wolfe and others including Glen

Coulthard and Audra Simpson, have noted that such market-oriented privatization schemes are part of a long genocidal tradition of seeking to "eliminate" Indigenous people's autonomous land-based existence.[88] These schemes stand in stark contrast to Indigenous practices and orientations toward land-based self-sovereign resurgence that reject colonial constructs of private property.[89]

Forever yours

All these dimensions factor into Belmore's performance. Settler colonialism has advanced by leveraging financialized mechanisms to transform land into property by eliminating Indigenous presence. Her temporary reclaiming of the bank's space aims, in part, to reveal the imaginary and imaginative powers at work by transforming a financialized space back into an Indigenous place. It is not insignificant that Belmore here opts to work with pennies as well, an almost worthless unit of Canadian currency that the state ceased to mint in 2012. Copper, which originally gave the penny its unique color and which has been a major target for ecologically destructive Canadian extractive interests for generations, has been, since before the invasion of Turtle Island, a very important material for many Indigenous cultures, used for a wide variety of cultural, spiritual, and economic purposes.[90] The toxins released by the mining, transportation, and refining of copper (as well as zinc, from which pennies were most recently made) have disproportionately affected Indigenous people thanks to centuries of environmental racism.[91]

Belmore's attempts to crush or pulverize this ubiquitous fetish object, stands in, perhaps, for Indigenous attempts to grapple with the poisonous financialized spirituality or belief-system of settler colonialism, which in the end is reducible only to the pathological logic of capital itself: accumulation at all costs.

If so, two, or perhaps three unpayable debts are at work in this piece. In the first place, Belmore's failure to crush the coins, and Greyeye's ambivalent, fractured dance, may be read as resonant with the way financialized settler colonialism, past and present, has sought to subsume or subscribe Indigenous people in a system that perpetually thwarts their thriving. As Paula Chakravartty and Denise Ferrera da Silva illustrate, the contemporary global financial order is not only built on legacies of racism and colonialism, but, because of that, creates racialized financial subjects doomed to a kind of perpetual failure that is nonetheless profitable for others.[92] In their reading, this financialized system places non-white people in a state of perpetual, unpayable debt, a debt incurred as a subject who was never intended to thrive or succeed within a white-supremacist economic system, even (especially) if that system now (self-servingly) declares itself a color-blind capitalist meritocracy.[93] Belmore and Greyeyes attempt to innovate Indigenous practices within a field of coins, in the shadow of the bank, surrounded by settler onlookers. Their inability to succeed or thrive then becomes evidence of an unspoken and unspeakable debt that settler colonialism imposes on Indigenous peoples and communities. As with the case of settler colonial schemes to "civilize" Indigenous people through the financialization of their lands, the gift is poisoned.[94] It follows on the heels of the way European colonists used the "gift" of Christian religion to destroy Indigenous cultural, political, and spiritual resistance and autonomy, the weaponized "gift" of blankets contaminated with smallpox as a means of biological warfare, or the way in which the Canadian government stripped Indigenous people of their rights over generations through the "gift" of enfranchisement (assimilation as Canadian citizens).[95] "Financial inclusion" here appears as the latest mystification of what could more fruitfully be seen as a multi-generational settler colonial campaign of revenge for the ontological crime of continuing to survive and occupy sought-after land.

Bankrupt

Yet at the same time this performance might also be said to seek to awaken the audience's sensibility to the unpayable debts owed by settler colonialism itself. With 13.5 million clients in a nation of 36 million, it is highly probable that the plurality of spectators at Belmore's performance had savings and investments in or debts with RBC. In this regard, all of Canada's five hegemonic banks are equivalent: settler colonial capitalist citizenship requires one be invested, one way or another, in both the symbolic and the real perpetuation of the financialized seizure and destruction of Indigenous lands via one's savings, investments, pensions, and other financial activity.[96] Further, the enjoyment of the built environment and of the rights of citizenship anywhere in Canada, and certainly in its financial capital Toronto, depends on a long history and legacy of financialized seizure of land and elimination of Indigenous presence.[97] Hence both the place of RBC Plaza and the material of the coins might be intended to awaken an awareness in the audience that they, too, are *the product and the reproducers of* a financialized form of settler colonialism, and that this system implies an almost sublimely huge moral and also economic debt.

For instance, the reparation settlement for the survivors of the Residential Schools alone (the largest for a class-action lawsuit in Canadian history, with upwards of 34,000 claimants) amounted to over $3 billion.[98] Were it to be seriously entertained (it is not), the monetary compensation and restitution for *all* historical harms, attempted genocide, and the systematic theft of Indigenous land would quite probably amount to a sum sufficient to bankrupt this G8 Nation.

Elsewhere I have mused on the political utility of settlers in Canada embracing this imminent bankruptcy as a methodology by which to imagine a world beyond both financialization and settler colonialism, which I think is urgently necessary.[99] For now I simply want to conclude by stressing that at stake in Belmore's summoning of the specters of unpayable debts is the question of in what currency, or through what terms, such debts might be repaid. As Coulthard has noted, in the name of "reconciliation" the Canadian government has made billions of dollars of new funding available in a kind of histrionic and hypocritical generosity: the money is, after all, derived ultimately from land and resources stolen from Indigenous people in the first place.[100] Indeed, even in spite of this "generosity," multiple levels of Canadian state administration have been found guilty in court of systematically underfunding Indigenous communities and people (especially children) relative to non-Indigenous Canadians.[101] By the same token, the colonial settler state has strongly encouraged (and at times blackmailed) Indigenous governments to accept profit-sharing agreements with extractive corporations for the (ab)use of their lands, even though the environmental and social impacts are ultimately destructive to those communities.[102] For these reasons, an increasing number of Indigenous nations and communities are resisting or rejecting monetary compensation or offers and, instead, insisting on their sovereign rights to control access and use of their territories, a sovereignty (which should not be mistaken for a replica of the Westphalian European model) they are willing to defend through civil disobedience, blockades, and, even, armed resistance.[103]

If this trend continues the settler colonial state of Canada will soon find itself unable to pay its debts for colonialism with its own minted currency: the currency itself is a key part of the system that exacts the violence that continues to incur the debt. If that is the case, amortizing that debt will need to take place by other means, through the cessation of the economic and social violence. But this is arguably ontologically impossible within the current order: the state and the form of financialized, settler colonial capitalism with which it is entangled cannot endure a terminal challenge to the twinned legal/political/economic logics of private property and territorial state sovereignty that such a cessation would implicitly demand. Repayment of the debt would quite literally require a revolution.

III. RACE, COLONIALISM, AND UNPAYABLE DEBT

If the above artworks have taught us anything it is that systems and structures of financialized power fabricate and enforce unpayable debts on those people and communities whom they subordinate precisely in order to cover over the unpayable debts they themselves owe to the subordinated. As Graeber argues, the unpayable debt of the subjugated is made to appear in quantitative, monetized terms precisely to help mask its origins in social violence and to individualize and pathologize the debtor to prevent them from creating bonds of solidarity within and beyond their communities, with those likewise encumbered.[104] Meanwhile, the debt owed by the systems and structures of financialized power are rendered qualitative and moral at best, irrelevant at worst, in any case unactionable.

But like an unquiet ghost, the deeper debt haunts: these profound unpaid, indeed *ontological* debts express themselves as contradictions and cataracts in the socio-economic and political fabric. Often, able to neither admit nor assuage the debt, those indebted systems take revenge in the form of punitive moralism or wanton cruelty: the hypocritical fetishization of the figure of the debt-free child; the passion play that blames Greek debt (and German wealth) on allegedly national cultural characteristics, but nonetheless abandons a whole population to penury; the poisoned benevolence of Canadian settler colonialism. Because ultimately these relationships are based on the exploitation and oppression inherent to the contradictions of capitalist accumulation in a financialized world, they breed resentment and are riven with crises which, as they deepen, require that the dominant systems unleash ever more structural and systemic violence.

One might assess these and other artworks on the basis of how well they can reveal these underlying dynamics. But more importantly, one might assess them to the extent they make visible, even for a moment, the potentials for solidarity, refusal, and rebellion within and between those who are both abject debtor and secret creditor to an unchosen, destructive system. The latter is the crucial work of the radical imagination within, against, and beyond financialization.[105] I will return to the prospects of generating a transformative avenging imaginary on the basis of unpayable debts in this book's conclusion.

Saidiya Hartman's magisterial book *Scenes of Subjection* provides us the resources to see the political and moral economy of unpayable debts in a different frame.[106] Following the work of W. E. B. DuBois[107] on the sabotage of post-Civil-War reconstruction and the renovation of a white-supremacist form of capitalism, Hartman details how in this period there emerged a new condition she calls "indebted servitude" to control Black labor and Black people. Debt served "to re-inscribe both servitude and the pained constitution of blackness": not only were many formerly enslaved people quickly (re)ensnared in punitive and ruinous debt relations including sharecropping, convict leasing, and other schemes for the exploitation of their labor, they were now also subjected to a set of moral exhortations to develop a consciousness of gratitude, diligence, servility, and humility.[108] Through an analysis of manuals written for (and sometimes by) freed people advising them on how to conduct themselves as free citizens, Hartman writes that "the cultivation of consciousness operated in the whip's stead as an overseer of the soul."[109] Once-enslaved Black people were now free to sign themselves into contracts of extortionate debt peonage and relentless exploitation to which they could be "held accountable," and contractual infractions were punishable by new legalized forms of forced labour.

The moral economy of debt was essential to the political economy of exploited Black labor, but the threats and practice of legal or extralegal punishment, rape, torture, and murder were also never far off. Indeed, Hartman notes that the "urging of servility" in the manuals "begrudgingly acknowledged the less than ideal labor conditions of the South and the averse racial sentiments to be negotiated and defused by the obeisance of the freed."[110] It is not simply that the freed needed to be warned against revenge toward their former owners; more accurately it was the revenge of the former owners, now cloaked as civil authorities (unevenly and heavy-handedly) enforcing laws and contracts, that needed to be mollified. Elsewhere in *Scenes of Subjection* Hartman catalogs the vindictive, sadistic, and spectacularized cruelty of white revanchism, including notably the terrorism of lynching. To my mind, this investment in normalized racial terrorism, which offers both financial dividends from the exploitation of Black labor and cultural or subjective dividends to those who fall on the side of the oppressor, expresses the quintessence of revenge capitalism.

"Emancipation instituted indebtedness," Hartman writes,

> Blame and duty and blood and dollars marked the birth of the free(d) subject. The very bestowal of freedom established

the indebtedness of the freed through a calculus of blame and responsibility that mandated that the formerly enslaved both repay this investment of faith [in them] and prove their worthiness.

She continues:

indebtedness was central to the creation of a memory of the past in which white benefactors, courageous soldiers, and virtuous mothers sacrificed themselves for the enslaved. This memory was seared into the minds of the freed. Debt was at the centre of a moral economy of submission and servitude and was instrumental in the production of peonage … in short, to be free was to be a debtor.[111]

Then, as today, Hartman makes clear that

in the language of liberal individualism, the ravages of chattel slavery and the degradation still clinging to the freed after centuries of subjection to the white race were obstacles to be overcome through self-discipline, the renunciation of dependency and intemperate habits, and personal restraint … [this was] a commitment to equality made ineffectual by an atomized version of social relations and the apportioning of individual responsibility, if not blame, for what are clearly the consequences of dominative relations.[112]

The unpayable debt in question here is one that acts not only in a punitively and disciplinary fashion, but also affords the debtor the compulsory (master's) tools to construct an appropriate economic and moral subjecthood, one that obliterates not just the desire but also the cause for seeking any justice beyond personal competitive striving. This framing of the debt of the freed subject is one that cannot be repaid because the freed subject is deemed morally deficient, tasked with striving to earn a place in a society built to exclude them and, indeed built by the coerced labors of the freed themselves for that purpose.

In this sense, Hartman notes that "as many former slaves asserted, they had not incurred any debt they had not repaid a thousandfold." Hartman continues, "In the counter discourse of freedom, remedy was sought for injuries of slavery, not through the reconstruction of the Negro – in other words, the refashioning of the emancipated as rational and docile individuals – but through reparations."[113]

With this in mind, we can revisit the example with which we began this chapter, of the subprime mortgage and its racialized dimensions. Ta-Nahesi Coates is one of the most popular voices linking the economic devastation of many Black people in the US to the afterlives of slavery, cataloging the ruination of Black people's and families' fortunes over successive generations through various forms of direct and systemic racist violence.[114] These range from the sabotaging of Black farmers' ability to succeed and upgrade their tools to the exclusion of Black workers from trade unions to the "red lining" and withholding of state-backed mortgages to majority-Black neighborhoods.[115]

Chakravartty and da Silva pose a set of difficult questions regarding the subprime crisis, particularly "How could the predatory targeting of economically dispossessed communities and the subsequent bailout of the nation's largest investment banks, instantly and volubly, be recast as a problem caused by the racial other?"[116] They argue that "the term subprime mortgage has become a racial signifier in the current debate about the causes and fixes for a capitalism in crisis," but that this needs to be understood in the longer arc of race at the cusp of financial and moral economies charted above by Hartman: "historical materialism alone cannot account for the ways in which capitalism has lived off – always backed by the colonial and national state's means of death – of colonial/racial expropriation."[117]

> Incomprehensible (moral) obligations and unpayable (monetary) debts – such as... those offered subprime loans – expose a political-economic architecture that has always thrived on the construction of modern subjects who lack mental (moral and intellectual) capacities. In other words, the analytics of raciality allow us to see how, since the last third of the nineteenth century at least, modern political-economic architectures – in Europe and in its colonies – have been accompanied by a moral text, in which the principles of universality and historicity also sustain the writing of the "others of Europe" (both a colonial and racial other) as entities facing certain and necessary (self-inflicted) obliteration. Just like this time around in the global financial capitalist casino, the house (the cozy state-financial capital home) cannot but always win because when betting on the other's (Black and Latino/a) inability to pay back its debts, it is betting on something it has itself brought into being.[118]

To close this chapter I would simply add that the condition to which Chakravartty and da Silva point – the racialized subject as fated to participate in a moral and financial economy predicated on their perpetual failure – seems to me to reveal the core logic of a system in which revenge is brought to the very core of its operations.

Interlude: Ahab's coin, or Moby Dick's currencies?

Figure 4 Ecuadorian eight Escudos doubloon, minted between 1837 and 1843. Image in the public domain.

I

The taciturn, brooding Captain Ahab, sequestered below deck on the Nantucket whaling ship *Pequod*, finally, several days after setting sail and with no hope of an easy return to land, emerges on deck to address his polyglot crew. How does he convince this anarchic mass, this many-headed hydra – devout New England puritans, Oceanic "cannibals," African princes, Indigenous Americans, suspicious Europeans, and more – to join him on his doomed mission of revenge against the eponymous white whale, Moby Dick? A coin: the eye of capital itself.

Holding up an Ecuadorean doubloon, worth $16 (roughly a standard whaling seaman's annual take home pay for a multi-year voyage), Ahab promises the glistening object to whichever crewman spots the elusive, vengeful, legendary whale first. Tantalizing them with its polished luster, he nails the coin to the mainmast of the ship so that its gaze and its lure might, until the end of the epic novel, discipline the crew and hold fast their fantasies.

The coin here might be read as a material allegory, or in some senses a synecdoche (a small part which represents the whole) of capital itself. First, it is the universal key to each sailor's heart, the promise of fulfillment and desire that motivates his labor. Capital operates not simply through brutal repression, nor even by universalizing desire, but by offering the coin as the indifferent means to different dreams. In a later chapter, the author, Herman Melville, traverses the imaginations of several of the mates and seamen on the *Pequod* who, in the course of their duties, gaze up at the longed-for coin, each seeing in it and the Andean iconography embossed on its face, a different reflection of their own diverse souls and souls' desires. The lure of the coin therefore unifies the crew in their manifold diversity. Yet the coin is literally nailed to the ship's main means of propulsion, the main mast, the *sine qua non* of the vessel. It works its magic in its promise, not its acquisition. It is the cyclopean gaze, not the possession of the coin, that holds the crew to its oath to Ahab to hunt his cetacean nemesis. And yet the voyage will not only wreak a terrible vengeance on many whales along the way (the method of hunting in that time was to lance and harpoon a whale and let it flee in terror and agony, pulling the boat behind until it tired, then to spear it to death, then to flay and boil it to distill its precious oils), it will also lead to the destruction of the *Pequod* and drowning of its crew at the hands (fins) of Moby Dick, the avenger of his species. The coin, then, also seals the fate of those who bow to its promise.

II

As C. L. R. James illustrates, there is in Herman Melville's depiction of Ahab and his 1830s voyage, a premonition of the twentieth-century totalitarian dictators that would arise out of capitalism's crisis 100 years after the book's events.[1] Ahab, though a fearsome and ugly figure, deformed not only by his earlier maiming by Moby Dick on a previous voyage but also by the all-consuming vengefulness that has become his only reason for living, is nonetheless a brilliant and charismatic orator, able to swiftly conscript the crew to set aside their desire for profit (whaling crews were, as Melville takes pains to explain, paid in shares of the value of whale oil they brought home) and join him in seeking a nightmare beast, known to have smashed whaling ships with what is characterized as a merciless and preternatural vengeance. For James, Ahab represents the seductive authoritarian nightmare of capital itself, a twisted man who, in a twisted system (like the gory, ecocidal whale hunt that provided a huge percentage of fuel and lubricant for the industrial modernity before advances in petroleum processing) is praised by his bosses (the Nantucket investors in the voyage) as a "grand, un-godly, god-like man."

In James's reading, Ahab's mad quest for revenge is not the exception to but the dark truth of the capitalist enterprise. Does not Ahab use every prized technique of oceanic capital to achieve his ends: the obsessive use of scientific measurement and navigation and the scientific management of his workers, the crew?

Michel Foucault, for one, identified the ship as the heterotopia *par excellence*: the space that is both within and outside the social order, a zone of exception and experimentation that nonetheless reveals the underlying patterns of power in society at large.[2] More recently Marcus Rediker has cataloged the way the ship, especially the slave ship, was the quintessential and prototypical site of capital accumulation and exploitation, a kind of model for the ways economic necessity, authoritarian power, rigid hierarchical discipline, racial ordering, patriarchal comradery and competition, and human cruelty would come to characterize capitalism as a whole, from the plantation to the factory.[3] This is to say nothing of the ship's crucial material role in transporting the cargos (including enslaved, indentured, or immiserated humans) between sites of exploitation and extraction.

This archetypal vehicle of discipline and exploitation was organized around the kind of preemptive revenge I have been noting throughout this book. In the first place, much of the discipline meted out on board for breaches of rigid decorum had a a sadistic, vengeful character. On a ship like the *Pequod*, there was no room for the niceties of penance and reformation: punishment for insubordination or failure to perform one's duties were dealt with through public, spectacularized violence meted out by the quartermaster or another representative of the autocratic captain, from consigning seamen to stocks and chains on the deck to face the agonies of the hostile elements and the taunts of his comrades to whippings and beatings to summary execution.[4] No matter the victim of the sailor's infraction, these punishments are inherently framed as revenge for an offense to the authority and order of the captain, and it is through the preemptive threat of revenge that his authority is secured. While the ship is imperial capitalism's alleged "state of exception" (the suspension of all liberalism's claims to fairness in the name of economic and military efficiency), it is the exception that proves the rule: the captain's authority here is simply a naked expression of the power of the state to take revenge in the name of accumulation.[5]

The vengefulness of the captain is also justified with recourse to the need to contain and control the crew, who are held by the captain and officers to be irrationally vengeful. Harsh discipline must be meted out because, in the absence of rigid order, the crew, stuck together in close confines for years, will fall to fights and quarrels over petty matters. They must be protected from their own vengeance, and kept in line, lest their own vengeful nature conspire in mutiny: revenge against the captain and officers who so abuse them.[6] Here again, an echo of a pattern already noted in other chapters of this book: the revenge of the powerful names itself law and order and regretfully takes revenge to allegedly prevent the revenge of the oppressed, who are cast as pathologically, irredeemably vengeful.

III

Thus, James in a sense encourages us to "provincialize" Ahab, to resist the urge to exceptionalize his monomaniacal vengefulness. He uses the fetish of the singular, shimmering doubloon to seduce the crew to his mission of exceptional vengeance against one particular whale, away from their enlisted mission of normalized vengeance against whales in general. Just as fascism reveals the ultimate horizon of capital's authoritarian and hyper-exploitative nature, so too does Ahab's fanatical quest reveal, rather than contradict, the underlying vengefulness of capital accumulation.

In the case of *Moby-Dick*, this contradiction is best encapsulated in Ahab's dialog with his First Mate, the pious Quaker Starbuck, who at least has the courage to challenge his captain. When taunted during Ahab's oration with accusations he might be afraid of the whale, Starbuck responds:

> "I am game for his crooked jaw, and for the jaws of Death too, Captain Ahab, if it fairly comes in the way of the business we follow; but I came here to hunt whales, not my commander's vengeance. How many barrels will thy vengeance yield thee even if thou gettest it, Captain Ahab? It will not fetch thee much in our Nantucket market."

> "Nantucket market! Hoot!... If money's to be the measurer, man, and the accountants have computed their great counting-house the globe, by girdling it with guineas, one to every three parts of an inch; then, let me tell thee, that my vengeance will fetch a great premium here!" [Ahab strikes his chest]

> "Vengeance on a dumb brute!" cried Starbuck, "that simply smote thee from blindest instinct! Madness! To be enraged with a dumb thing, Captain Ahab, seems blasphemous."

Here, it appears that Ahab is defying the logics of capitalism, decrying the reduction of the world to economic motives and calling to a higher virtue to justify his quest. Indeed, sensing Starbuck's theological disposition, and being a master manipulator and demagogue, Ahab uses the opportunity to stage a scene of pantomime philosophy. He responds:

> All visible objects, man, are but as pasteboard masks. But in each event – in the living act, the undoubted deed – there, some unknown but still reasoning thing puts forth the mouldings of its features from behind the unreasoning mask. If man will strike, strike through the mask! How can the prisoner reach outside except by thrusting through the wall? To me, the white whale is that wall, shoved near to me. Sometimes I think there's naught beyond. But 'tis enough. He tasks me; he heaps me; I see in him outrageous strength, with an inscrutable malice sinewing it. That inscrutable thing is chiefly what I hate; and be the white whale agent, or be the white whale principal, I will wreak that hate upon him. Talk not to me of blasphemy, man; I'd strike the sun if it insulted me. For could the sun do that, then could I do the other; since there is ever a sort of fair play herein, jealousy presiding over all creations. But not my master, man, is even that fair play. Who's over me? Truth hath no confines.

In this staged dialog at the very crux of the novel (staged by Ahab as part of his seductive theater and staged by Melville as part of his enigmatic allegory) we have the encapsulation of the two contradictory yet mutually supportive fantasies of capital itself. On the one hand, Starbuck makes the argument for calm, rational, calculative business, of measured risk, of paying back one's debts to the Nantucket investors. This Godly matter of business is contrasted to the anathema of Ahab's *jouissant* vengeance, his perverse surplus of passion. Yet, of course, the "gentle commerce" that Starbuck proposes is itself horrifically vengeful. It depends fundamentally on the normalized vengeance of capitalist shipboard labor discipline. It is also a mission of truly horrific systemic vengeance against the whales the *Pequod* and its industry seek to transmute into oil and profit: animals that, even in *Moby-Dick* (and the scores of contemporary and historical sources it cites), are evidently highly sentient, social, communicative, and passionate beings.

And yet in contrast to Starbuck's bourgeois moralism, Ahab's treatise reveals the other soul of capital: a raw will-to-power and a vindictive hatred for that which refuses to submit to its rule, a sense of unquenchable insufficiency, a gnawing hollowness. Ahab's speech might be a manifesto for the entrepreneur as much as for the authoritarian: the world is illusion, truth is a lie. Individual ambition, agency, will, and vitality are all that matter. At once, Ahab calls on the capitalist principle of "fair play" to justify his right to seize reality for the taking, but in the same breath announces even fair play itself is not his master. If ever we had a literary warning of the way capitalism rots out the corpse of liberalism in which it festers, it is the calculating, imperious Ahab's announcement that the "truth hath no confines."

Upon quelling Starbuck in this way, Ahab seals the conspiracy of the *Pequod* by ordering the ship's steward to bring a measure of grog (watered rum) to toast the oath. He orders his harpooners and mates to drink with him from the sockets of their harpoons (where the blade attaches to the rod) and swear their vicarious vengeance against Moby Dick.

IV

The name of the vessel is far from innocent: it refers to a once-mighty Indigenous nation whose territories were near the present-day Hartford, Connecticut (not far from Nantucket, the *Pequod*'s home port and a capital of the whaling industry). As we shall see in Chapter 3, the decline of the Pequot people came in a quintessential moment of colonial revenge politics, when a Dutch trader kidnapped their leader for ransom and through it seized that nation's treasure of wampum: rare painstakingly crafted purple and white beads that Indigenous nations used for a wide diversity of spiritual, cultural, diplomatic, and economic purposes but which the colonists mistook for a primitive form of their own fetishized money. Wampum, once a technology of peace, became a weapon of war as colonists used their control over its coastal sources of production as a means to leverage genocidal power over the Pequot and other nations along the Eastern shore of Turtle Island (North America).

I don't know how well Melville knew this story, though he was a keen (almost obsessive) student of American history and seems to have been interested in numismatics. In any case, the naming of the ship *Pequod* nonetheless summons a specter of a kind of unpayable debt. Of course, it reflects a long-standing settler colonial tradition of first committing genocide and then having the audacity to name pets, sports teams, streets, vehicles, and military technology after the vanquished who, though in life they were castigated as bloodthirsty, semi-evolved, disposable, and ignoble savages (among other things, pathologically and primitively fixated on vengeance) can safely be recuperated as symbols of those celebrated virtues (steadfastness, nobility, belonging, solidarity, ferocity, courage) that settler colonists wish to claim – claim, of course, precisely in spite of the fact that all such high-minded principles were in horrific abeyance during their erstwhile acts of conquest.[7]

Thus the very name of the ship *Pequod* indexes some deeper current of revenge than is sensed merely in the pathology of Ahab's monomania. The voyage, from the beginning, is haunted by a ghost of a kind of nascent revenge, or a fear of revenge, from those so brutally revenged against in the gory foundations of American capitalism, of which the *Pequod* now, in the novel, is a synecdoche. Inasmuch as the Ecuadorean doubloon itself resonates with the ghosts of the millions of men, women, and children (whole civilizations) sacrificed to the Spanish Empire's Andean gold mines from which the coin is wrought, so too does the ship resonate with the unpaid and unpayable debt to the Pequot and their kin, on whose lands the ship itself was built, from which it was provisioned and set sail, and on which has been built Starbuck's sacred market for the oil of murdered whales.

V

What of those murdered whales? Melville takes pains to humanize these huge sea mammals, expounding at length on their typical gentleness, sociability, curiosity, and intelligence. This, in stark contrast to the crass comradery and at times sadistic fraternal culture of their human hunters. The general pacifism of whales is also painted so as to better frame the pathology of Moby Dick, the grotesque and huge white sperm whale who is Ahab's nemesis. In humanizing other whales, Moby Dick's violence, cunning, courage, and vengefulness is cast as monstrous in stark relief, the perfect foil for the "god-like, un-godly" Ahab.

A sensitive and thoughtful author such as Melville must have been horrified, while on the whaling voyage that inspired the novel, at the terror unleashed by the industry on cetaceans, and on the ways its monstrous economic logic made monsters of the men conscripted to its service. *Moby-Dick* also illustrates the way this monstrous industry and its workers also cast its quarry, the whale, as monstrous, not so much because whales were in fact intentionally threatening to their hunters (the exceptional case wherein a sperm whale attacked and sunk a ship was remarkable enough to make headlines and inspire the novel) but because, in casting them as monsters, the hunt could retroactively justify itself.

One reading of *Moby-Dick* is of an author seeking to present a vengeful exception that proves the rule: Moby Dick's destructive vengefulness crystalizes, in impossibly concentrated form, the monstrousness of the whale, its preternatural and inhuman instinct, a justification for treating it as a beast, a resource. This would, for instance, be Starbuck's argument when he calls the whale a "dumb thing" driven by the "blindest instinct" and therefore not worthy of Ahab's "blasphemous" revenge. The blasphemy here is to attribute a soul and a will (and thus a capacity for revenge) to an animal that, in Starbuck's protestant/bourgeois cosmology, is little more than a resource to be exploited. It is, to the last, unclear, if Ahab truly sees his nemesis. As he makes clear in the above passages, in a certain sense his desire for revenge is not against the whale but against the *idea* of the whale.

There is no alternative ending to *Moby-Dick* where, rather than being caught up in his own cordage as he attempts to spear the whale and hurled into the sea, Ahab kills his quarry and returns to his young wife and son in Nantucket. Ahab is nothing but revenge. It is his unflinching embrace of this fantasy that makes him such a perverse character: unlike the capitalist whaling industry of which he is a part, Ahab refuses to veil his desire, to subscribe to the myths of commerce, religion, or liberal dogma, those pastboards that otherwise mask the relation to the real.[8]

Yet beyond Starbuck or Ahab's envisioning of the whale, we have a depiction of the animal or monster that is vengeful in a way that only humans can be vengeful: calculating, sadistic, pathological. We know that other animals do enact forms of retribution; some even appear to premeditate it, or use it as a means to shape social organization. But there is, nonetheless, something particularly human about this thing we call revenge. To name revenge as a human characteristic is to honor the universality of its appearance in the cultural and religious texts of all known human civilization while, at the same time, not losing sight of my key point throughout this book: that revenge, both as a category for understanding human action and a set of socially acceptable or unacceptable acts, takes radically different forms depending on the social order. Revenge is not only something individual humans fantasize about or enact; it is, vitally, a way of describing a certain set of processes within and that reproduce *systems* of exploitation. The perpetuation of the conditions and relations of exploitation rely on (often sadistic) revenge against the oppressed, often preemptive acts of revenge (where no original infraction has occurred), justified in the name of preventing the revenge of the oppressed. In such systems, if revenge is seen as a pathology (as it is in our current day), it is ascribed to the oppressed as their sick fixation, their all-consuming passion, precisely in contrast to the patient, forgiving, wise, just, or necessary "justice" of the oppressor or their agents (their law).

Under revenge capitalism this formula takes another turn: the vengefulness of the system is not only in the explicit and intentional acts of cruelty and oppression that enforce the relations of exploitation. A kind of vengeance also emerges from the core of the system itself, driven not by the bloodlust or sadism of any particular agent (all the agents might be earnest, saintly people like Starbuck) but from the way the system takes on a kind of logic of its own as the sum effect of a million acts of self-interested and competitive accumulation.

The whale hunt itself is a good example: none of Starbuck's prized investors at the Nantucket market, other than Ahab, have a hatred of whales or a desire to wipe them off the face of the planet, which is essentially what the whale hunt was doing at the time. From a certain angle and distance, the whale hunt was a sadistic, vengeful campaign of ecocide. Had other economic factors not intervened, the industry would have hunted the sperm and other whale species to extinction, something that would have also destroyed the whaling industry that relied on them and all the other industries that, in turn, relied on whale oil, from industrial lubricants to margarine to gun oil (necessary for the weapons of empire) to modern illumination (oil and candles). Again, Ahab's single-minded, suicidal fixation on the whale is the exception that proves the rule for the industry (and capitalism) as a whole.

VI

Moby-Dick, written about the outset of fully-fledged industrial capitalism, may be the first example of a narrative that, by now at revenge capitalism's chaotic financialized zenith, is all too common: the revenge of nature.

As Michael Fuchs illustrates in his essay on animal revenge film, it is only with a fully "modern" sense of human agency that we can project onto animals a sense of justice and the settling of scores that, while all too human, was hitherto reserved for God.[9] The vengeful animal, or nature itself as a vengeful force is, of course, our human fantasy, one accelerated in recent years by the terrible realization of humanity's impacts on the more-than-human world.[10] There are many ways to read this projection. Fundamentally, while it may beguile us into imagining we fear, respect, and honor "nature" and our baleful impacts on it, it is an anthropocentric and narcissistic fantasy: the vengeful animal or natural force is given human drives and desires precisely to accentuate the separation of supernatural humanity from base nature, a separation that lies at the very root of capitalism's destructive cosmology.[11] Hence, Moby Dick's vengefulness is a projection of human vengefulness, not whale vengeance (if there is such a thing).

Of course, Moby Dick would be entirely justified in his vengeance. It is not at all unlikely that many members of his pod were slaughtered by ships like the *Pequod*. Today we are aware that sperm whales are capable of complex communication over the span of thousands of kilometers: some scientists believe they are capable of interlacing the globe with a web of sonic communication.[12] Sperm whale brains are four times the size of those of humans and their lifespans are at least as long as ours. If so, Moby Dick would have listened to the destruction of his kindred for decades as fellow cetacean correspondents around the world went silent, or shrieked in pain during the days it took them to bleed to death, all the while pulling their tiny murderers behind them in their boats.

And yet as tempting as it is to cast our lot with Moby Dick, the avenger of his species, and delight in the recompense for our all too human accumulative sadism, this itself is a fantasy, a projection, and not simply because *Moby-Dick* is a novel (a novel, it is true, loosely based on real events). It is a fantasy precisely because it, like the whole genre of revenge-of-nature films, performs a double movement that obfuscates and ultimately reinforces the system (of capitalist ecocide) it would appear to critique. On the one hand, as mentioned, it reifies and celebrates human agency, mastery, and exceptionalism by projecting it onto the non-human animal. At the same time, it exonerates humanity as a whole, from actually taking responsibility for the abolition of the ecocidal systems we have created: nature will take care of itself. We are helpless in the face of Moby Dick's revenge, which is actually our own revenge on ourselves for what we have done to him and his kind.

There is a kind of death drive here that Herbert Marcuse and Erich Fromm, each in their own way, associate with a fear of freedom.[13] What these authors call the "reality principle" is produced by social orders such that, long after those orders are unnecessary (if they were ever necessary at all) we come to be terrified of their absence, of seizing the freedom and possibility for paradigmatic socio-economic transformation for fear we will lose the structures to which we have become habituated. As has often been repeated, it has become easier to imagine an apocalyptic end of the world than an end to capitalism.[14] In this case, we dream, over and over, of a revenge we know ought to befall us precisely to endlessly forestall having to take action and make societal and economic change that would avert the cause for that mythical revenge. In the kind of vengeful human (metahuman) subjecthood we project onto Moby Dick and other of nature's avengers, we paint ourselves as helpless in the face of our urges. Like the bloodthirsty whale, we cannot help what we do, and thus we deserve to be annihilated by that which we have created.

3
Money as a medium of vengeance
Colonial accumulation and
proletarian practices

This chapter proposes that, in spite of the claims of neoliberal theorists who frame capitalist money as a singular social technology of peace, it can fruitfully be understood as a medium of systemic and structural violence and revanchism. I begin by recalling the early history of the (vindictive) monetary colonization of Turtle Island (North America) before telling three stories about the way proletarians responded to the vengeance of capitalism by appropriating and repurposing money as a platform for imagination and solidarity.

Jackie Wang's *Carceral Capitalism* paints a vivid picture of the way that neoliberal financialized racial capitalism flourishes through what she calls "exclusion through financial inclusion."[1] As we saw at the close of Chapter 2, the subprime loans debacle saw the systematic targeting of the hopes of poor and racialized – notably Black – borrowers for sabotaged, extractive loans that, ultimately, left most poorer and more precarious than they began. Wang connects this to the way in which prisons in the US function as vehicles not only for private investment but also for the management of surplussed populations. She explores and the way austerity-wracked municipalities increasingly turn to predatory fines and fees to make up for chronic budget shortfalls, which leads to often deadly altercations with police and prison systems for those who cannot pay. All of these examples, for Wang, are mechanisms by which the overarching crisis of capitalism in an age of financialization is displaced through the channels cut by centuries of white supremacy. Yet like so many other moments of this system, these renovated operations of racial capital speak the language of color-blind inclusion through the magic of disinterested markets.

Money, we are encouraged to believe, has no prejudice. It is the great neutral equalizer, obedient only to the laws of supply and demand. As Melinda Cooper notes, the key architects of neoliberalism were centrally concerned with how the magic of markets might help America to rise above its history of racism and unleash a true meritocracy.[2] Today, the belief in money's inherent or ideal neutrality animates the enthusiasm for new cryptocurrency schemes that would use emergent digital technologies to finally "liberate" money from the grip of the state.[3] The belief in money's neutrality has also inspired the rhetoric and massive public, private, and philanthropic investment in schemes heralded under the banner of "financial inclusion," including attempts to get the world's poor to take our micro-financed loans, use financial savings apps, and more.

Underscoring these approaches is the notion that money is ultimately a technology of peace, that the spread and integration of global markets are like inexorable waves in whose face borders, prejudices, tyrannies, and ideologies are destined to erode and crumble. Yet what if, as Wang's analysis of exclusion through inclusion suggests, the opposite is true? What if capitalist money is a technology of systemic and structural revenge?

In this chapter I will explore this concept through a series of stories. I start with the story of wampum, small white and purple beads traded and used for a multitude of purposes by numerous Indigenous civilizations in the Northeastern part of Turtle Island (North America) before, during and after the European colonial invasion. Though it was in many ways a medium for peace, diplomacy, and reconciliation, Europeans (violently) mistook it for "primitive" money and weaponized it as a tool of colonialism. This episode in many ways haunts modern forms of fiat money and offers us an important counter-narrative to the (neo)liberal story of money's peaceful and bucolic origins, myths to which I return in the second part of this chapter. We then turn to three almost-lost stories of what I call the "hidden ledger" of proletarian money sabotage: small collective acts of defiance against capitalism by those whom it oppressed and excluded who took its emblem and weapon (money) into their own hands and used it as a medium of solidarity and revenge. These stories, I suggest, offer us a chance to recognize the vengeful systemic violence inherent to capitalism's "gentle commerce" and an alternative genealogy of resistance and refusal toward an avenging imaginary.

My ambition in this chapter is at once both simple and ambitious. I want to set forth a suite of stories that imply a very different way of thinking about money, the better to understand it as a crucial element of what I am calling revenge capitalism: a tendency within capitalism toward reckless, needless vengeance that not only operates at the level of the individual human cruelties germane to the enforcement and reproduction of oppression, but also operates through the logic of the system itself, without any necessary malice or cruelty on the part of its human agents. My desire here is not to categorically prove that capitalist money is, in fact, a tool of revenge (though that it often enough is) but rather to tell a disquieting parallel story about money that will sit uneasily alongside conventional neoliberal narratives of money as a medium of peace, and even alongside more strenuous and systematic Marxist and critical narratives of money as the lifeblood of capital.

THE WEAPONIZATION OF WAMPUM

When Europeans invaded the area now encompassed by New York and New England, they found a diversity of Indigenous nations organized into complex and shifting alliances and connected across vast distances by enduring trade routes.[4] That Europeans (in the case of this territory: the British, Dutch, and, to a lesser extent, French) saw these civilizations as fundamentally inferior and the land and its resources as theirs for the taking is well established. But in their early years these extractive colonial economies, organized by private corporations to send wealth back to the metropole, required that European forces forge alliances and trade relationships with the nations they were soon to destroy, enslave, and immiserate.[5]

Part of the challenge was that, while Europeans brought many desirable trade goods that Indigenous people could not manufacture (guns, metal pots and knives, and rare decorative objects) they were ill at ease with Indigenous trading customs which were generally based less on mutual competitive acquisitiveness and more on custom, hospitality, reciprocity, and social complexity.[6] While different Indigenous cultures had diverse ideas about what we would call "ownership" they did not easily map onto the European obsession with exclusivist "private property," especially in matters of land.[7] To say these cultural differences "led to conflict" would be a half-truth; more accurate to say that the conflicts that naturally arise in any intercultural zone were taken by the Europeans as a pretext for war, murder, and punishment.[8]

A fine example is the European "discovery" of wampum: small purple and white shell beads used by Indigenous people of the region for a wide variety of purposes not limited to spiritual and secular regalia, trophy for victors of sports and games of chance, marriage and funerary rites, and specific kinds of trades and exchanges. Importantly, when strung together in strands or "fathoms," wampum served as a common mnemonic device for recording history and treaties.[9] Wampum was particularly prized because of its scarcity: the shells could only be harvested at certain times of the year on specific beaches controlled by specific nations who painstakingly refined them into beads before trading them inland.[10]

Wampum's use as a diplomatic and pacific technology is emblematized in its vital importance to the Haudenosaunee Great Law of Peace, the constitution of the then five (now six) nation confederacy which is governed by what many consider to be the oldest surviving democratic constitution in the world.[11] The story of the Confederacy's origins, sometime in the 1300s, is tied to the use of wampum to subdue and heal a monstrous necromancer whose spirit had been corrupted by revenge and to bring into alliance the leaders of five nations ruined by vengeful warfare with one another.[12] Though the Haudenosaunee home territories are hundreds of kilometers inland from the coastal nations that harvested and manufactured wampum (and the two were frequently at war), wampum became a vital part of Haudenosaunee civilization.[13] The exchange of wampum was a crucial part of many diplomatic, political, and spiritual processes. As numerous Haudenosaunee thinkers and anthropologists note, wampum was particularly important in its capacity to give gravity to spoken words: many solemn oath-takings, from marriage to treaty-making, from the retelling of history to the sharing of stories.[14] It also has medicinal properties, such as the ability to cure grief and stave off vengefulness, and it was used to pay ransoms and blood debts.[15]

As David Graeber notes, in spite of the fact that the Haudenosaunee were well known as ambitious and fearsome warriors, wampum was ultimately a creative technology for the production and reproduction of peace, a means through which individual and collective social creativity and innovation could be expressed in the interests of maintaining relations within the confederacy and beyond it.[16] I want to stress the importance of wampum as a flexible social technology, one of whose key functions is the transmutation of vengeance into social accord.[17]

Wampum's ameliorative functions were, in a strange way, its downfall. As noted, it was frequently used as the means to pay a ransom for a warrior captured in battle.[18] It was to this end that, in 1622, the early period of European colonization, the Pequod people near what is now Hartford, Connecticut, offered a French trader working for the Dutch West India Company named Jacques (sometimes recorded as Jacob) Eelkens some 140 fathoms of wampum for the return of their chief Tabotem, whom Eelkens had captured while the former visited on matters of trade.[19] Eelkens was furious with Tabotem that the Pequod would not supply him with sufficient animal furs that the trader could satisfy his corporate masters' quotas and so took his hostage to compel the Pequod to be more forthcoming. 140 fathoms represented almost 10,000 beads, each of which was painstakingly manufactured using stone and bone tools and traded to the Pequod, presumably for items of equivalent scarcity and value: in other words, this was a kingly ransom indeed.[20] But at this time the Dutch cared little for wampum, which they saw as a fetishistic trinket idiotically beloved by people they saw as fundamentally inferior.[21] Eelkens returned only Tabotem's head to his people.

This initial act of revenge is the grim origin of wampum's use as currency in New England and New Holland and indeed it was used so widely, and European gold and silver currencies were so scarce in this period, that wampum became legal tender in both colonies well into the seventeenth century, as well as the main trade commodity of the fur trade. Eelken's revenge against Tabotem and the Pequod for failing to deliver to him what he believed he was entitled to, which masqueraded as justice, is another quintessential example of the revenge-from-above I am exploring in this book. More vitally, it represents an alternative origin story to modern money.

Eelkens turned his "primitive accumulation" of a king's ransom of wampum beads into a means to leverage more furs from the Pequod and other nations in the sphere of what K-Sue Park calls the "contact economy."[22] As colonial brutality and disease took their deadly toll on Indigenous nations, and as European conquest seized more and more coastal lands, already-existing and newly emergent rivalries deepened among and between Indigenous nations who were increasingly made to compete to harvest a dwindling supply of furs in order to secure European imports including guns and ammunition, dry goods, and liquor.[23] The latter was intentionally used by European traders (traded at a loss or given for free) as a means to produce favorable trading conditions, in spite of explicit warnings from European missionaries that addiction was ravaging Indigenous communities.[24] In this context, the European traders in both colonies were able to insist that wampum become the main and in some cases exclusive currency of the fur trade; especially convenient because they now controlled the coastal territories where wampum shells were collected.[25]

Throughout the latter seventeenth and early eighteenth century wampum was essentially weaponized as a means to compel and cheapen Indigenous labor and extract resources from the interior, with colonists controlling the supply. Indeed, Europeans commissioned Indigenous people and early settlers to manufacture wampum with newer European techniques, and out of conch shells now imported from Caribbean colonies.[26] There is even evidence that colonists began to forge or counterfeit wampum from glass or ceramics.[27] Much of this was undertaken in an entrepreneurial fashion, frequently by working class colonists, so much so that both Dutch and British colonies at various times had to pass laws regulating the quality of beads.[28] As

European power and influence grew, the commoditization of wampum spread inland, as did competition between Indigenous nations for furs. With the seizure of more Indigenous lands and the forms of social and ecological destruction colonialism unleashed, Indigenous nations became increasingly dependent on imported European goods.[29] Wampum, which was once a technology of peace, became a technology for a kind of systemic, decentralized vengeance of nascent capitalism.

By the eighteenth century colonial power was such that it was possible for its administrators to demand tribute ("taxation") from Indigenous nations in wampum.[30] The colonists also declared the right to try Indigenous people in their courts and fine them according to their criteria, fines payable in wampum.[31] Traditional wampum regalia handed down over generations was broken up into beads to pay these fines, as were the belts and strings of wampum that told the story of centuries of Indigenous history and diplomacy.[32]

Legacy

This story of punitive "financial inclusion" is revealing in its own right and because it is arguably the origin of two quintessential American institutions that, today, have been globalized.

Jessica Cattelino argues that the imagined figure of the pre-monetary and economically immature "New World Indian" was central to the philosophical understandings of money, economics, and commerce for many of the most influential "Western" philosophers, notably John Locke (whose influence on Adam Smith and other seminal political economists is difficult to underestimate).[33] The (false) notion that Indigenous people were primitively pre-economic not only served to exclude them from the capitalist economy built on their stolen lands, it also created a romantic myth of universal prehistory and progress against which modern forms of political economy defined themselves.

Legal historian and theorist K-Sue Park argues that the notion of alienable land and the practice of foreclosing on housing in revenge for non-repayment of loans was pioneered in the seizure of Indigenous lands through the wampum economy, as were the modern practices of extortionate debt.[34] Furthermore, the idea that land could become a liquid asset, which stemmed from these practices, was crucial to the ability of the nascent American colony and, later, nation to develop its particular (now globalized) legal-economic framework.[35] In other words, it's not only that America was built on stolen Indigenous land; it's also that the method of that land's theft, commodification, and financialization became the legal and economic foundation for the evolution of American capitalism.

Literary and cultural historian Marc Shell makes a similar argument about the origins of American money.[36] Framing wampum in the contact economy as a project of both Indigenous and colonial innovation, he traces the way this early form of colonial currency, even after it was discontinued as legal tender, had a strong influence on a particularly American history of financial innovation. He illustrates that the experience of wampum allowed colonists to recognize that the value of money is built on relationships, trust, and diplomacy, rather than the allegedly inherent value of the underlying commodity, thus enabling some of the innovations with paper and credit money that financed the American Revolution. Later, the recurrence of the metaphor of wampum for money, and the appearance of wampum and Indigenous people on American money and financial instruments (like stock certificates) indicates an enduring legacy.[37] In this sense, the ghost of wampum, and the colonial violence to which it bore witness, haunts modern money to this day.

Money's vengeful peace

Thus vengeance by financial inclusion has a long pedigree. But this approach contrasts profoundly with the dominant discourse, then and now. The dominant view is that financial inclusion is a pathway to peace, prosperity, and progress. The gradual inclusion of more and more of humanity in a formal, regulated and liberal economy is alleged to represent perhaps the final conquest of many of our species' most destructive inheritances.

One of today's most popular proponents of this view is conservative financial historian and media personality Niall Ferguson who opens his triumphalist *Ascent of Money*:

> money is the root of most progress ... the ascent of money has been essential to the ascent of man ... financial innovation has been an indispensable factor in man's advance from wretched subsistence to the giddy heights of material prosperity that so many people know today.[38]

Accordingly, "poverty is not the result of rapacious financiers exploiting the poor. It is has much more to do with the lack of financial institutions, with the absence of banks, not their presence"; summoning up the specter of gangs, mafias, and other informal, extortionate (notoriously vengeful) lenders he asserts that it is "only when borrowers have access to efficient credit networks can they escape from the clutches of loan sharks, and only when savers can deposit their money in reliable banks can it be channeled from the idle to the industrious or from the rich to the poor."[39] "This point," he continues, "applies not only to the poor countries of the world [but also] the poorest neighborhoods in supposedly developed countries – the 'Africas within.'"[40]

Such statements will come as no surprise from an author whose next books were an explicit apologia for the British Empire and a bullyboy paean to "the West" as the seat of progress in an otherwise dark world. Thus they are symptomatic of the persistence of the imperial and racist worldviews which see "non-Western" cultures (those Africas "without" and "within") as both eternally indebted for their newfound economic freedom and somehow, at the same time, doomed to betray it.

From Ferguson's (Lockean) perspective, money is a natural and beneficial outgrowth of the human capacity to specialize and trade, allowing for the development of more and more "complex" forms of social organization. This insight was popularized by Adam Smith and has become an almost unquestionable pillar of modern thought.[41] Money is a neutral and natural tool, more or less a direct expression of human nature. While various regimes can manipulate, contort, abuse, or constrain money, its evolution proceeds, especially (for Ferguson) when paired with modern forms of capitalism and liberal governance. In this sense, Ferguson sees today's financial order as more or less the natural evolution of the earliest forms of money and therefore on some level just and inevitable. It delivers us freedom, prosperity, individual liberty, and socio-cultural progress, a benign medium through which humanity's allegedly natural competitiveness and acquisitiveness can be safely harnessed for the greater good.

Running through this discourse and others associated with it is a fundamental belief that the free market represents the apogee of the Enlightenment liberal project, which is, in a way, cast as the antithesis of revenge. It goes something like this: once upon a time there was a war of all against all and revenge ruled. Then the pre-modern sovereign arrived and elevated revenge to law and preserved his sole right to claim it and adjudicate disputes. His enforced peace allowed for the specialization of labor and the development of primitive markets, which increased the wealth and sophistication of societies and also offered a platform for international trade. But the lust for power and rivalry between claimants to sovereignty led to the curtailment of economic and personal freedom. That is, until a special variety of historical, technological, and intellectual elements converged in Europe in the late eighteenth century, opening the door for the French and American revolutions, the birth of human rights, and the development of market economies. Since that time, while rulers and regimes have sought to limit personal and economic freedoms, liberal democratic capitalism has persisted, now to such a point that it has the technological capacity to truly globalize and, vitally, unseat or tame the sovereign once and for all, providing through market mechanisms the antidote to revenge. On the one hand, as peace and abundance grow, the material privations and pressures that give rise to resentment and envy will decline. On the other, to the extent that revenge is rooted in an inherent human struggle for recognition or a dispensation for competition, the market is the ideal place to allow and encourage these drives to play out: market-mediated competition is good for everyone as it drives progress, innovation, and efficiency.

I have taken some liberties in distilling this argument for the sake of clarity. It is one that has been made in many ways, and with important nuances. Stephen Pinker's recent bestselling *The Better Angels of Our Nature: Why Violence has Declined* is one of the more sophisticated and methodical articulations of a similar set of arguments, though one marred by a near-complete omission of systemic and structural forms of violence.[42] (One then doesn't have to count, for instance, the tens of thousands of suicides of farmers in India who are beset by the vengeance of debt[43]). Perhaps the most explicit scholarly discourse to entertain the idea of money as a medium of peace has occurred under the banner of "the capitalist peace" which takes as doxa that liberal democratic states are less warlike and suggests that it is capitalist market competition, rather than democratic institutions, that are responsible.[44]

The notion that the globalized free market is or will or might supersede the functions of the sovereign state is articulated from a wide variety of positions. Joseph Vogl for instance has observed the way the sphere of finance has subordinated the key institutions of the state, developing what he calls the "sovereignty effect."[45] The central claim of Michael Hardt and Antonio Negri's influential *Empire* is that, increasingly, sovereignty has moved from the level of the nation-state as the container of rival capitalist interests to a decentralized networked form of global capitalism. This new form of capitalism is less interested in a kind of disciplinary power to exploit socially-necessary labor time for the production of surplus value and more driven by the proliferation and interlacing of mechanisms for the capture of "biopolitical production," communicative capacities, and the reproduction of social life.[46]

These latter authors are, obviously, much more pessimistic about the prospects of the global rule of free markets and (rightly) deeply skeptical about the conflation of liberal notions of democracy, freedom, and individual choice with capitalism. Rather than see "financial inclusion" as the triumphant march of progress and liberty, they see it as the consolidation of an even more fearsome if less obvious tyranny, and I agree. My argument throughout this book is that the form of global capitalism that today rules is not the kindly king returned from exile, but a vengeful tyrant.

Counternarratives

Two counternarratives are worth keeping in mind.

The first is presented by Graeber, who illustrates how the bucolic just-so story of money's origins in barter and, evolution into a neutral tool, in spite of its popularity, has little to no anthropological or historical support.[47] Indeed, Graeber argues that it would be more accurate to see money not as an evolution of peaceful trade but as a kind of crystallization of the violence of debt. Societies where power relations solidify into durable forms frequently blur the line between moral and economic debt as a means to normalize social hierarchy. It is this extortionate and exploitative debt which is the original source of money, an origin story which helps us better explain the various ways that money has continuously been used as a tool of compulsion, including in our own times. In this sense, money is a kind of encrypted form of vengeance: what appears as a neutral and innocent object or concept is actually the bearer and enforcer of a fundamental retributive social violence.

The second stems from Marx's theory of money. Arguably, Marx generally agreed with the liberal genealogy of money as emerging from barter but, with the ascent of capitalism, a fundamentally new form of money emerges as the incarnation, the medium and the lifeblood of capital itself.[48] Many non-capitalist societies have used money in various forms, sometimes highly complex forms including speculative forms we associate with finance. Many non-capitalist societies have also been dramatically unequal and based on the exploitation of the labor of an underclass. And many non-capitalist societies also have a ruling class that perpetuates its power through force and influence. Only under capitalism are all three of these features brought together: money defines the power of the ruling class and commands the labor of the exploited. Indeed, money intercedes throughout society, reshaping more and more social relationships. But, importantly, for Marx it is not money itself but the particular way money is used to harness and command abstracted labor time that is specific to capitalism, in part because it does so to ensure its own endless reproduction and accumulation.[49] A kind of meta-intelligence or "logic" of capital emerges above and beyond the particular desires or choices of this or that capitalist; indeed, it emerges precisely from the inherent and necessary competition between capitalists.[50]

Capital expands endlessly and inevitably seeks to bring more and more aspects of the world into its orbit, but it also necessarily produces crises, first and foremost for its exploited creators, proletarians, whose own reproduction is reduced to the barest minimum, and sometimes less than that. As capital drives competing capitalists to cut costs, workers' wages are cut or fall behind inflation, mechanization introduces less autonomy and greater dangers, the body is abused, social relations are mined, and, as we shall see, sometimes whole populations are abandoned when their exploitation proves unprofitable.[51] To this we can also add the wars that emerge from contradictions between various factions of the ruling class, the policing and prisons used to keep workers in line, and the wastage of social wealth on luxuries for the rich.[52] In this sense, capitalist money represents the crystallization of a kind of pathological inhuman systemic vengeance on its own (re)producers: the proletariat. Money is not capital, but it represents, circulates, and enforces capitalist relations. It is, ultimately, the alienated and exploited energies and potentials of the working class now returned to them in punitive, extortionate, and, indeed, *vengeful* form.[53] And yet, ironically, it is frequently the case that, rather than take seriously the structures of capitalist exploitation, we fixate on the arcane mechanics of money, as if small adjustments to its operations will rectify the economy. Calls to restore the Gold Standard or the recent craze for Bitcoin and blockchain technology are only the most notorious forms of a much more general myth that would encourage us to believe that "fixing" or "disrupting" money is the key to overcoming the pathologies of capitalism. Yet massive investments in "financial technology" (FinTech) and a celebratory rhetoric of "hacking" money (as one might hack into a computer network) offer a radical gloss on what essentially amounts to developing new methods of monetizing and financializating ever more spheres of life.

THREE STORIES OF PROLETARIAN VENGEANCE AGAINST MONEY

In the remainder of this chapter I want to turn to three examples of practices whereby the oppressed and exploited have taken a small kind of revenge on money. From these I think we can learn something about what financial innovation or money hacking might look like from below.

They represent entries into what anthropologist James C. Scott calls a "hidden transcript" of power, or which I, in reference to their particular monetary characteristics, call a hidden ledger.[54] For Scott, arguments about the cultural hegemony that the powerful wield usually rely on the testimonies, observations, and records of the powerful, which are oblivious to the actual thoughts, sentiments, and practices of the oppressed. These accounts tend to vastly over-state the acquiescence of the oppressed, whereas, in actuality, the relationship is typically marked by the proliferation of infra-political "arts of resistance" which can include things like tactical laziness, performative stupidity, parodic obsequiousness, sly jokes, encrypted stories of resistance, and other cultural and material practices which are subtle enough to evade detection and punishment from the oppressors and their enforcers but meaningful enough to build solidarity among the oppressed. Scott encourages us to look to the hidden transcript of these arts of resistance if we are to truly understand social struggle, in part because, all at once, these seemingly insignificant puffs of wind can drum up a revolutionary storm which appears to come from nowhere.

I have selected three almost mythical moments in the history of capitalist and colonial modernity because I think they represent a very different vision of what "financial innovation" could look like which do not in any way participate in the general trend toward trying to "correct" money so that capitalism might function properly. All three examples emerge from contexts in which the oppressed and exploited feel money to be little more than a lash, who seem to share no optimism that money could or should be anything else, and who do not fall prey to the dream that somehow money could be a friend. In each case, money acts vindictively on the bodies and communities of poor, oppressed, exploited, or abandoned people and, in appropriating, cutting, manipulating, and wrecking money, they enacted a kind of avenging imaginary. If modern money on some level is the icon of the unholy marriage of state and capitalist power, then the hidden ledger I am indexing here represents a dream of freedom or exodus.

Convict love tokens

Love tokens are a subset of popular money interventions enacted largely by the working class in Britain and America in the eighteenth and nineteenth centuries.[55] Largely in response to states declaring the nominal exchange value of coins beyond or contrary to the actual metallic substance, proletarians began to seize upon coins, especially devalued ones, as canvases for other sorts of commerce. This is in contrast to the brutalizing indifference of the emerging capitalist economy, which rendered workers disposable and interchangeable with one another, and which enforced a wage relationship through the equally indifferent medium of money. Using proletarian money "hacks," one could impress a unique stamp of one's indelible individuality on the effaced surface of a coin of the realm. Copper coins were transfigured by anonymous artists into testimonies of love or fidelity, a small gift made of the same material that tore so many proletarian lives apart.

Among the most poetic and revealing examples of this practice were convict love tokens, most of which were forged by or at the behest of British prisoners awaiting the punishment of "transportation," either in decrepit jails (notably, London's notorious Newgate) or below deck on overcrowded ships set to ferry them to Australia or other British colonies.[56] Were they fortunate enough to survive their incarceration and voyage, these proletarians, most of whom had been convicted of petty crimes by uncompassionate, hasty judges, would typically land and be auctioned to local farmers, capitalists, and public officials as indentured servants; they were violently transmuted into cannon fodder for the expansion of the British Empire.[57] Many of the female convicts were essentially made into state-sanctioned sexual slaves.[58] In the unlikely event of surviving their brutal sentence, some were permitted to buy passage back to England, but most couldn't or did not.[59]

While incarcerated in Britain, some prisoners carved or commissioned the carving of a love token as a keepsake for a loved one from whom they were soon to be separated, probably forever: a lover, a parent, a sibling, or a friend. These mementos were evidence of their existence in relationship to one another. As in the present, most of the acts for which proletarians were convicted were crimes of poverty and desperation: theft, prostitution, insubordination, vagrancy, and, importantly, forgery and counterfeiting.[60] While the eighteenth and nineteenth centuries are remembered for the economic growth and power of the British Empire, these massive technological and economic transformations typically hit the working class as disasters.[61] The "disruptive innovation" of new manufacturing methods could throw hundreds of thousands of workers into the street at a time. The constant political squabbles between various elite factions led to the passing of trade and sumptuary laws that would cause commodities that were common one day to become scarce the next and vice versa, triggering massive shifts of wealth at the top of society and shifts in life and death at the bottom.[62]

Figure 5 George Cruikshanks's *Bank Restriction Note*, 1819. This satirical rendition of a Bank of England note highlighted the lethal punishment for counterfeiting. Image in the public domain.

In *The London Hanged*, radical historian Peter Linebaugh makes clear that, for elites throughout the eighteenth and nineteenth centuries, economics was not, as myth would have it, a benign and neutral affair.[63] On the contrary, it was a system enforced by authoritarian power. The close friendship between John Locke and Isaac Newton, remembered today as heroes of philosophy and science respectively, was forged during their joint management of the nascent capitalist economy, Locke in the realm of policy and Newton as an early but formative Governor of the Bank of England. Both agreed that no punishment was too severe for proletarians who dared defy the state's control over the money supply, and they therefore helped pass a bevy of laws that criminalized the slightest economic infraction. George Caffentzis has detailed the lengths to which the British government went to enforce what it considered the proper use of money, to prevent coin clipping (shaving off the edge of a coin to garner the metal) and counterfeiting.[64] Linebaugh argues that so many were the capital crimes associated with the "misuse" of money at the dawn of modern capitalism and the modern state that we should rightly understand this period as a Thanatocracy, the rule of death. George Cruikshank's *Bank Restriction Note* of 1819 – a satirical print sold on the streets – comments on the horrors unleashed on the working class convicted not only of creating but even of handling counterfeit money by accident.[65] But who could blame them? The Bank

Figure 6 An early convict love token carved by or for a Thomas Tilley, who was convicted of counterfeiting money, 1786. Image in the public domain.

of England notes of the day were laughably easy to imitate and, for those starving on the streets of the world's wealthiest cities, the temptation to take into their own hands the seemingly magical power of the Governor of the Bank to sign wealth into existence with the stroke of a pen must have been irresistible.[66]

It is difficult to read Linebaugh's account of the legal and punitive regimes of early English capitalism without being enraged by its petty vindictiveness. First it made proletarian lives practically unlivable through the legalized seizure of lands and repression of struggles for better living conditions. Then, to add insult to injury, it criminalized a huge swath of survival activities and rendered up the victims to the hangman to serve as grim exemplars for their peers.

While the punishment for such infractions against the Crown was nominally death, most convicts had their sentences commuted to "transportation." As cheap as it was for British elites to make gruesome public spectacles of the execution of proletarians, it was still more profitable to consign them to indenture and transport them. The ocean, disease, overwork, or heartbreak would likely do the work of the executioner anyway.[67] It would not be an exaggeration to say that most judges and lawmakers were enthusiastic financial and ideological investors of colonial expeditions, and the colonies demanded cheap labor.[68] The desperate, traumatized, and deracinated survivors would become the shock troops of settler colonialism, with all the horrific violence the process entailed.[69] The means and ends of the whole gory enterprise were capitalist forms of state-backed money.[70]

Convict love tokens represented proletarians taking money back into their own hands and radically transforming it into a medium for their own tragic solidarity, a tiny rebellion or revenge against the very medium of their immiseration. An artisan of such tokens would painstakingly efface the image of the King or other royal symbolism – the very nexus of state and capitalist sovereignties – to create a smooth surface. Less sophisticated, cheaper makers would create words or even crude images by punching dozens of small holes in the coin. More skilled artists carved into the surface of the coin itself.[71] The ghostlike messages are often simply a name and a date. Sometimes there is also a description of the crime for which the carver or commissioner of the carving had been convicted. Other times the token directly addresses a loved one, begging them not to forget. Occasionally startlingly intricate designs appear.

This story reveals a proletarian view of money as a weapon wielded against common life. There is no utopianism here, just rancor, terror, and revenge. From the bottom-up perspective, and despite its alluring nature, money is not a medium of social or economic innovation; it is a curse, a trap, and a poison. The physical effacement of coins is a desperate antagonism to a capitalism that renders the proletarian body a worthless machine to be exploited and disposed of. To simply carve one's name on the King's coins is a human rebellion against an inhuman system. In this sense, this proletarian financial innovation reclaimed from the sovereign, in a small, micropolitical way, the right to revenge. In Western ruling class political thought (Hobbes, Locke, Rousseau) sovereignty allegedly arises to monopolize revenge and prevent society from succumbing to endless and escalating cycles of retribution. The sovereign insists on the right to adjudicate claims to harm and undertake vengeance against wrongdoers not for an infraction against this or that wronged person, but for an infraction against the common peace. That common peace is likewise represented in the image of the sovereign on the coin, the medium of peaceful, mutually advantageous trade, trade which relies on laws to enforce contracts and prevent theft. The acts of the proletarian coin carvers was a kind of inchoate refusal of the whole narrative emblematized in the sovereign-stamped coin.

Second, by transforming coins into a medium of relationality, proletarian artists reverse-engineered the capitalist alienation of labor power. For Marx, money is the ultimate manifestation of the commodity form.[72] Capitalism transforms thinking, feeling, relational human beings into mere sellers of a standardized commodity – abstract labor power – for which they earn a wage, with which they buy "back" the products of their (collective) labor power: commodities.[73] Money both orchestrates and intermediates this process, but also in a sense represents it.[74] Money is the hieroglyph of alienation. Both the young and the old Marx agree that money is the false bond with the rest of society one carries around in one's pocket, what I have elsewhere proposed as a holographic shard of a larger totality, containing an uncanny glimpse of the whole in the fragment.[75] By transforming money into a medium of social intercourse, of human relationality, of pathos and proletarian poetry, the convict love token refuses the mystification of society in money and instead reiterates the work of sociality, of social reproduction, that is locked or encrypted in money.

Figure 7 American "Buffalo Nickel," minted between 1913 and 1938. Image in the public domain.

Figure 8 George Washington "Bo" Hughes, The "Dicer" Hobo Nickel, 1939. Image appears courtesy of Chris Dempsey of hobocollector.com.

Hobo nickels

Hobo nickels were crafted by itinerant Americans forced into a life of vagrancy in the aftermath of the First World War (when millions of decommissioned soldiers – many of them physically and psychologically wounded – and their families were essentially abandoned by the state), and later during the Great Depression.[76] From 1913 to 1938 the United States Mint produced a distinctive "Indian Head" or "Buffalo" $0.05 piece (so named for the relief image on the obverse and reverse, respectively), which became a favorite canvas for carvers. Both the image of the man (a fictionalized amalgam of many different Indigenous people and cultures) and of the buffalo were larger than most similar depictions on other coins, and the copper alloy from which the coin was minted presented a relatively pliable material if one had minimal tools.[77]

While proletarians almost immediately began to "hack" the coins to create love tokens and similar artifacts, the heyday of the hobo nickel came during the 1930s, when an increasing number of proletarians were forced to abandon their homes and "ride the rails" in search of food, shelter, and work amidst wholesale economic collapse. The carved nickels often showed portraits of the carver or his commissioner (we do not know of any female carvers, though we do know of women hobos)[78] by means of altering the "Indian Head" on the obverse, while the buffalo on the reverse became a boxcar, a horse, a turtle, or a hobo with an iconic pack on his back.

Hobo nickels appear to have served many purposes, though much is unfortunately lost to history.[79] There appears to be evidence that, through their artistry, hobos increased the coins' exchange value, selling them or bartering them for goods and services (from food to shelter) that would cost more than the coins' (ef)face(d) value of $0.05. There are reports of hobo nickels being given as gifts in return for even mundane kindness, such as a farmer letting a hobo sleep in his barn, or a woman giving a hobo a meal, regardless of the estimated value. There are also rumors that the nickels were tokens of solidarity among hobos, a unique calling card and means of communication passed from one hand to another as their bearers made their way back and forth across the nation. And, however doubtful they seem, there are even rumors that hobos added coded messages on these tokens, as they were known to mark buildings and other infrastructure with sigils to warn or encourage future travelers.[80]

The identities and biographies of only a handful of original hobo nickel creators are known, notably George Washington "Bo" Hughes who lived an itinerant life from the time he left home aged 15 in roughly 1915 until the time of his disappearance in the early 1980s.[81] The son of formerly enslaved parents, Bo's craft was taught to him by another famous carver, Bertram "Bert" Wiegand. While Hughes created nickels until the time of his disappearance, his most sought-after work was carved in the early phase of his career. Frequent beatings by railway police as well as having to endure frigid winter nights in meager shelters or on trains left his hands in a near ruined state. This was compounded by a carving accident in 1957 which, in his last decades, left him unable to do more than merely punch out crude diagrams on coins rather than carving images.

The hobo nickel gives us a glimpse into a proletarian practice of secretly avenging the crimes and cruelties of a system of capitalist monetary privation and exploitation. Here, the medium of money itself becomes an opportunity to craft a whole new infraeconomy, wherein these tokens come to express, communicate, and reproduce a very different set of non-market values and relationships. We know so little of the use and transit of hobo nickels (except as collectors' items and numismatic curiosities) that we cannot know the rules of this game, but at least two things seem clear. The first is that the hobos were obviously not seeking to build an alternative market economy, and they seemed to have no ambition to challenge or replace the existing capitalist-state money system either. Second, if there were rules to the economic game of the hobo nickel, these rules were evidently extremely flexible. Was it a gift economy or a barter economy? Was the hobo nickel a commodity or a sacrament, a joke or a coded message? Perhaps none of these, or perhaps all. What seems evident at the very least is that the hobo nickel was a medium of solidarity, joy, and creativity at the margins of the capitalist economy.

Drawing on Scott's discussion of the "hidden transcript" and the "arts of resistance" of the oppressed, I propose that the proletarian currency "disruptions" and "hacks" presented in this chapter might be understood as part of a "hidden ledger." Miranda Joseph has illustrated the importance of forms of counter-accounting to movements for economic and collective liberation.[82] The examples explored here represent some of the many forgotten, ignored or suppressed attempts by the oppressed to express value otherwise. Collectively, this hidden ledger would challenge our unfounded optimism in top-down monetary innovation and echo the haunting revelation of Walter Benjamin that

> There is a secret agreement between past generations and the present one. Our coming was expected on earth. Like every generation that preceded us, we have been endowed with a weak Messianic power, a power to which the past has a claim. That claim cannot be settled cheaply.[83]

Figure 9 Kahn and Selesnick, *Eisbergfreistadt* (exhibition view), 2008. Image appears courtesy of the artist.

The myths of the Eisbergfreistadt

It is said that, in October 1923, at a moment of almost complete economic catastrophe in Germany, an iceberg made its way from the North Pole through the straits between the North and Baltic Sea to arrive at the nation's port city of Lübeck, a one-time Hanseatic capital. Appearing as if through a portal from another cold, pure world, this strange and barren visitor came at a moment when society had all but collapsed. Due to the vindictive reparations Germany was made to pay in the wake of the First World War, inflation in the country became so severe that people had to take wheelbarrows full of bills to stores to buy the most basic commodities. Government-issued notes, even in denominations of billions of Marks, were quickly deemed worthless. The wealthy sought to remove as much gold and hard foreign currency from the country as possible as the state mandated its right to raid personal deposits at private banks to pay its foreign debts. This was an economic catastrophe that made a grim and deadly pantomime of the typical uncertainties of capitalist prices and money supplies.

Figure 10 Kahn and Selesnick, *Eisbergfreistadt* (Notgeld), 2008. Image appears courtesy of the artist.

As a result, municipalities like Lübeck began to issue their own cheaply manufactured, mass-printed Notgeld: emergency money intended for temporary use to enable commerce and taxation in the absence of any useful legal tender.[84] Throughout the heyday of Notgeld, from 1921 to 1923, hundreds of thousands of different, often extremely creative and colorful notes were produced, sometimes for use as functional – if unreliable – currency, often (and increasingly after 1923, when their use as "money" was banned by the national government) as a collector's item and as a way for the local municipality to raise funds.[85] Because it offered so many artists and citizens an opportunity to mint their own money with their own chosen symbolism expressing their own individual and collective values, Notgeld became a particularly vivid social canvas.

In the present-day, artist duo Kahn & Selesnick offer a parafictional depiction of the fabled 1923 event when the rogue iceberg became lodged in Lübeck's harbor for about a month, during which time the municipality, in what must be a somewhat tongue-in-cheek move, declared sovereignty over it, naming it Eisbergfreistadt (the Free City Iceberg) – a strange, barren, and rapidly melting temporary autonomous zone.[86] The artists present a range of beguiling historical documents that indicate that, until it finally split and its remnants were washed back out to sea in November, citizens not only visited the iceberg out of curiosity, they appear to have increasingly used it as a literal and metaphorical platform to imagine new relationships and new political and economic orders.[87] It could almost have been a spectacle orchestrated by the contemporary surrealists, a public dream amidst a common nightmare. And, indeed, Kahn & Selesnick offer that the Eisbergfreistadt was commemorated on several Notgeld notes. These exhibited a rare aesthetic exuberance and imaginative panache during a time when many were starving amidst literal piles of money; when money was in fact being burned for warmth and desperately sewn into clothing for insulation. Some of this Notgeld appears to have been issued by the Eisbergfreistadt itself, a conjectural, melting free state minting its own currency through the power of imagination alone.

Eighty-five years later, amidst the financial crisis of 2008, Kahn & Selesnick created, assembled, and organized materials related to the mythical Eisbergfreistadt incident in an immersive exhibition.[88] Replicas of the "original" Notgeld pour out of a suitcase, are stacked neatly in a wheelbarrow, and are stitched together into garments distributed around the exhibition. Meanwhile, the bills appear in panoramic paintings, in staged and archival photographs, in vitrines and affixed to the walls. A huge replica of one of the bills hangs face up from a pulley on the gallery's ceiling, counterbalanced on the other end of the rope by a stack of flat rocks. Paper birds and airplanes made of the Notgeld flock about the gallery, suspended by thread. A house of cards, made out of bundles of Notgeld, sits ominously on a plinth.

Much could be said about the Eisbergfreistadt, both in terms of its moment in history as well as Kahn & Selesnick's exhibition. The artists operate at the fraught threshold of fact and fiction to generate the radical imagination. I am less interested in if the events actually occurred than in what the myth might make imaginable. My interest stems from the way they seem to gesture toward an alternative horizon for money if we were to reject a genealogy of top-down money invention and engineering, and instead paid attention to the ways in which the poor and the exploited have appropriated money as sly resistance. What does it mean to create a currency for a temporary autonomous zone?[89] From the perspective of almost any mainstream or heterodox economic school of thought it is a futile or purely aesthetic exercise. The zone doesn't need money: it can't sustain an economy and it will immanently melt back into the ocean. And yet what was perhaps revealed in the Eisbergfreistadt episode and exhibition is that, when money is detached from functionality and from the dreams of the economic architect, when it is allowed to become part of an economy of creative social improvisation, money can become a medium of collective joy, and a kind of proletarian minor utopianism.[90]

The Eisbergfreistadt Notgeld, if it really existed in fact or if it exists purely as a fiction was (and in a way is) essentially a public plaything, a shared resource for a *virtuosity* of the commons where, even amidst some of the darkest, most chaotic moments of people's lives, a shared wonder emerged from the fabric of the cooperative human imagination.[91] This is a reflection of what Cornelius Castoriadis calls the tectonic magma of the radical imagination; that substance of destructive and creative potential out of which all social formations, institutions, and orders are congealed, but that also periodically sweeps away those remnants.[92]

CURRENCIES OF THE UNDERCOMMON

There have, of course, been intentionally radical artistic and political appropriations of money. At the turn of the century, suffragettes famously

Figure 11 Joseph DeLappe, *In Drones We Trust*, 2014; *Hands Up Don't Shoot!*, 2014–15; and *Sea Level Rising*, 2015: crowd sourced, participatory rubber stamp currency interventions. Image appears courtesy of the artist.

carved "VOTES FOR WOMEN" on British shillings as part of an escalating repertoire of direct actions.[93] In the 1970s, the Brazilian artist Cildo Meireles stamped banknotes with subversive messages and passed them back into circulation to avoid censors and repression by the reigning military Junta.[94] More recently, American artist Joseph DeLappe created and distributed rubber stamps that imprint money with political messages.[95]

The proletarian money-hacks and currency disruptions explored in this chapter are typically categorized as exonumia: money-like objects that do not function as money. "Exo" derives from the Ancient Greek prefix for "out," often used to refer to the outside or the alien; "numia" refers to money by way of a reference to customary practices, a root that also gives us the legal, political, and philosophical notion of "nomos" or "law." We can interpret the practices noted here as ones that exist and persist outside – or, maybe more accurately, within, against, and beyond – laws, customs, and practices of the conventional, exploitative, unequal capitalist economy. We might understand these as some of the currencies of the undercommons, as Fred Moten and Stefano Harney frame it: those quotidian practices of proletarian planning, of pragmatic yet imaginative solidarity. Ironically, the capitalist economy depends on the bedrock of decommodified social care that these undercommons represent, but which it also strives to contain, control, delimit, and criminalize.[96] In this sense, exonumia is the money of the internalized alien, or of the alienated.[97] For Marx, money represents the method, the lifeblood, and the culmination of a system of capitalism that alienates us from our species-being, our cooperative and imaginative potential. These exonumismatic practices represent a kind of revenge of the alienated, in a small but revealing way. It is the specter of our own cooperative and creative potential.

Scores of convict ships were lost at sea on their way to the colonies, many of them to mutiny. Many hobos, including George Washington 'Bo' Hughes, disappeared without a trace. It is rumored that, when the Eisbergfreistadt drifted back out to sea, there were a number of people who had, impossibly, made the barren, melting chunk of ice their home, presumably preferring its topographical austerity to the unnecessary, all-too-human austerity of post-war Lübeck. Not all were accounted for after most were rescued. Imagine now a parallel universe where all these exiles from the history of capitalism's vengeful accumulation met. What currency would they have invented together, these convicts, hobos, and debtors? And, what wisdom can we adopt from their stolen future to change our own seemingly foreclosed present?

Interlude: Khloé Kardashian's revenge body, or the Zapatisa nobody?

I

The theme of the Entertainment Network's popular "reality TV" series *Revenge Body with Khloé Kardashian* is simple: contestants/participants audition to be featured working with a personal trainer over a short period to meet ambitious goals for transforming their body as a means to get back at someone or something that has hurt them.

In the initial episodes, most of the contestants were women unhappy with bodies they considered overweight, who were seeking to transform to take revenge on men who spurned them. As the series unfolds, the reasons and targets for this vengeful transformation shift, as do the contestants. In some episodes, revenge is sought against nasty or belittling parents, siblings, bullies, or bosses. Sometimes the revenge is waged not against individuals at all but against the contestant's past traumas or against nebulous social expectations.

The notion of a revenge body makes a kind of intuitive sense within a society that persistently frames social problems as individual burdens and which blames individuals for what are systemically and structurally compounded misfortunes, a society in which the punitive demands to conform to patriarchal beauty norms are not framed as a source of oppression but an invitation to individualistic "empowerment." It is a vindictive system, in a sense, that in turn provides its own catalysts for non-transformative fantasies of "revenge" that, by and large, end up reproducing the status quo.

Like much reality TV, the goal of the show's producers is to place the contestant in a gauntlet of stressful situations to heighten the drama. The show is formulaic: initial studio interview with the contestant reveal their back story. They are then led to a set where the show's multi-millionaire celebrity star, Khloé Kardashian, deigns to offer three minutes of her time to hear the contestant and sympathize with their plight. Next, the contestant is introduced to a personal trainer who, in the core segments of each episode, puts the contestant through an intensive workout regime aimed at helping them meet their stated goals, usually for weight loss. (Occasionally, especially for male contestants, the goal is muscle gain or physical self-confidence.)

In spite of the saccharine claim of support and care for the contestant and rhetorical goals of empowerment that the program manifestly espouses, the gym scenes are shot and cut to make the antics of people not conventionally imagined as athletic seem entertaining, or at least titillating. To heighten the drama, we are treated to shots of the contestants panting, exhausted, falling, and even weeping as the trainer encourages, berates, cajoles, or even laughs at them. All for the best, we are told: the episode ends with a "reveal" party where the contestant's friends and family are assembled, along with, if possible, the person or people on whom they are taking their "revenge." The contestant enters wearing tailored clothes and shows off their "revenge body" and we are treated to the spectacle of the enthusiasm of their loved ones, an emotive heart-to-heart dialog between the allegedly successful avenger and their trainer, and, if we are very lucky, a confrontation with the now-ashamed tormentor.

II

The show is, ultimately, highly exploitative in a sly way, which offers the viewer a kind of sadistic, bombastic, and emotionally stimulating spectacle while claiming that everyone (the producers, the trainers, Kardashian, and the viewers themselves) is on the side of the avenger. A hybrid televisual artifact made in and for the digital age, much of *Revenge Body*'s reach exists online, on forums like Reddit and YouTube. In the user-generated comments threads, the two-faced nature of the spectacle is revealed. While some fans delight in echoing the manifest sentimentality of the show, which sympathizes with and wishes the best for the contestants, many others express the show's latent id: a kind of caustic fat-phobic, often misogynistic *jouissance* that snipes and mock, the alibi being that the contestant has already chosen to make a spectacle of themselves.[1] The program cunningly opens itself up to both approaches, and indeed I would suggest it functions precisely because it entices each audience member to simultaneously savor both sentiments: a kind of sympathetic pity and a vindictive loathing.[2] It is a narcissistic fantasy: on the one hand, we are offered a resource to help us imagine ourselves to be the kind of spectator who empathizes with the struggle of the abject contestant as they seek to transform themselves to overcome the legacy of trauma and ostracization; on the other, we project onto that contestant our own self-doubts about our failures, desirability, and disposability in an increasingly austere, vengeful society.

Revenge Body with Khloé Kardashian's propaganda value for a neoliberal empire that makes each of us feel like a permanent failure, a doomed body, is precisely its utter banality. Like most reality TV created to fill daytime airtime, the program is a meticulously sanded and smooth experience, calibrated to hold attention gently but firmly, offering a narcotizing mix of stimulating human drama and comforting predictability, something that (as we shall see in Chapter 5) Geert Lovink associates with what he calls "platform nihilism."[3]

III

The poetic revenge promised by the program is rarely even realized by the original tormentor. It is rare that the person or people on whom the contestant wishes to take revenge by personal transformation are willing to participate. But even so, the overarching thematic of the show participates in the saccharine pop-psychology of what I have been calling reconcilophelia. The overarching manifest message is that, in spite of the fact that revenge is the most enticing part of the show's conceit and the only thing (other than Kardashian) that separates it from the many similar offerings, revenge ought not to be outward-facing but rather a matter of personal redemption. Revenge is only acceptable if it becomes a motivation for individualized transformation of the body and soul. Don't take revenge on those who wronged you, transcend it by "working on yourself," specifically on your body, specifically your fat.[4] Much of the discourse around fat in the show (the main villain, in actuality) takes liberally from pseudo-scientific and self-help rhetoric which suggests that fat is the result of poorly processed grief or trauma. Other times, fat is represented more conventionally, as the result of poor personal habits. In either case, the antidote to fat is self-discipline and self-denial. The contestant is invited and encouraged to redeem themselves through punishing exercise and dieting, motivated by a sense that the outcome will be a kind of revenge on the Other that the Other may (very likely) never know or acknowledge.

The notion of a revenge body is relatively recent, first popularized in the mid-2000s by tabloids that sensationalized the weight loss of once-heartbroken women stars. Here, presumably, the determination of these icons of conventional patriarchal beauty to relentlessly modify their body to even better approximate the socially-constructed ideal was a laudatory way to deliver a poetic justice to the (exclusively) male stars who dumped them.

As with celebrity culture more generally, the biography of stars becomes a kind of allegory by which the rest of us are intended to learn the hegemonic values of our society. In this case, a number of lessons are at work. In the first place, of course, there is a lesson about feminine beauty and success. As much as the outward claim of *Revenge Body* is that all bodies are inherently beautiful, and that the goal of the show is to help contestants find their inner beauty and confidence through hard work, the latent ideology of beauty is so obvious it hardly needs to be stated: fat is not only the result of trauma or poor lifestyle, it is itself a trauma. Fat is a lifestyle choice, and an abject one. The (naturally and unnaturally) sculpted bodies of Kardashian and the personal trainers represent the ideological image of god-like perfection against which the mere mortal contestant is judged and always found wanting, but everyone's so nice about it.

In spite of its implicit claims to "empower" women, and its featuring of a celebrity (Kardashian) who frames herself as a self-possessed entrepreneur, the show trades heavily on the hegemonic norms of gender and sexuality, even when it features non-heterosexual individuals or couples as contestants. Women's and men's attempts and desire to better approximate conventional gender expectations are celebrated as worthy and laudatory goals. Evidently Kardashian's time is so valuable she only appears briefly in each episode to knit her brow and nod as the constant (urged, no doubt, by the producers) detail their traumas and insecurities. Then, placing her hand on their knee, the multi-millionaire heiress offers some vaguely related tidbit from her celebrity family's well-known (indeed, highly televised) biography. Occasionally, Kardashian, like a modern-day Marie Antoinette, bestows a gift on the would-be avenger; in any case the show itself and the services of the trainer are framed as Kardashian's magnanimous offering to these little people.

IV

The thematic of the program is also, fundamentally, one of neoliberal and financialized self-improvement. Revenge here is an investment in the self, the perseverance contestants are told to exhibit is offered as a token of their inherent value. The transformation of the contestant's body is presented as the key to a form of self-worth that will, it is suggested (often explicitly), lead to happiness, wealth, love, and acceptance. Here we have a spectacle of a truly financialized work-of-the-self, a kind of privatized biopolitics.

The revenge body of the show is not a killing body or a vindictive body but a self-transforming body, and a body which transforms itself (often at brutalizing personal cost) toward a set of norms. Yet frequently it is deviation from these norms, or unwillingness to attempt to achieve these norms, that led to the cause for revenge in the first place: the quintessential boyfriend who dumped the contestant because he thought her too fat. In a kind of perverse reversal, the show reorganizes revenge to comply precisely with the demand or accusation that led to the injury in the first place.

Isn't it always thus, though? In the neoliberal capitalist idiom, in the shadow of a system that is endlessly taking revenge on us in a myriad of ways, we are invited to imagine our personal revenge in precisely the terms offered to us by that system. The bullied or fired worker dreams of becoming the boss. Indeed, the latest wave of digital hyper-exploitation germane to the "gig economy" is sold to workers as a kind of revenge against what is presented as an older, formal, hierarchical employment economy: be your own boss, work hard, and eventually you will be richer, happier, and more successful than the boss who once bullied and harassed you. Apocryphal tales of the culture of Wall Street and investment banks speak to the way new recruits are hazed, harassed, hyper-exploited, and abused to make them hungry for a form of revenge that will impel them up the corporate ladder to one day lord it over their inferiors in turn.

V

What goes unquestioned and unremarked are all the systemic and structural factors that impinge on the contestants, the forms of unspoken, indeed unspeakable, revenges they endure. The majority of the contestants, for instance, are poor or working class, in part because of the financial incentives the show must offer its contestants, in part because perhaps middle class and professional participants would fear losing face by appearing on a "low-brow" television show, in large part because, as numerous scholars have categorically shown, obesity is disproportionately a condition of the disenfranchised.[5] This sociological factor is completely invisibilized in the program with its relentless focus on the individual as a classless agent of their own betterment. Outside the temporal frame of the show is the question of if the contestants are able to maintain their sought-after body, something that has proven statistically unlikely largely because poor and working class people often lack access to affordable healthy foods and fitness facilities, and are often caught up in living and working conditions that militate against their health.[6]

Also outside the frame of the show is the vindictive and ever present disciplinary cruelty of bodily gender norms, which define beauty around so narrow a set of body types that failure to approximate the ideal is both inevitable and deeply punishing for the vast majority of people.[7] They are especially but not exclusively vengeful against women. Feminist scholars have, for generations now, observed how these expectations encourage women and girls (and we might say, more broadly, people of any gender who are expected to orient themselves toward hegemonic constructions of femininity) to take a kind of daily, unceasing revenge against themselves for their inevitable failure.[8] It is in precisely these expectations that *Revenge Body* trades that it reinforces, yet which, on the surface, it appears to disavow.

VI

This internalized revenge is in some senses the very thematic of the show. Michel Foucault famously suggested that Jeremy Bentham's panopticon prison instilled in the inmate a kind of mental projection of the invisible guard and thus would police their behavior, their very soul, long after release.[9] So too does *Revenge Body* instill in the contestant a kind of neoliberal political-economic aesthetic. The contestant is taught that the slings and arrows of the world can be met through an investment in the self, a process of sometimes grueling personal bodily transformation, and, indeed, the pain of that transformation is a kind of evidence of its success. Revenge, then, is first and foremost a revenge against the self, a self-punishment aimed not at abolishing the source of the injury but transcending if not becoming it.

What, by contrast would a reality show called *Avenging Body* look like, by which I mean a show that, rather than fixating on a form of revenge within the moral economy of oppression that caused the injury, dreamed of a form of collective vindication that abolished the source of that injury? Of course, no such show could exist: it would contradict the entire logic of the genre, and the culture industry that created the genre. Though a paltry and sorry excuse for a revenge fantasy, *Revenge Body* is one of a wide range of mass produced cultural artifacts that seizes upon the experience of alienation and disposability integral to what I am calling revenge capitalism and offers an almost narcotic tonic.

While *Revenge Body* is fixated on weight loss through conventional exercise and commercialized regimens centered around gyms and personal trainers, its ethos resonates with a much wider fixation on the perfection of the body under neoliberal capitalism that takes a plurality of forms.[10] Among these are a wide range of commercialized or semi-commercialized practices that see the cleansing, purification, or care for the body as an estimable personal responsibility, and that frame this imperative as a form of personal empowerment (yoga, mindfulness, minimalism, etc.).[11] As we have already seen, while this discourse is often one of personal liberation, the practices are typically based on a kind of revenge against the constantly-failing body, not only the body that refuses to adhere to the conventional standards of beauty but also the body that refuses to be sufficiently productive, sufficiently mobile, sufficiently healthy, or sufficiently happy. Within a system that structurally militates against all these virtues, or transforms them into commoditized practices in which the vast majority can ill afford to invest (financially or in terms of time or self-discipline), we can observe that, across the field of revenge capitalism, there is a kind of bodily self-vengeance, wherein the body that fails to improve itself, fails to perform, fails to compete, is a liability worthy of pain.

VII

It was in the face of this that an interesting encounter occurred at the First International Gathering of Politics, Art, Sport, and Culture for Women in Struggle convoked by women of the Zapatista Army for National Liberation (EZLN) in their territories in the Mexican state of Chiapas over three days in March of 2018, attended by 5,000–8,000 delegates (all women and trans people) from over 50 nations and some 2,000 Zapatista women. Writing of the gathering, the North Carolina feminist and anti-capitalist platform El Kilombo's delegation summarized a key tension that emerged:

> Many of the workshops proposed and led by non-Zapatista attendees were focused on struggle understood as challenging the limitations imposed on self-expression and the individual female body. These workshops involved, on one hand, a wide variety of ways of using movement, voice, and art in order to heal, honor, or express oneself, and on the other, topics that address (what presenters imagine to be) the realities of the female body including reproductive rights and experiences as well as corporal self-knowledge and self-care.[12]

While steadfastly refusing to separate these practices from a broader feminist agenda, the delegation echoes the sentiments of many of the hosts and guests that "it seemed that in the presentations of many attendees, self-expression and the body appeared entirely divorced from the questions of collective self-organization and structural transformation." "The danger in focusing on forms of individual expression," they write,

> is that they can easily remain within the realm of a cathartic and ephemeral release, and that this can stand in for the long, arduous

process of building alternatives to a capitalist system that has proven itself adept at accommodating and even manufacturing these forms of release.

The delegation continues:

> The risk inherent in the focus on corporal self-knowledge and self-care is that it can delink the necessary understanding and defense of our bodies from the structures that impose corporal controls on us in the first place and mask the reasons why the struggle over "the body" is so central to a project of emancipation to begin with. Here it is helpful to remember that capitalism has made control over women's bodies compulsory in order to reproduce itself on whatever terms necessary for the system at a given time, whether that is obligatory procreation, forced sterilization, coerced reproduction to produce workers, postponed reproduction in order to work, or generalized sexual objectification. But reclaiming our bodies in this context is not about gaining control over our individual bodies – that particular understanding has only led us into a reality where some women in some places have been able to gain substantial control over their bodies and reproductive choices, while other women's bodies are ravaged by poverty, police repression, overwork, and the vulnerability to violence that accompanies a life lacking in resources. This includes those who have had to give up control over their own reproductive life and domestic sphere in order to perform waged labor in someone else's.

VIII

In contrast to the gathering's guests' individualizing focus on the body, the Kilombo Women's delegation turns to explore the thought and action of the Zapatista hosts who "began by theorizing the triple oppression they experience under the capitalist system for being poor, being indigenous, and being women." The hosts gave a "multi-generational account of the Indigenous history of colonization, slavery, violence, rape, forced labor, forced marriage, military harassment, and many other forms of violence and repression." This narrative confirmed the "conviction that nothing other than the actions of the oppressed themselves have ever or will ever move us toward liberation." The hosts then "laid out their struggle as the EZLN, and as women of the EZLN, to organize themselves and to build a series of autonomous institutions on recuperated lands that would allow them to take collective control over their lives."

The delegation recounts the way that, starting with early declarations against patriarchy and machismo in the EZLN's earliest founding documents in 1993, the intervening quarter-century has seen Zapatista women build, through solidarity, an integral place for self-empowering women within the wider revolutionary movement, including securing leadership roles for women in the governance structure in the territory's five semi-autonomous jurisdictions, within local communities, and within other elements of society. "These advances," the delegation summarizes

> were made possible not through avenues of individual expression and protection, but through the struggle to transform their concrete material conditions – in land use, food production, health, education, and conflict resolution – a transformation both generated by and generative of an understanding of self-organization and self-government so deeply socialized across the community base and collective consciousness that it gives rise to unique and constantly evolving forms of practice.

They cite the speech of *Ingsurgenta* Erika, who was delegated to speak for the intergenerational collective of Zapatista women who hosted the gathering: "You should know that it wasn't always men who exploited me, robbed me, humiliated me, beat me, scorned me, and murdered me. Often it was women. And it still is." The delegation notes that

> while the Zapatista women critique and counter sexist and patriarchal practices at every level of their resistance, their thought and actions help us to see the limitations of those forms of feminism where the imaginary of struggle does not go beyond the displacement of men and the desire to take their place ... in the Zapatista framework there is an understanding of patriarchy not as a women's issue or a men's issue, or even primarily as a gender issue, but rather as a systemic form of domination and inequality that structures all social relations and licenses the domination of men over women, but also of men over other men and women over other women.

IX

The delegation concludes with the following reflection, inspired and informed by the Zapatisa theorization of gender and oppression.

> in the current system we are offered only weak substitutes for [a deep and authentic] sense of self. We have been sold many forms

of "freeing" ourselves from oppressive conditions that necessarily pass through the process of becoming *somebody* – of achieving recognition or a place in the limelight. These are enticing forms precisely because so many women and others have been silenced in or erased from our collective consciousness and memory. But those places and lights are not only increasingly fleeting but largely circumscribed and proscribed by and for the system itself. Neoliberal capitalism offers no shortage of opportunities for individual recognition and self-promotion disguised as freedom ... We think the Zapatistas are showing us a process of becoming, all together, *nobody*, of creating a largely invisible and mostly anonymous social power from below with a far more profound response to exploitation, dispossession, repression, and humiliation than the symbolic and select somebodies permitted by capitalist structures. In the EZLN's words, "when the powerful refer to others, they disdainfully call them 'nobody.' But 'nobody' makes up the majority of the planet." We must of course protect and respect the individual bodies – women's and men's – that are violated in so many different ways through the absurd horrors of the capitalist system. But in that effort the only body that can free us is the social body, constituted by those anonymous acts of collective self-organization capable of birthing a new way of life.

Here, I believe, is a key to helping us cultivate an *avenging body*. In the becoming-nobody of the Zapatistas we recognize that, rather than a vehicle for personal gratification or liberation, the body is a fundamentally interconnected phenomenon, intimately linked to other bodies and to the ideas, cultures, practices, and collective desires that make up the lifeworld and the field of struggles. The avenging body does need seek individual acceptance within their reigning system but, rather, recognizes that each nobody yearns for the abolition of the system that makes each body into a constantly-failing would-be somebody.

4

Our Opium Wars

~~Pain~~, race, and the ghosts of empire

We must study how colonization works to decivilize the colonizer, to brutalize him in the true sense of the word, to degrade him, to awaken him to buried instincts, to covetousness, violence, race hatred, and moral relativism ... a universal regression takes place, a gangrene sets in, a centre of infection begins to spread, a poison has been instilled into the veins of Europe and, slowly but surely, the continent proceeds toward savagery.

Aimé Césaire, *Discourse on Colonialism*[1]

But yester-night I prayed aloud
In anguish and in agony,
Up-starting from the fiendish crowd
Of shapes and thoughts that tortured me:
A lurid light, a trampling throng,
Sense of intolerable wrong,
And whom I scorned, those only strong!
Thirst of revenge, the powerless will
Still baffled, and yet burning still!
Desire with loathing strangely mixed
On wild or hateful objects fixed.
Fantastic passions! maddening brawl!
And shame and terror over all!
Deeds to be hid which were not hid,
Which all confused I could not know
Whether I suffered, or I did:
For all seemed guilt, remorse or woe,
My own or others still the same
Life-stifling fear, soul-stifling shame.

Samuel Taylor Coleridge, *The Pains of Sleep*[2]

This chapter was prompted by the startling statistic that one of the best predictors of shifts in American voting patterns, at the county level, from Barack Obama in 2012 to Donald Trump in 2016, was the increase in so-called "deaths from despair," notably those associated with drug overdoses, which have risen precipitously since the turn of the century almost single handedly thanks to the flood of prescription opioids and its aftermath. These drugs, and their illegal street replacement (primarily heroin and fentanyl) are responsible for the most grievous human-caused public health crisis in American history, directly responsible for the deaths of over half a million people and the addiction and immiseration of millions more. New reports have, somewhat misleadingly, tended to stress the disproportionately white face of this epidemic, remarkable because most other public health disasters disproportionately affect people of color.

If, as I have argued in Chapter 1, the Trump phenomenon is an exemplary case of revenge politics that is, itself, the byproduct and expression of a deeper trend toward revenge capitalism, in this chapter I want to examine the dense intersections of race, accumulation, pain, drugs, and empire that are all too often lost in the discussion around the American opioid epidemic. I am interested in the way whiteness figures in public and medical narratives of pain, the way (revenge) capitalism comes to feast on the ruins it has, itself, created and the way notions of addiction and anesthetization can help us better understand these workings in our moment.

I

The temple

Around 15 BCE Caesar Augustus commissioned the construction of the Temple of Dendur on the upstream banks of the River Nile in the area that today is covered by Lake Nasser.[3] Augustus had his image prominently engraved on the outer walls of the temple in the garb of an ancient Egyptian pharaoh making an annual offering to the local gods Isis and Osiris, whose marriage symbolized the cycle of fertility of the Nile valley. The Roman emperors knew that power was sustained not merely through military domination and not only by gaining the consent of the governed, but also by exploiting dependencies; in this case, the reliance of the local population on ritual offerings to ensure the annual return of the generative waters to an otherwise arid region.

Two millennia later, on March 10, 2017, that same Temple of Dendur is surrounded by bodies lying prone, empty pill bottles scattered around them.[4] In the Sackler Wing of the Metropolitan Museum of Art, in the world's new imperial capital, New York City, the temple was re-erected in 1978. It was relocated in 1963 through a UNESCO-facilitated program whereby the Egyptian government led by Gamal Abdel Nasser awarded many such doomed temples as gifts to nations who had helped Egypt finance the monumental Aswan Dam, their ancient sites soon to be submerged by the iconic mega-project.[5] Aswan defied the ancient gods and brought the Nile's rhythms under human command, and also demanded the forced relocation of countless Nubian villagers in Egypt and Sudan.

The bodies that now lie prone are protesting another human-created flood, another empire. The Sackler Wing, like dozens of museums around the world, bears the infamous name of a family estimated to be among the richest in America, generous if narcissistic philanthropists whose fortune derives almost entirely from the privately held company Purdue Pharma: the patent-holder, aggressive marketer and beneficiary of OxyContin, the prescription opioid infamous for hooking America.[6]

The house of Sackler

The honorary leader of the protest is the artist Nan Goldin, well known since the 1970s for her unflinching photographic portraits of those marginalized from New York's booming real estate and tourist culture – drug users, queer folk, and drag queens. In late 2017, following a series of revelatory articles about the Sacklers and their "empire of pain" in *Esquire* and the *New Yorker*, Goldin announced that she too was recovering from a destructive addiction to OxyContin, which had initially been prescribed to her by her doctor for post-surgical pain.[7] Like so many doctors, hers had been beguiled by the research provided by Purdue and its competitors that promised prescription opioids as miracle drugs: a non-addictive painkiller that could be liberally prescribed.

Along with other opioid manufacturers, Purdue was a key player in a profound movement to lobby doctors to reimagine pain itself. Whereas throughout modern medical history pain was considered an unavoidable reality of illness, and addictive opioids reserved for the terminally ill, a new alliance of pharmaceutical companies and compliant researchers began to propound the notion that pain was unnecessary.[8] Indeed, they fostered research that encouraged physicians and care providers to take treatable pain so seriously that it be considered the "fifth vital sign" (along with pulse, body temperature, respiration, and blood pressure), the almost sacred *sine qua non* of clinical diagnosis.

Goldin, like millions of others, became an increasingly desperate addict, crushing the pills to defeat the patented time-release mechanisms, gaming her prescriptions to access the drug at multiple pharmacies, and replacing or augmenting the drug with street heroin.[9]

Her struggle became the material for a new photographic series and candid revelations about her addiction, which helped to catalyze the activist group PAIN Sackler. This group has joined with other movements in New York, like ACTUP, with experience in targeting the reckless profiteering of the pharmaceutical industry and shaming the Sackler family through performative actions like the die-in at the Temple of Dendur, the jewel in the crown of the family's philanthropic efforts. By demanding that the Sacklers use their ill-gotten wealth to fund rehabilitation programs, PAIN Sackler has crystallized recent debates on how to approach a contemporary "artworld," whose most prominent patrons are the corporations and oligarchs of a global capitalist empire.[10] Protests against the sponsorships of London's Tate Britain by British Petroleum and of the Metropolitan Museum by the far-right Koch brothers bear witness to precarious arts and culture workers struggling to defy the "art washing" of corporate images and cast a wrench into the gears of bourgeois vanity whereby creativity itself, as well as the treasures of non-Western civilizations, become branded monuments to the destruction of today's civilizations and environment in the name of profit.[11]

There is a whiff of vengeance in the PAIN Sackler protests. After all, as the heirs to the Sackler fortune argue, Purdue was only one of several large companies to push the drug. If they hadn't done it, others would have eagerly taken their place. Why aren't the protesters targeting the other companies that manufactured, marketed, or distributed prescription opioids? It wasn't *their* fault that people misused the drug, Purdue argues, which after all was created and marketed as a gift to the world, capable of relieving the agony of millions of afflicted bodies.

There is a grain of truth to these claims, though they neither exonerate Purdue nor should they discourage protesters from continuing to leverage the stain of the Sackler name on the world's most prestigious cultural institutions to draw attention to the ongoing crisis. But, as we shall see in more detail, the opioid crisis is, if anything, a plague of revenge capitalism that must be understood as emerging from and contributing to interlocking systems of exploitation, extraction, racial (dis)ordering, and chronic *social* pain. Culpability is widespread, but firms like Purdue must be targeted less because they are morally corrupt (all corporations are inherently morally corrupt, after all: they exist purely to earn profit) and more because they are organisms adapted to and reproductive of an artificial socio-economic ecosystem that produces such monsters.[12]

II

Free trade is Jesus Christ

"Free trade is Jesus Christ, and Jesus Christ is free trade" supposedly announced Sir John Bowring, a near perfect encapsulation of the apotheosis of *homo economicus*.[13] Bowring was a reputed scholar (an acolyte of utilitarian philosopher and inventor of the panopticon prison, Jeremy Bentham) and reformer who advocated liberal causes during his time as a UK Member of Parliament. His pivotal role as governor of Hong Kong and key player in the Opium Wars came about ironically as a result of his ruin by financial speculation, which led him to take up the Asian post in service to the Empire from 1854 to 1859.[14] His association of free trade with divine providence cunningly combined white-supremacist conservative religious values with liberal notions of cosmopolitanism and the progressive rationality of the market: the retrograde Chinese Empire must, he argued, be forced to accept the bitter-sweet medicine of British-produced opium at the point of the bayonet if need be, so as to be able to gain the civilizing influence of commercial trade. Never mind that the scourge of opium addiction was withering away the lives of millions of Chinese people, that its cancerous spread through the Qing Empire was corroding the social and political fabric.[15] Never mind that the opium itself was produced in India under drastic and well-nigh totalitarian conditions by and for the British East India Company.[16] It was the fulcrum by which British and other European powers half a world away could exploit and drain the resources of the world's wealthiest and most populous nation.[17]

It is at turns ironic and dispiriting to observe the strong parallels between, on the one hand, the arguments of the nineteenth-century lobbyists and defenders of the opium trade in the British parliamentary deliberations on the matter and, on the other, the arguments of Purdue Pharma's lawyers combating the wave of class-action lawsuits targeting the firm.[18] Were England not to exploit this market, it would go to the French; English merchants should not be held accountable for the misuse of a neutral commodity; it was the job of the corrupt, ineffective, and decadent Qing Empire to look to the drug trade in China, not interfere in free trade; and for the British parliament to interfere in the free trade of its merchants would both set a dangerous precedent for civil freedoms and, ultimately, threaten to quench the very dynamo of the capitalist empire: competitive economic liberty and entrepreneurialism. But the opium trade filled the coffers of the British Empire and single handedly fixed its once-massive trade deficit with China, and many, many members of the English bourgeoisie gained huge wealth from it.[19] Its profits were key to the establishment of huge global firms like HSBC (once the Hong Kong and Shanghai Banking Corporation – infamous today still for being the banker to the world's narcos), the industrial and logistics conglomerate Jardines (in which Bowring was an investor and his son a partner), P&O shipping (now part of the Maersk), and the mining giant Rio Tinto.

The sleep of reason, the nightmare of liberalism

The liberal justifications for the poisonous opium trade and the conduct of its key supplier, the East India Company, are a key subject of Lisa Lowe's invaluable investigation into the ways that nineteenth-century Anglo-American liberal thought allowed for the passage of world racial capitalism from an earlier moment of formal, military colonialism and slavery to an (no less violent) empire of free trade and allegedly free labor. Against liberalism's triumphant narrative, that today undergirds the specious historiographic assumptions of neoliberalism's champions who posit capitalism as the apogee of liberal humanist freedoms (see Chapter 3), Lowe insists on providing a genealogy of liberalism's imbrication with racialized financial, legal, and extrajudicial violence to challenge the dominant "economy of affirmation and forgetting."[20]

Succinctly, she summarizes:

> modern liberalism defined the "human" and universalized its attributes to European man, it simultaneously differentiated populations in the colonies as less than human. Even as it proposes inclusivity, liberal universalism effects principles of inclusion and exclusion; in the very claim to define humanity, as a species or as a condition, its gestures of definition divide the human and the nonhuman, to classify the normative and pathologize deviance ... liberal ideas of political emancipation, ethical individualism, historical progress, and free market economy were employed in the expansion of empire [and] universalizing concepts of reason, civilization, and freedom effect[ed] colonial divisions of humanity, affirming liberty for modern man while subordinating the variously colonized and dispossessed peoples whose material labor and resources were the conditions of possibility for that liberty.[21]

The specters of this constitutive violence are still with us in both the concept and the lived actualities of race and racism.

> Race as a mark of colonial difference is an enduring remainder of the processes through which the human is universalized and freed by liberal forms, while the peoples who created the conditions of possibility for that freedom are assimilated or forgotten. The genealogy of modern liberalism is thus also a genealogy of modern race; racial differences and distinctions designate the boundaries of the human and endure as remainders attesting to the violence of liberal universality.[22]

Bowring's apocryphal slogan, associating at once Christian religion, imperial hubris, white supremacy and free market capitalist liberalism, became a justification for the Second Opium War (1856–1860), a cynical expedition to avenge the audacity of the Qing Empire daring to seize a British ship thought to be a pirate vessel.[23] In reality this incident was understood by all parties as an attempt by the Qing to regain some sovereignty and prevent the further importation of opium. In revenge for this affront, British and French forces, after rampaging through several major cities, plundered and destroyed the emperor's marvelous Summer Palace outside Beijing, popularizing in the European press a word recently appropriated from Hindi: *loot*.[24] The treasures of the Chinese Empire that survived the drunken and destructive carousing of the soldiers, were systematically divvied up by officers and crated and shipped to Paris and London, where they entered into family and public collections, were sold as exotic curios, or were given as gifts to secure political favors. Priceless Chinese artifacts, representing the legacy of 4,000 years of Chinese civilization, flowed steadily out of China in the era of that nation's "great humiliation" spearheaded by the narco-capitalist Western exploitation of the Opium Wars.

Among the most famous and prolific twentieth-century collectors of the sorts of artifacts that were looted were the three Sackler brothers who founded Purdue Pharma. It would appear that some of the artworks that were presumably looted during the Opium Wars, or exported as a result of this economic terrorism, are today housed in the Sackler Wing of the Met near the Temple of Dendur. Some might be in the galleries that surround the Sackler courtyard at London's Victoria & Albert Museum, or in the Sackler Chinese collections at the Smithsonian in Washington or at Princeton University.

Several months into the Second Opium War, Bowring and many of the other European members of the Hong Kong colony fell seriously ill when arsenic was added to bread baked at a local Chinese-owned bakery.[25] Bowring's wife and several others were said to have eventually died from the poison. While the bakery's owner and workers were eventually exonerated at trial, the poisoning was attributed to a Qing war crime and presented in Europe as evidence of the depravity of the Chinese civilization. In the aftermath thousands of Chinese workers in Hong Kong were exiled or compelled to flee, fearing vengeance.

III

The house of Sackler is not in order. In the 1960s the three brothers, sons of Jewish immigrants to the New York borough of Queens who made good as medical doctors, were unified in their support for the building of the Met's Sackler Wing. A few years later the eldest of the three, Arthur, split with his brothers and his side of the family divested themselves of Purdue stock before the company introduced OxyContin.[26] This fact is often cited in public statements by Elizabeth Sackler, Arthur's daughter, one of the most prominent patrons of feminist art and a scholar and activist for the repatriation of sacred artifacts to Indigenous people in what we currently call North America.[27] Arthur is nevertheless remembered as the father of modern medical marketing, the high-pressure and seductive sales techniques that companies like Purdue used to popularize branded pharmaceuticals.[28] Indeed, Arthur's test case for these techniques was a previously mass marketed narcotic, Valium, notorious for becoming the drug of choice to numb the boredom, anxiety, and social pain of post-war middle class white women onto whose shoulders fell the burden of reproducing the idealized patriarchal suburban home and its associated forms of domestic terrorism.[29]

The infamy of the Sackler name cannot be so easily diluted.

Rock bottom

The opioid crisis is arguably the largest human-caused public health crisis in American history. Since its onset at the end of the twentieth century at least half a million people have died from opiate-related causes. The Center for Disease Control explains that

> Doctors wrote 72.4 opioid prescriptions per 100 persons in 2006. This rate increased 4.1% annually from 2006 to 2008 and 1.1% annually from 2008 to 2012. It then decreased 4.9% annually from 2012 through 2016, reaching a rate of 66.5 per 100 persons in

2016. That year, 19.1 per 100 persons received one or more opioid prescriptions, with the average patient receiving 3.5 prescriptions.[30]

The report also estimates that at least 4.7 of every 100 Americans "misuse" prescription pain relievers, contributing to the estimate that, in 2015, prescription opioids were involved in at least 63% of the record-setting 52,404 recorded deaths from drug overdoses in the world's richest country. Indeed, it is a prime cause in one of the most startling statistics in recent years: the now steady year-over-year decline in the life expectancy of white women, among the healthiest demographics.[31]

In 2007 Purdue Pharma was forced to settle a multimillion-dollar lawsuit brought by the West Virginia Attorney General for essentially misleading doctors and other health professionals into believing that the drug was safe to prescribe generally for pain.[32] While the company admitted no wrong-doing, this began a slow turn against the drug. But as the flood of prescription opioids receded and legal supplies began to dry up, many users turned to illicit street drugs, notably the notoriously and lethally potent fentanyl, which is typically manufactured in semi-legal laboratories in China and is so concentrated that mass quantities are relatively easy to smuggle into the US among the tonnage of other imports along that world-defining logistics route.[33]

The narcotic of racism

The modern history of opium is the story of colonial war and its vengeful afterlives. Opium also left its mark on the heart of the British Empire, trickling back to England despite the (highly ironic) attempts of parliament to prohibit the importation and sale of the drug. As early as the mid-nineteenth century opium distilled into morpheme was a key tool of battlefield medicine and offered doctors and nurses a humane way to end the lives of soldiers whose bodies were torn apart by the horrors of industrializing warfare (the hypodermic needle was introduced in 1844). Addiction to the drug, not only among wounded soldiers but among traumatized care providers, wended its way back to London and other cities where already concern was building about the appearance of opium dens.[34]

Then, as now, the scourge of the drug was blamed on racialized "outsiders," notably people presumed to be of Chinese ancestry, often accused of smuggling opium into England and America (the irony) as a kind of revenge for the shame of China's subjugation.[35] Within the racist worldview such opaque vengefulness was unjustified but typical: as with other non-white people, the Chinese were cast as pathologically vindictive, but inscrutably so. Propaganda pamphlets, daily papers, and politicians all warned that even when Chinese people appeared obsequious and good natured (probably fearing that to act otherwise would result in harm or murder) they could not be trusted.[36] At the same time, opium addiction in the imperial metropole was cast as the regrettable price (or sometimes punishment for the sins) of imperial benevolence.[37]

In the United States, waves of opium and morphine addiction raged across the devastated postbellum landscape after the American Civil War and the urban fabric after the close of the First World War.[38] There, too, the plague of opioid addiction was presented as a moral rot introduced or facilitated by unscrupulous foreigners. The threat of opium, in particular the threat that it might be used to sexually enslave white women, was a key element of the horrifically vengeful anti-Chinese racism, including riots, pogroms, and freelance terrorism, that helped to unify the American republic around the myths of white supremacy in a period of class discord at the turn of the century and indeed well into the twentieth century.[39] This is perhaps especially ironic and tragic given that the presence of the "cheapened" lives of Chinese "coolie" and other migrant labor in the United States and other settler colonies was, as Lowe makes clear, a direct result of the opium scourge destroying the Chinese social and economic fabric. This led to the desperate exodus of a now-"surplussed" population, facilitated largely by the same merchant capitalists who were profiting from the forced import of opium into China in the first place.[40]

War and money

Today, the scourge of opioids is often linked to the return of American soldiers from deployment in the War on Terror. The ability of the Taliban to withstand almost two decades of warfare from the most powerful military the world has ever known is in no small part due to their control over the illicit distribution networks for Afghanistan's opium plantations, the fruits of which were widely sought by bored or traumatized American troops stationed in the region.[41] Here, heroin appears as a kind of balm of imperial masculinity: culturally and institutionally inhibited from directly addressing the existential pain and mental anguish of having witnessed and performed gruesome acts of war, the soldiers turn to an anesthetic.[42]

Today's prescription painkillers are also made of a derivative of the poppy, but while Afghanistan provides perhaps the lion's share of the world's illicit opioids, the active opioid agent in OxyContin and other prescription drugs probably did not come from Afghanistan, but more likely from the highly securitized fields of Tasmania, the Australian island where genocide against the Indigenous Palawa people, deemed savage enemies of progress, was mercilessly exacted since the nineteenth century.[43]

OxyContin and other prescription painkillers were widely prescribed by army doctors for the same reason that they were prescribed to athletes, financiers, surgeons, and traveling musicians on the home front: they allowed for the continued extraction of skilled and specialized labor time beyond the body's conventional limits, working through the pain.[44] As Laurent De Sutter notes, capitalist accumulation has always relied on, perhaps even been defined by, the incorporation of narcotics, which dull the pain of its toll on the body and render it ready for ever-greater levels of exploitation.[45]

IV

Race, pain, and forgetting

The faces of the opioid crisis are diverse: urban or rural, of all complexions, young and old. It involves bored suburban teenagers raiding their parents' medicine cabinets for a quick high, indebted retirees transformed into drug dealers when they realize the street prices for their prescribed painkillers could supplement their impossibly meager pensions, injured or idled workers seeking public disability insurance and using opioids to help combat a sense of abandonment and alienation, and overworked doctors ignorant of or denied the ability to offer holistic therapies, reaching for a panacea or being threatened or pressured by their patients for a fix.[46]

While those suffering addiction come from all ethnic backgrounds and tax brackets, the story of prescription opioids like OxyContin usually concerns the rot of the American white heartland: the staggering rates of prescription and addiction throughout the deindustrialized Rust Belt and Appalachia region.[47] The fact that the disproportionate majority of deaths and suffering are exhibited by white people is one reason the political discovery of the opioid crisis in the second decade of the twenty-first century has tended to stress users as innocent victims in need of rehabilitative services.[48] This, in stark and infuriating contrast to earlier waves of drug crises like street heroin or crack cocaine, which disproportionately ravaged urban Black communities in the twentieth century, or to the height of the AIDS epidemic, which disproportionately affected intravenous drug users and men who have sex with men.

Whereas these groups are, in the cultural politics of racial capitalism, suspected of deserving the plague inflicted upon them, the opioid crisis is presumed to have struck the innocent, hard-working, law-abiding representatives of white American quintessence.[49] Neo-Nazis are even revivifying anti-Semitic conspiracy theories of poison-peddling "Jewish doctors" with reference to the Sackler family heritage.[50]

While a huge number of Black people suffer dependency on opioids, Black people in the US appear to have been less affected by the crisis than many observers expected, given the general pattern whereby systemic racism elevates susceptibility to public health risks.[51] But this is thanks to a dark web of causes that all derive from systemic and structural racism. Many Black families in the US lack access to doctors and medical insurance plans that would provide them with opioid prescriptions, a major influence on the statistics, as too is the lack of pharmacies or their stock of opioids in predominantly Black neighborhoods.[52] A number of observers have noted that, while reliance on government aid is common for many American citizens, it is more frequently (successfully) claimed by white people in the form of the seemingly more noble package of assistance for "disability," whereas thanks to structural forms of racism it is more common that Black people are encouraged to claim stigmatized forms of social assistance or "welfare"; the former often comes with pharmaceutical subsidies, whereas the latter does not.[53]

But even still, several recent studies have demonstrated that doctors ignored, downplayed, or distrusted Black patients' testimonies of pain.[54] Some doctors felt that their Black patients were more likely to abuse or resell opioids than patients of other ethnic backgrounds. These statistics add credence to broader arguments that the medical establishment is so saturated with racist prejudices that doctors either misjudge the intensity of Black people's testified pain or implicitly believe that Black people can (and therefore should) endure greater pain.[55] This presumption inherits the legacy of American medical pioneers like J. Marion Simms, the "father of modern gynecology," who conducted excruciating surgical experiments on enslaved and free Black women without anesthetic in the nineteenth century, and the broader history of at times sadistic medical experimentation on Black people.[56]

Our pain

The power of pharmaceutical giants and health care conglomerates in America continues to face no serious challenge. But on a fundamental level the opioid crisis has spurred a questioning into the nature of pain itself. Many of those to whom opioids were prescribed suffered from ailments with no name, or forms of chronic pain that are difficult (and, more importantly, costly) to diagnose and treat. Opioids provided doctors with a miracle drug that made patients suffering from a wide range of maladies "feel better." And, indeed, as addiction rates grew doctors came under increased pressure to provide prescriptions, thanks in part to the leverage patients can have over doctors through their corporate employers or various complaints mechanisms that see medical care as a "service." But while companies like Purdue and their affiliated lobbyists and researchers encouraged doctors to interpret patients' reported pain as a direct expression of a physical phenomenon (except, as noted, in the case of many racialized patients) the reality is of course more complex.

Pain cannot be measured except through the testimony of they who suffer and pain is obviously at least partially psychological. It's also profoundly but indirectly social.[57] Many of those to whom opioids were prescribed were indeed in pain, but that pain was linked to the neoliberal conditions of un(der) employment, loneliness, alienation, lack of purpose, and sense of hopelessness, especially in deindustrialized areas. Yet while rates of opioid prescription and "misuse" are often associated with the capitalist "sacrifice zones" of Appalacia and the Rust Belt, it also plagued the suburbs or exurban zones of normative American white life.[58] While often a drug user's first prescription was to treat the pains of surgery or workplace injuries like carpal tunnel syndrome, on a demographic level it was clearly being used to treat some deeper, more existential, shared pain.

Demographer Shannon Monnat's research has found that voting for Donald Trump in 2016 (relative to his Republican candidate predecessor in 2012) was highest in counties that had elevated rates of mortality related to drug and alcohol abuse and suicide: so-called "deaths of despair" attributed to poor, deindustrialized, rural and largely white populations.[59] Journalists and researchers of the opioid epidemic confirm the trend based on systematic though anecdotal investigations: somehow the opioid crisis is connected to the rise of a kind of vengeful, nihilistic politics highly indexed to the long-standing cultural and material patterns of a white-supremacist nation and by the realization of the death of the American dream for its one-time and would-be beneficiaries.[60]

During his campaign and since his election, Trump has has found that great political capital can be extracted from the opioid crisis. In spite of much bombast, his administration has disastrously failed to respond to the public health emergency, in part because (as is typical) it has hand-picked some of the most notorious corporate lobbyists from the industry that created the crisis to now oversee its repair.[61] But Trump has leveraged long-standing racist tropes to, once again, displace responsibility for the crisis onto convenient Others. At several international trade meetings Trump has thrown away the agenda to berate the Chinese government for failing to control the export of fentanyl.[62] Trump's justification for the proliferation of notorious concentration camps across the country for irregular and illegalized border-crossers, including children, has been time and again justified by claiming that migrants are "bringing drugs" into the US, seemingly a reference to the importation of black tar heroin from Mexico.[63]

From a certain distance, this rhetoric and the cruel policies it justifies appear as acts of warrantless, unjustified vengeance. Certainly the rhetoric echoes that used in previous moments of the American Empire to cohere a national imaginary around racist tropes that valorize a normative whiteness, betrayed by its craven leaders, beset by poison-peddling foreigners bent on demonic, envious vengeance. If the forgoing examples are any indication, such vilifications of the sadistic non-white Other has long been a technique by which a coherent notion of "whiteness" and white supremacy is sustained, sustained in the face of its ontological lack (there is, of course, biologically speaking, no such thing as whiteness) and cracks and fissures in its ideological foundation as the realities of (largely top-down) class warfare make themselves known.

From one angle, the Trump phenomenon and the revenge politics it represents is the rage-filled conductive scream of a society in pain. From another angle it is the dope-sick panic of whiteness itself, that great anesthetic which, as a psycho-sociological formation, was always used to dull the senses to the pain of others. Like all addictions, whiteness's effectiveness constantly diminishes with use, demanding an ever-higher dose. The veins recede into the arms, abused too many times by the needle. You begin to fear sleep for the nightmares that will come. Digestion and evacuation become unreliable. The days drift together. The shame of being willing to sell your most precious things (liberty? justice? freedom?) for a fix. And that shame becomes the pain to flee to fix to flee to fix. It's all your fault. It's all your fault. It's their fault. It's all their fucking fault. You'll die without it. You'd kill for a hit. You'd kill for it …

V

Capitalist anesthetics

Revenge is both the method and the symptom of a form of capitalism that feeds on its own ruination, whether it is the criminalization and hyper-incarceration of those dispossessed by previous waves of capitalist exploitation and extraction or the speculative thriving in the aftermath of disaster.[64] The opioid crisis, likewise, was the result of capitalist speculation on the material and spiritual ruination of American racial capitalism.

In her enlightening reading of the final passages in Walter Benjamin's celebrated "The Work of Art in the Age of its Mechanical Reproduction,"[65] cultural theorist Susan Buck-Morss has convincingly argued that her Marxist predecessor's concern for the fate of aesthetics under industrial capitalism was not, as is commonly imagined, primarily oriented toward art. Rather, Benjamin had in mind the politics of what Buck-Morss calls the "capitalist sensorium": the way rapid urbanization, industrialization, and technological change in the late 19th and early 20th centuries both depended on and shaped the transformation of proletarian bodies as sensing, feeling entities.[66]

She points to the rise of new entertainment technologies, new sonic experiences both artistic (movies, phonographs, radio) and ambient (the din of the factory or city), and the casualized bodily violence of factory work and urban life. These took a slow toll on the laboring body and often enacted swift bodily harm in accidents. She observes that the rise of industrial capitalism was defined not only by new aesthetics in the field of mechanically reproduced culture, but also by the proliferation of pharmaceutical and non-pharmaceutical *anesthetics*: methods by which proletarians could dull their torqued sensing bodies to survive the accelerating mediatic and haptic violences of capitalism. These include the use of narcotics, but also the narcotizing qualities of mass culture: cheap sentimentality, Manichean narrative closure, bombastic aesthetics, reckless melodrama, and the like. In Benjamin's other writing, he explores in detail how the complicity of the middle classes in Germany, England, and France was purchased with the hallucinogenic temptations of consumerism in the arcades and later department stores of the growing metropolis: secured spaces of capitalist pleasure walled in from the grime, smoke, poverty, and strife that produced them.

This, for Buck-Morss, is the key to understanding the haunting final lines of Benjamin's essay, where he meditates on the rise of fascism in his time. Fascism, while doing nothing to alleviate the pain and sensory overload of the proletariat, gives thrilling expression to their suffering, often in the very same media. The hyperbolic participatory spectacles which overwhelm the senses and the maximalist, affectively consuming pageantry of fascism represented the "aestheticization of politics", not just the transformation of politics into hyper-nationalist spectacle, but a politics calibrated to exploit the fractured, wounded, rewired sensorium of the industrialized, self-anesthetizing proletarian body. Benjamin argued that such a body (and body politic) comes to delight in the spectacle of its own annihilation, eagerly careening toward a self-destructive orgy of violence, the immolation of the individual in the forge of the vengeful mass.

Buck-Morss ends by reiterating Benjamin's urgent invitation, in the name of the socialism that opposes barbarism, to imagine the "politicization of aesthetics": not simply the creation of avowedly or explicitly "political art," but the politically considered mobilization of the aesthetic sensing subject of the new capitalist sensorium. Benjamin rightly worried that nineteenth-century bourgeois models of the monadic, rational, self-contained subject as the seat of aesthetic and political judgment were inadequate to understand or liberate a mediatized proletariat that had become a very different animal indeed.

Recent neuroscientific discoveries about the plasticity of the brain reinforce his point.[67] The task before us, then as now, is to mobilize ourselves as animals capable of rewiring ourselves, just as it is to recognize how deeply and profoundly we have been rewired by the everyday traumas of our economic and social systems, systems whose fractured, accelerated, digitally mediated sensorium makes that of Benjamin's era look almost humane by comparison. As we will see in the next chapter, Silicon Valley tech firms sell advertisers the knowledge of how much user attention, parceled by the millisecond, it takes for the brain to recognize a brand image, meanwhile brokering data about our most visceral and spontaneous reactions (eye movements, variations in scrolling speeds) to the highest bidder.[68] More generally, these technologies impact and shape the sensory capacities we must generate to survive in a new landscape of work and exploitation in which we are each tasked with leveraging every ounce of "human capital" (skills, relationships, hobbies) to compete in renting our time or assets to fickle micro-employers.[69] For millions whose labor is no longer necessary to capitalist accumulation – the surplussed – anesthetics dulls the pain of essentially being relegated to the status of prematurely dead in the eyes of the system.

VI

The cosmology of homo oeconomicus

Jamaican philosopher and social critic Sylvia Wynter provides a radically new interpretation of opioids as the key chemical for the regulation of social and political life, albeit she is interested in particular in the endogenous production of opiates, which is to say those manufactured by the brain itself.[70] While exogenous opiates, notably those extracted from poppies and refined into heroin, OxyContin, and other drugs, have been cultivated and used by humans for millennia, their effectiveness as a mind-altering substance depends on the way they attach to synaptic opioid receptors in the brain that are a crucial part of the way thought and other actions are motivated and rewarded. Wynter, drawing on recent insights from neuroscience, posits an *alchemical* model of "being human as praxis": we are the only species (it would seem) that has the ability through storytelling, narrative, and that field of activities we call "culture" – what Wynter calls "The Word" – to shape the way our own brains function. Wynter, drawing on Fanon, identifies humanity as a *sociogenic* species: one capable of and therefore responsible for a profound form of collective freedom and agency. Our "genres" of mythmaking and storytelling are foundational to the entire way we live together because they produce a mythos wherein we come to understand our own agency and our sense of community and kinship with others, what she terms the "referent-we." This mythos is defined by a symbolic system which associates certain people, traits and behaviors with "symbolic life and death": more than simply desirability and distaste but a deep shared affect keyed into our sense of survival and reproduction.[71]

Sociogenic systems, though they are reproduced and reinforced by social intercourse, are typically unconscious of themselves: they produce a whole cosmology with its own rules for truth and value which, even though they shape the remit of philosophy and science, are opaque to those who live within them. This is no less so for our current global capitalist, hetero-patriarchal, neocolonial order. Wynter sees this order as the nightmare of the way the Enlightenment notion of rational man (what she calls "Man 1") has given way to the universalizing mythos of *homo oeconomicus* ("Man 2"): the self-maximizing, acquisitive, accumulation-driven subject. Though it is a particular mythological archetype produced within and reproductive of the world system, it is taken for eternal and projected back into human prehistory and across the vast span of human experience as the norm.

This cosmology is, fundamentally, racist and borne of the colonial world order. It is not simply that the Enlightenment (Man 1) in Europe emerged in the shadow of global conquest and bourgeois empowerment, or that its even more austere off-spring/usurper (Man 2, *homo economicus*) was forged to legitimate and enable the ruling class, Western European conquest of nature and the world's other civilizations. All those who appear (in the eyes of the masters of this mythos) to *fail* to embody the allegedly natural virtues and characteristics of *homo oeconomicus*, or who impede his self-maximizing, profit-seeking competitive behavior (which is to say racialized and colonized peoples), are cast as fundamentally inferior human models, as are the various cultures and civilizations whose mythoi is not centered around *homo oeconomicus*. We have observed this earlier in this chapter, when the British justified their poisoning of China with opium as the inherent right of *homo oeconomicus* to pursue trade and triumph in the face of a retrograde people.

For our purposes, it is crucial to hold fast to Wynter's insistence that these processes are defined by the brain's opioid-receptor network. She outlines this process with reference to the placebo/nocebo effect: the shockingly powerful way that the brain can be induced to alchemically transform itself due to what are essentially narratological inputs. It has, for instance, been widely found that the placebo effect induced when a doctor or researcher authoritatively tells a patient that the sugar pill they are taking is a curative drug is almost as powerful as (sometimes more impactful than) the drug itself.[72] This is especially the case in terms of many psycho-pharmaceuticals. Likewise, studies have revealed that the profound power of the nocebo effect – essentially when the authoritative figure tells the patient that the (real) drug or therapy they are taking is ineffective, and thus renders it so. The exact biochemical and psychological dynamics of this effect are still widely debated but it is generally accepted that the opioid-receptor system is highly important to it.

Hacking homo narrans

To clarify, Wynter is not advocating a sociology of biological determinism; quite the opposite. She is precisely arguing *against* the way Darwin's thought has been conscripted (for instance, in fields like behavioral economics and evolutionary psychology) to argue that contemporary capitalist human behavior is just an expression of biological destiny. Instead, she is arguing that this Social Darwinist metanarrative is a cosmology that, though it claims to stand outside history and comment on the truth of universal human nature, is itself only one (particularly dangerous and uniquely imperialistic) instance of the almost infinite capacity of humans as *homo narrans*: storytelling, mythos-creative, alchemical beings. Biological determinism, in other words, is a story we tell ourselves largely to justify and reproduce power relations and our habituation within them. Such metanarratives are not only ideologically beguiling, they actually shape the ways in which we are habituated to produce and receive endogenous opioids.

To put it in other terms, we "hack" into our own opiate-reward placebo/nocebo systems through storytelling, mythos-building collective work and, in so doing, reshape how we make kin and define kind. Then we retroactively and necessarily imagine that this process is "natural," inevitable, or supernaturally determined. Our myths shape our alchemical powers by defining the way we associate certain practices, people, ideas, and behaviors with symbolic life (triggering the placebo effect) or death (triggering the nocebo effect). This, in turn, manifests in a logic of selection and deselection, though by these terms Wynter means something more than merely mate-selection: she is speaking to the much broader notion of how we define (and are defined by) the "referent-we": the notion of to whom we belong (and, conversely, who does not belong).

To conclude this chapter, then, I will offer three speculations by way of the opioid epidemic in the US and elsewhere.

The first is that, while according to Wynter's framework, capitalism/colonialism/patriarchy has always "hacked" into the opioid-receptor placebo/nocebo system by which alchemical humanity reproduces itself through story and mythos (as do all systems, in some way), I would argue that today's mass commercialization of synthetic opioids represents a profound and world-historical shift in this process. For Wynter, the rule of *homo economicus* globally has profoundly reshaped the feedback loops between behavior, culture, and the alchemical placebo/nocebo (opioid) processes of the human body-mind. Already those traits, characteristics, behaviors, dispositions, symbols, and ideas that serve to reproduce the logic *homo economicus* are rewarded. They resonate with the dominant political and social narratives of our day are coded as life-affirming, good, beautiful, just, and true (in ways we have been observing throughout this book in terms of the valorization of financialization). Habituated already to this narrative, its appearance in a variety of forms triggers the placebo release of endogenous opioids; those people, traits, behaviors, ideas, and practices associated with its opposite have the inverse effect, triggering the nocebo effect.

Hence we might better understand, for instance, the seemingly improbable rise to power of far-right political strongmen who, even while all are not themselves successful businessmen, seem to embody the ethos of *homo economicus*, thereby triggering a kind of encoded injection of self-produced drugs. Hence, we too might better understand the rancorous loathing of so many toward those whom the system has rendered "surplus" (refugees, the homeless, the unemployed) who appear as the antithesis of the independent, powerful, competitive *homo economicus* (they are seen as disgustingly dependent, sickeningly powerless, uncompetitive) and also as threats or encumbrances to the success of *homo economicus*.[73] This helps explain the particularly visceral and vengeful loathing against surplussed populations by those not-yet-surplussed.

We are in an era (call it globalization, neoliberalism, financialization, neocolonialism) where the subjecthood of *homo economicus* is now universalized as the horizon for all people the world over and its adoption, we are told, is the only means to assure our individual survival. In this way, the logic of Man 2, once reserved exclusively for the wealthiest white elites, is now recoding all of us and reshaping the placebo/nocebo opioid-receptor interface. But this phase of capitalism/colonialism/patriarchy goes one step further still with the mass production and mass manufacturing of *synthetic* opioids, their strength thousands of times more powerful than anything our brains can produce on their own.

It is obviously not simply that this order of narcocapitalism addicts us to shots of synthetic opioids to reward us for behaviors aligned with the mythos of *homo economicus*, although that reality is perhaps not so far off. Rather, opioids travel through a biomedical industrial apparatus that claims to cure our pain, but for which the psycho-social dimensions of pain are largely opaque. In contrast to earlier models of "legitimate" opioid use, largely reserved for terminally ill and chronically debilitated patients, today's prescription of opioids is aimed largely (at least nominally) at "returning" the human subject to a functioning capitalist actor, to help them better approximate the behavior of *homo economicus*. Whether prescribed after surgery to help the patient recover or for those who suffer chronic pain to help them function, the logic of the late capitalist opioid is one of stabilizing the subject of pain the better for participation as a competitive, independent, self-maximizing subject. Indeed, advertising for OxyContin and similar prescription opioids has tended to stress its benefits in helping a user "get back to normal," without, of course, acknowledging that 'normal' is poverty, alienation, and slow death.

White surplus

If the demographics of the opioid epidemic are any indication, this drug has targeted precisely those who are most expected to approximate and emulate *homo economicus*, which is to say white men living in the United States, but who are for a variety of reasons foreclosed or inhibited from doing so. From a certain perspective, the universalization of *homo economicus* as a model was always a ruse: by virtue of its very competitive, accumulative logic, personification of *homo economicus* is only really accessible to a tiny minority; ideologically it functions to conscript the sentiments and behaviors of many, but can only reward the few. Yet, as has been argued elsewhere at length, this mythos also profoundly masks its own impossibility and, instead, offers its adherents only the tools to understand this general failure as a personal liability. The pain that synthetic opioids treat, then, is a kind of dark (or white) inversion of the existential pain that gave Fanon and DuBois (and Wynter) such insights into their own double-consciousness. In the case of these thinkers a leap of thought became possible in the impossible, painful space of inhabiting an abjected (Black) body in a white-supremacist cosmology. In the case of the quintessential white heartland target of the opioid industry, the pain is different: being unable to thrive and emulate *homo economicus* in a system where it is framed as your birthright and responsibility.

In the case of Fanon, DuBois, and Wynter, the body itself is riven by the experience of, on the one hand, being habituated to the normative placebo/nocebo opioid-reward system of white-supremacist capitalist patriarchy and, on the other, being cast as the very abject nadir of that cosmology. The generative double-consciousness emerges from being enrolled in a form of life in which you were never meant to be alive. The struggle to think and feel beyond the instilled placebo/nocebo system generates pain, but also possibility.

For the targets of today's opioid industry and its aftermath, the pain is different: these are the normative subjects who are expected to thrive, to compete, to accumulate, to participate, yet they die, chronically.

A final related point. As intimated somewhat poetically earlier, I would seek here to extrapolate on Wynter's work to frame whiteness itself as an opioid whose effectiveness is dwindling in the face of mounting psycho-social pain. We have already seen that the cosmology of *homo economicus* is one that, built on white supremacy and capitalism, casts Black people and other subjects of empire as abject outsiders associated with symbolic death, inherently deselected within the logic of the system. In the long tradition of critical race studies, whiteness must be understood not as a phenotypical descriptor or even a cultural marker but, rather, a political category by which various populations and subjects are brought into alignment with the projects of colonialism/capitalism/patriarchy. Various people and groups variably gain access to claims to and privileges of whiteness depending on historical variables, but the underlying logic is that, fundamentally, whiteness is projected as the zenith of human achievement and evolution, the proper subjects of the system of liberal humanism (Man 1) and of *homo economicus* (Man 2). In Wynter's terms, whiteness itself, and those traits and behaviors associated with whiteness, are favored in the placebo/nocebo opioid-receptor feedback loop habituated by white-supremacist capitalist patriarchy.

If this is the case then, in line with the early observations of DuBois and others, the so-called wages of whiteness are both profoundly material and also *alchemical*. To be admitted into whiteness is to be selected, to be associated with intelligence, beauty, moral virtue, competitiveness, and desirability. The constant re-inscription of whiteness, the daily way one is born again into whiteness through a million tiny acts, reinforces this feedback loop, just as it enables white people to compete and hypothetically thrive in a competitive white-supremacist capitalist world. As I alluded earlier, whiteness, among other things, can be observed to function as a social anesthetic (literally a dimming of feeling), dulling the sympathetic imagination such that its beneficiaries inure themselves to the pain endured by others in an economy of race and racialization. Perhaps all systems of power and domination produce their own cultural anestheses that inure the privileged to the pain of the oppressed. In the case of whiteness, this anesthetizing effect helps explain a range of activities, from vindictive violence to casual insouciance, by which non-white people are made to endure conditions of premature death and heinous exploitation.

And yet what do we make of a moment when, as Keeanga-Yamahtta Taylor puts it, "the wages of whiteness are not so great that they can stop millions of ordinary white people from literally drinking and drugging themselves to death, to escape the despair of living in this 'greatest country on earth.'"[74] There is a secular stagnation in the global capitalist economy as a whole, where returns on capitalist investments seem not to render sufficient surplus value for non-financialized systemic reproduction.[75] This stagnation, in turn, has led capital on a desperate global quest to seek ever more profitable venues for exploitation and has also led, along with other factors, to systematic disinvestment in the social web through privatization, cutbacks, mergers, and more. We might also say that there has been a kind of secular stagnation in whiteness itself. In pharmacological terms, one is left chasing the high: the old drug no longer offers the escape it once did.

This in part helps frame the opioid epidemic: as the opioid of whiteness proves less and less effective as a kind of remedy for class exploitation, a new synthetic drug, highly indexed to whiteness, takes its place. But so too does a rancorous political and social violence and vehemence toward a now seemingly irrational loathing and fury at those deselected souls who are now blamed for the worsening white condition.

Interlude: V's vendetta, or Joker's retribution?

I

As I detailed in Chapter 1, one key dimension of actually existing revenge politics is male violence directed against women (often intimate partners and family members) or against those queer, trans, non-binary, and other people who refuse to conform to dominant ideologies and expectations of gender and sexuality.[1] Hegemonic masculinity, then, in some sense organizes itself around revenge, around the potential to declare a kind of state of exception wherein such violence is warranted, necessary, normal, and justifiable. As Silvia Federici illustrates in her studies of witch trials (both historically and in the present) we must not separate gendered violence as it plays out on the level of individual people's lives from the broader political-economic systems and structures that have relied and that continue to rely on the extraction of reproductive labor in the unpaid realm of the home.[2]

The unlikely 2019 blockbuster *Joker* plays on, appears at times to critique, and in many ways reproduces this underlying thematic. Its sympathetic depiction of the slow turn of a lonely, sick, working class man to murderous violence was initially seen by many critics as a paean to the most violent elements of hypermasculine revenge politics, notably the virulently misogynistic so-called "Incel" (involuntary celibate) online subculture.[3] The film follows an awkward but gentle middle-aged white man, Arthur Fleck, who works as a clown and lives in a tenement with his mother, and struggles with mental illness. Set in the fictional Gotham City in the 1980s, the dawning age of of the neoliberal social abandonment transforms Fleck into the sadistic supervillain of the film's title.

Yet while many critics have lauded the film for its vivid portrayal of the way rapacious financialized capitalism impoverishes and neglects the poor and those in psychological distress,[4] it is important to recognize that this system itself appears nowhere in the film, and with two exceptions the literal faces of those who betray and abandon Fleck are all women, most of them Black women. The film's first and last scenes of dialog involve Fleck in the care of two imperious Black women: in the first, his overworked, jaded, and unsympathetic social worker who, later in the film, reveals that the program he relied on for his psychopharmaceutical medication, and her own job, have been terminated. The final scene finds Fleck in a mental institution, psychotically toying with a Black female psychiatrist whom, we are led to believe, he then either murders or imagines himself murdering. In the course of the film it is revealed that his beloved mother has raised him in a web of lies about his childhood and the family's relationship to the allegedly benevolent billionaire Wayne family (Bruce, the future Batman, is its scion). These lies have been calculated to hide her own debilitating mental illness and her shame at allowing her past boyfriends to horrifically abuse Fleck as a child, memories which he has suppressed. For her failures, Fleck murders his mother. We are also left to wondor about the way the film implies the murder and sexual violence Fleck exacts on his neighbor, another Black woman, about whom he has constructed an elaborate fantasy of a caring, supportive relationship, only for it to be revealed that she hardly knows who he is.

Much is made in the film about Fleck's revenge against men: three young, drunk financiers who harass him on a subway car; the brutish co-worker who gets him fired; the late-night talk-show host, Murray Franklin, Fleck's idol, who brings the sick man on his show as an object of ridicule; even, indirectly, the patrician Thomas Wayne, whom Fleck for a time believes is his father, who is murdered along with his wife at the end of the film by someone inspired by Joker's nihilistic example.

The film relies upon and dangerously normalizes or echoes a narrative that frames masculinized vengeance as the natural, regrettable, and in some sense inevitable outcome of women's (especially racialized women's) failure to provide sufficient feminized caring labor: had the social worker been less cynical and impatient, had Fleck's mother been able to overcome her own narcissism, had a random Black woman on a bus been kinder to our hero, had Fleck's neighbor consented to his awkward, harmless advances and his benign fantasy, his transformation into a monster might have been prevented.

I agree with critics of the film who note that it does the important work of revealing that human evil is not, as previous cinematic iterations of the Joker myth imply, something that emerges *sui generis*, with no backstory.[5] This backstory of the Joker reveals that his violence is the result of society's failures and inequities. And yet the face of these injustices is a feminized and racialized one. Women are presented as hapless and often uncaring or narcissistic conduits of systemic injustice who fail to cushion Fleck from the blows. Though the film climaxes with Fleck's transformation into the Joker with his revenge against

Franklin, whom Joker shoots during a live broadcast, and (indirectly) against Wayne, these men are presented as agents of their fate, as paternal figures who, to the last, exert their will in the world: Franklin persuasively but unapologetically argues with the armed Joker; Wayne, who previously rebuffed Fleck's sad entreaties for acceptance as his illegitimate son, dies trying to protect his wife and young son, from one of the Joker's devotees. They die, in other words, "as men."

II

The worry that the film's presentation of the rise of the Joker would inspire copycat crimes was understandable, given that a previous cinematic incarnation of the supervillain had inspired a deadly massacre at the debut of a Batman film in Aurora, Colorado, in 2012.[6] But the assailant in that case had identified with a very different character than the one so evocatively depicted by Joaquin Phoenix in 2019. Health Ledger's Joker in the 2008 film *The Dark Knight* may have been a nihilistic psychopath, but he was every bit the nightmare version of hegemonic, hyper-capitalist masculinity: a self-made man fully in control, a mastermind who sadistically toyed with innocent people's lives, a judicious investor in his own criminal ventures, a dark genius who was always one or two steps ahead of the police and even with the quintessential avenging businessman: Batman. The real-life Colorado mass murderer, an awkward, unpopular, alienated young man (not, ultimately, unlike Phoenix's Fleck) found in Ledger's Jocker the apotheosis of a kind of agentful, vengeful masculinity he, like all of us raised men in this society, was taught to adore and emulate. The false choice of masculinity under revenge capitalism is to be caught between Batman (the suave but vengeful boy-king who takes the law into his own hands to save it) or the Joker (the nihilistic icon of the will-to-power). Both see through the veil of social norms and niceties, and presume to know how the world "really works," and take individuated masculine action to rectify or destroy.

By contrast, even in his moments of vengeful glory, Phoenix's 2019 Joker appears out of control, a victim, a strangely feminized subject to whom the world *happens*. Even his metamorphosis into the supervillain is in a sense accidental: his murder of Franklin on live TV, as well as his previous panicked murder of the three financiers, has catalyzed riots of the inchoate dispossessed of neoliberal Gotham who don masks and makeup echoing Fleck's workaday clown costume. In the final scenes, Fleck is freed from police captivity by his newly-found followers and is embraced by them as the city burns around him, though even this, we are led to believe, may be a sad fantasy.

III

This final scene, where a masked swarm, inspired by a singular male hero, anarchically takes to the streets to take vengeance on a system that has oppressed them is reminiscent, perhaps directly so, of the climax of the Wachowski sibling's 2005 hit movie *V for Vendetta*, based on the celebrated 1984 comic written by Alan Moore and illustrated by David Lloyd. Here, the hero known simply as V – a victim of a fascist regime's biological experiments which accidentally bestow him with supernatural strength and agility – consummates a year-long plot of political revenge by orchestrating the spectacular destruction of the British Parliament building, inviting the otherwise cowed and fearful public to join the ritual disguised in his garb: an ever-smiling, mustachioed Guy Fawkes mask, capotain hat and black cape. In *V for Vendetta* the fascistic regime has risen to power in England thanks to false-flag operations of biological warfare used as a pretext for a campaign of political and ethnic cleansing. Throughout the film, the Shakespeare-quoting, debonair V, who never removes his mask, systematically assassinates the leaders of the regime and authors of his personal misfortune while, at the same time, staging daring acts of terrorism, including destroying public monuments and hijacking the regime's communications and surveillance systems.

Both *V for Vendetta* and *Joker* are means by which Hollywood, for all its contradictions as a capitalist industry, both processes and co-opts social movements symbolism, but, at the same time, provides semiotic and narrative resources for popular mobilization. The earlier *V for Vendetta* was produced in the early 2000s in the wake of the so-called Alterglobalization Movement and during some of the world's largest ever demonstrations against the Bush-led "War on Terror." It was no doubt inspired by a preceding decade where masked protest had become a mainstream media spectacle, notably inspired by the Kafiya-wrapped militants of Palestine's Second Intifada and the charismatic example and theorization of the mask by the Zapatista Army for National Liberation and its enigmatic, suave, and poetic spokesperson, Subcomandante Marcos. Major counter-globalization protests in Seattle and Genoa had seen masked protesters as protagonists of anti-systemic struggle. The masks in all these cases were first and foremost practicalities to protect the protesters from identification and reprisal by the state, as well as from tear gas. But they were also symbolic: as Subcomandante Marcos made clear from the very appearance of the Zapatistas in 1994, the mask was a sigil for universality and unanimity among the oppressed.

This is who we are.
The Zapatista National Liberation Army.
The voice that arms itself to be heard.
The face that hides itself to be seen.
The name that hides itself to be named.
The red star who calls to our humanity and the world to be
heard, to be seen, to be named
The tomorrow to be harvested in the past.

Behind our black mask,
Behind our armed voice,
Behind our unnamable name,
Behind us, we are you.

Behind we are simple and ordinary men and women, who
represent all races, painted in all colors, speak in all languages,
live in all places.
The same forgotten men and women.
The same excluded,
The same untolerated,
The same persecuted,
We are you.[7]

IV

The use of the Guy Fawkes mask popularized by *V for Vendetta* as
a protest technology appeared a few years after the film's release
at a strange set of coordinated protests by the hacktivist tendency
Anonymous at the prominent storefront edifices of the Church of
Scientology around the world. Anons (as they dubbed themselves)
wanted revenge against the Church for seeking to "censor the internet"
by threatening massive "lawfare" if a video of Church celebrity
Tom Cruise was not removed from platforms like YouTube.[8] In the
video, Cruise made a series of laughably absurd statements about the
benevolence and supernatural powers of the Church, which Anons
delighted in ridiculing. Fearing reprisal from the notoriously litigious
and allegedly vengeful Church, the Anons cautioned one another to
mask their faces and many chose to order cheap Guy Fawkes masks,
famous among them not only because of the film but also because of an
early in-joke meme. The masks supplied a poetic resonance with *V for
Vendetta*'s final scene of anonymous uprising, meant that, by the time of
the so-called Arab Spring and anti-austerity Movements of the Squares

in Europe in 2010, the mask had become a mainstay of protest aesthetics and a practical tool for activists in repressive atmospheres.[9] It reached massive mainstream appeal thanks to the appearance of Occupy Wall Street in New York's financial district in 2011 and its spread to cities and towns across America and around the world: the mask became in some ways the sigil of the movement.

Nearly a decade later it remains a key artifact in global protest, notably in the recent uprisings in Hong Kong where protesters were deeply aware of the power of the Chinese government's digital surveillance arsenal. Yet in recent months it has been joined by the appearance of protesters around the world donning makeup to echo that of Phoenix's *Joker*, in protests in Beirut, Santiago, Hong Kong, France, and elsewhere.[10] Perhaps this appearance is simply a flash in the pan, a temporary borrowing of Hollywood iconography that seeks to capitalize on the runaway popularity of the film. But it is tempting to read the identification with Phoenix's Joker as a sign of the times.

Beyond its utility as a cheap and disposable means to disguise one's identity, the Guy Fawkes mask offered its wearer a reference to a kind of public myth with two faces. On the one hand, to wear the mask was to be associated with the film's hero, V: a superhuman avenger who presented himself as the culturally enlightened mastermind who, like Ledger's Joker, was always several steps ahead of "the system," a perfected hypermasculine revenge agent who, like that earlier Joker, saw through the lies, propaganda, and false moralism of the reigning order and, acting outside it, transformed history. This Nietzschean superman was the only one capable of giving agency and meaning to the drone-like victims/accomplices of the fascist regime, to wake them from their comfortable nightmare, through violence if necessary. The endlessly bemused face of the mask indexes a kind of supreme, aloof knowingness.

On the other hand, the Guy Fawkes mask as an icon of mass uprising recalled the final scene of the film in which the anonymous masses flock into the street and non-violently overwhelm the army and police of the decapitated fascist regime, unstoppable in their number, unified in purpose. I would offer that the success of this mask relies on both contradictory tendencies together, in ways that are both consonant with and also surpass the general neoliberal cultural politics of the day.

From one angle, the Guy Fawkes mask represents an aegis of collective liberation, in the spirit of the Zapatistas. It represents a utopian grasp for an unprecedented collectivity, a kind of avenging cooperative agency that defines itself through mass action in the streets. It signals the relinquishing of the fetish of consumer and possessive individualism and the abnegation of a patriarchal notion of agency, where singular, fearless men change the world. It's worth considering that, in spite of the superhero's perennial popularity as an avenger of justice, we have yet to see protesters don Batman masks.

From another angle, however, the avenging hero here is a flattering reflection of the kind of agency, intelligence, individualism, and will-to-power of the perfected masculine subject of neoliberalism. In Alan Moore's original comic book depiction V is a perverse character, crazed and vindictive in exact proportion to the fascist system that wrought him, an avenging angel of anarchy, the nightmare of authoritarian order. In the film, as the curmudgeonly and iconoclastic Moore lamented, V is in a strange way the avenger of liberal capitalist democracy, the petty bourgeois' preferred self-image vivified, an erudite entrepreneur, motivated less by revenge than by a benevolent desire to restore democracy, the rule of law, and the gentle commerce of capitalism.[11] The uprising V triggers at the end of the film is ultimately messianic: whereas in the comic the story ends in riots and chaos, the film ends as the liberated masses remove their masks to watch the fireworks of the Parliament's detonation, their work done for them by the conquering hero, their father.

V

What, then, to make of the appearance of Joker at today's protests? One might speculate that it signals a sympathy or identification with Joker the lesser: the emaciated, suffering Arthur Fleck buffeted by the cruel winds of austerity in the first part of the 2019 film. Perhaps the makeup is worn in order to dramatize the tragi-comic shared condition of living in a moment of neoliberal capitalism that, on the one hand, insists that we are each responsible for seizing our own fate and, on the other, transforms life into a series of fateful disasters. Perhaps the makeup signals its wearer as a kind of vengeful ghost, abandoned by society and left to wander in the streets.

Equally, however, the Joker makeup might signal an embrace of the more nihilistic chaos unleashed at the end of the film, the descent into a kind of destructive *jouissance*. Here, the abandoned and surplussed of revenge capitalism offer themselves up as vehicles for revenge against its agents and edifices. Perhaps this form of masking is actually a reference to Ledger's Joker: the sadistic, nihilistic mastermind. But my hunch is it is far more pessimistic. It is, in a sense, not an overidentification with the entrepreneurial will-to-power, but with its abject counterpoint: the rock-bottom loser, who has given up all hope in the neoliberal promise, but cannot dream of anything beyond revenge.

5
The dead zone

Financialized nihilism, toxic wealth, and vindictive technologies

This chapter is about the dead zones that grow around the world and inside each of us under revenge capitalism. It's about the numb but panicked apathy, the overstimulated stagnation, and the blindered fixation on unfulfilling survival that strips us of our empathy and imagination.

In the news cycle, dead zones name the rivers, lakes, and coastal areas blighted of life, thanks largely to the massive influx of synthetic nutrients like fertilizers from industrial-agricultural runoff or poorly treated human or animal waste. But dead zones here also refer to the mind-numbing vindictiveness of neoliberal bureaucracies, the soulless cores of gentrified cities, the social breakdown around mining camps, and the existential and cognitive condition of oversaturated vacancy that has become so normalized in an age of social media. Indeed, taken in sum, the dead zone ultimately references the nihilistic political ecology of financialized capitalism.

In general terms, my conceptualization of the dead zone describes as unintended but disastrous collective consequence of the kinds of market-oriented behaviors encouraged by financialized capitalism. In this paradigm, economic exploitation and social order is not simply orchestrated "from above" but instilled in and activated through many individuals, each of them motivated by the pressures to compete in a society where everyone is expected to transfigure themselves into a speculator, which seeks to recode all relationships as risks, and where we are taught to imagine everything of value as an asset to be leveraged.[1] In aquatic dead zones algae flock to areas flooded with the toxic nutrition of human waste or industrial-agricultural runoff, who bloom enthusiastically but end up, in so doing, destroying the interdependent thriving of the ecosystem. In an analogous fashion, in this moment of financialized capitalism produce near-apocalyptic and irrational (vengeful) impacts by encouraging the individual competitive and speculative behavior of a variety of actors, each of whom feels compelled to act by the same force of which they are a part.

My theorization of the dead zone here builds on and expands the exploration of the metaphor by David Graeber and Henry Giroux, who each in their own way grasp its potency, if not its full richness as a means to talk about the way power works on the imagination.[2] My intent is to draw a wider arc, suggesting that the term helps us describe a crucial aspect of what I have been framing as revenge capitalism, and perhaps its most perplexing but important aspect at that: the way in which systemic revenge transpires not simply or exclusively through the sadistic or vindictive intentions of any individual but emerges from the aggregate and often competitive or contradictory activities of millions of economic actors (not all of them human).

More generally, my intention in this chapter is to illuminate the way that the paradigm of the dead zone, and the process which I will call dead zoning, manifests in mutually reinforcing ways throughout the financialized world, not only in terms of the heartbreaking destruction of human and non-human landscapes, but also throughout the field of psycho-social life.

I. INTO THE DEAD ZONE

In Stephen King's bestselling 1979 novel *The Dead Zone* John Smith, a jovial public school teacher, wakes up from a five-year coma in 1975 to a world that is subtly but radically changed, in possession of supernatural powers. The car accident and brain damage that led to the coma now mean that skin-to-skin contact gives Johnny visions, sometimes of other people's past, sometimes of their future. Yet his preternatural insight cannot help him shake the feeling of being "out of step and out of tune" with reality.[3] But it is perhaps this condition of being outside of time, in the "dead zone" that gives Johnny his powers, powers he ultimately uses to save humanity from annihilation, or so he thinks.

The dead zone of the film's title refers to several things at once: first, the area of Johnny's brain damaged by the accident and, later, the location of a malignant tumor which, on the one hand, has altered his mind but, on the other, is the source of his visions. Second, the dead zone names the feeling that Johnny experiences when a vision takes hold of him, as if he was drained of life and subjectivity, the better to fully enter the thoughts of another. Third and most importantly, the dead zone names the opaque areas of Johnny's premonitions: details that are tantalizingly out of reach or, more vitally, aspects of the future that cannot be foretold. As the novel progresses we learn that these dead zones are aspects of the future that will depend on Johnny's own actions in the present: he cannot see these parts of the future because they are in his hands to change.

I see this novel, and, to a lesser extent, the 1983 film adaptation, directed by David Cronenberg, as an enigmatic but important parable for our times: our protagonist awakens to a profoundly reactionary age, having slept through the many minute social, political, cultural, and economic shifts that brought about the new paradigm. He finds himself with profound but unreliable powers and must, ultimately, make a fateful choice to sacrifice himself to prevent future apocalypse, to avenge the present-day murder of the future.

The asleep and the awake

There is a subtle allegory here for the fate of America at precisely the pivot of the neoliberal, financialized era.[4] Johnny has slept through the oil crisis, the severing of the dollar from the Gold Standard, and the US-backed *coup d'etat* in Chile that would make that nation the testing ground for neoliberal "shock therapy." Though few would have known it at the time, he also slept through the publication of the Black-Scholes formula for the pricing of derivatives, which would radically transform global finance, as well as the first steps in the computerization of global trade. Large firms were increasingly integrating computers and complex data analytics into their operations, including in the field of logistics that allowed for more complicated manipulation of increasingly globally integrated supply chains. Johnny therefore is trapped in a transition from Keynesianism to neoliberalism that theorists were only able to fully grasp in hindsight, but that King grasps precisely in his own authorial dead zone, in what Fredric Jameson has called the political unconscious where those structural transformations to capitalist totality that defy direct description make themselves known, obliquely and often unintentionally, in art.[5]

These many consequential structural and systemic transformations are, as usual, unknown to the novel's characters, but the narrative does focus on the seismic political shifts over the 1970s that, in the real America, would lead to the election of Ronald Reagan in 1981.[6] In the novel, the right-wing revanchist reaction against the protests of the late 1960s and early 1970s comes in the form of the clown-like candidacy of Greg Stillton. Throughout the novel we are treated to glimpses of Stillton's rise to power: on the surface, a colorful, populist, glad-handing buffoon; behind closed doors a merciless bully and extortionist, surrounded by a security team of neo-Nazi bikers.

When he and Stillton shake hands at a campaign rally, Johnny enters the dead zone: a hazy vision of an anguished future of violence, death, and fear. Later it is revealed that Johnny recognized that Stillton's religious zeal and cowboy politics would, if empowered by the Presidency, lead to a nuclear holocaust. Johnny struggles with the implications of his vision and its ethical calling, something complicated by the abstract and incomplete nature of the premonition thanks to the dead zone: the way the future might be influenced by Johnny's own actions. Our protagonist ultimately determines he must kill Stillton. But while attempting the assassination at a campaign rally, Johnny misses his mark and is fatally shot by Stillton's neo-Nazi security detail, but not before Stillton grabs a baby from the audience to use as a human shield, a depraved act that is caught on film and ultimately leads to Stillton's political ruin.

There is much to take away from this powerful, bestselling novel (and, to a lesser extent, its film adaptation) as an oracle for our own times. I am certainly not the first to note the parallels of Stillton's clownish populism with the rise of political power of Donald Trump since 2015: the similarities are profoundly unsettling.[7] But there is more at work here.

To be in the dead zone is to know something is profoundly amiss, terrifyingly so, and yet to be unable to name it. It is to know that something world-changing must be done, yet not knowing what to do. It is to have a premonition of sacrifice but not know at which altar. It is to be filled with a kind of slow-motion dread that one is a small part of a massive current that is headed for disaster. It is the awareness that "we have been endowed with a weak Messianic power, a power to which the past has a claim, [and] that claim cannot be settled cheaply."[8] We must avenge a stolen future.[9]

II. DEAD ZONES OF THE IMAGINATION

If the metaphor of the dead zone is familiar it is perhaps because it refers to the outcome of a now well-known biological process known as eutrophication, one which has affected rivers, lakes, and coastal areas around the world, leading to sometimes gargantuan aquatic areas heartbreakingly denuded of life. Perhaps the best-known example is the huge dead zone in the Gulf of Mexico, primarily caused by the accumulated runoff of industrialized agriculture that flows down the Mississippi River and its tributaries.[10] Importantly, eutrophication, whose Latin root refers to an overabundance of food, is not caused because of an accumulation of toxins that poison life (though that, too, is a problem for the Gulf of Mexico and other aquatic systems). Rather, it is the result of too much nutrition in the water, predominantly thanks to the introduction of massive quantities of synthetic fertilizers, including nitrogen and phosphate, and animal waste.[11] These micronutrients foster the growth at the microscopic part of the food web, frequently leading to huge algae blooms on the surface of the water. While sometimes these algae release harmful toxins the bigger problem is that they blot out the light to plants and other organisms below. As these other organisms die and decompose, the oxygen in the water is consumed and not replaced and without oxygen organisms are starved for life. It's not only that these organisms then die: it's that their death disrupts the whole ecosystem and food web, meaning it is extremely difficult for the aquatic zone to regenerate life even after the initial process of eutrophication subsides. It may take decades, centuries, or even millennia for the complex aqua-system to once again foster the density and diversity of life that had been the norm.

While eutrophication is a "natural" phenomenon which has been occurring in long cycles for billions of years, today the transformation of global food systems toward intensified and typically export-oriented production has created a worldwide crisis. I would frame the dead zone today as a creature of what Donna Harraway, Anna Tsing, and their colleagues call the plantationcene: the particular ways the world has been reshaped, since the mid-fifteenth century, by the colonial and proto-capitalist model of the plantation, where the labors of humans, animals, and other organisms are reorganized on a model of dispossession, forced transportation, scientific management, and profit-oriented production.[12]

The allegory of the dead zone has been most capaciously theorized by Graeber as part of a larger investigation into the power of bureaucracy in terms of "dead zones of the imagination."[13] Graeber seizes on the polyvalence and evocativeness of the term to describe a number of interconnected phenomena. On a first level, he is alerting us to the well-known mind-numbing banality of bureaucracies and their seemingly fanatical devotion to rules, protocols, reporting, metrics, and paperwork that seems to leave almost no latitude at all for the imagination and, indeed, usually see the imagination as a kind of threat to efficient and orderly operations. Second, Graeber uses the term "dead zone of the imagination" to call attention to the way the academic anthropological and sociological gaze seems to slip off banalized and unsexy sites of study (like bureaucracies), even though they have massive power and consequences for a huge number of people, and in spite of the fact that almost all of us are in some way caught up in them.

But Graeber uses this as a jumping off point for a much more profound and general point about the asymmetries of what he calls interpretive labor and the realities of structural violence. In Graeber's interpretation, which he develops out of feminist social criticism, structural violence refers to the "forms of pervasive social inequality that are ultimately backed up by the threat of physical harm" that "invariably tend to create the kinds of willful blindness we normally associate with bureaucratic procedures. To put it crudely," he continues, "it is not so much that bureaucratic procedures are inherently stupid, or even that they tend to produce behavior that they themselves define as stupid, but rather, that they are invariably ways of managing social situations that are already stupid because they are founded on structural violence."[14]

Graeber identifies many sites of structural violence within our society, ranging from the insouciant, megalithic, and seemingly vindictive healthcare bureaucracies of the contemporary United States and Britain to the overarching structures of a patriarchal society, which, while it may claim to guarantee women's full legal and political rights, remains deeply unequal and oppressive. But, importantly, for Graeber this kind of bureaucracy thrives not in the public but the neoliberal private sector, where corporations see opportunities to extract wealth in a labyrinth of rules, fees, penalties, and forms of asset stripping.

Pedagogies of vengeance

A fine example of structural violence is cataloged by Henry A. Giroux in his damning indictment of the way neoliberalism has transformed public schooling in the United States into:

> "dead zones of the imagination," reduced to anti-public spaces that wage an assault on critical thinking, civic literacy and historical memory. Since the 1980s, schools have increasingly become testing hubs that deskill teachers and disempower students. They have also been refigured as punishment centers, where low-income and poor minority youth are harshly disciplined under zero tolerance policies in ways that often result in their being arrested and charged with crimes that, on the surface, are as trivial as the punishment is harsh. Under casino capitalism's push to privatize education, public schools have been closed in cities such as Philadelphia, Chicago and New York to make way for [privatized] charter schools. Teacher unions have been attacked, public employees denigrated, and teachers reduced to technicians working under deplorable and mind-numbing conditions … Trust, imagination, creativity and a respect for critical teaching and learning are thrown to the wind in the pursuit of profits and the proliferation of rigid, death-dealing accountability schemes.[15]

Echoing a theme taken up by Graeber, Giroux illustrates how the reduction of schools to dead zones of the imagination is a public–private partnership under neoliberalism. Whereas the conventional imaginary of bureaucracy conjures up images of inefficient, petty, and vindictive public servants working for faceless government ministries, the reality today is that the routinization, banalization, and metrics-obsessed character of many of today's institutions is largely thanks to the way they have been opened to private sector "competition," either through direct privatization or the applications of market-crafted standards, measurements, incentives, and punishments. Ironically, these reforms (in education, health care, social services) are typically justified in the political arena with reference to the kinds of bureaucratic nihilism they claim to *solve*, but in fact exacerbate.

If we were to apply Graeber's analysis to Giroux's examples we might say that neoliberalism frames a series of structural violences that transform "public" education into a venue for further structural violence against teachers and students. This structural violence produces a dead zone of the imagination in at least two ways: first, in the sense that the school system abandons any pretense to providing care for young people's holistic growth and simply becomes a kind of machine for vocational drilling, social sorting, and habituation to quasi-authoritarian boredom. Second, the dead zone is produced in the students themselves thanks to the way the pedagogy of the institution comes to mirror and reproduce the broader ideology of neoliberalism. Giroux notes that:

> Neo-liberalism is a disimagination machine that remakes social identity by turning civic subjects into consuming and marketable subjects. As a public pedagogy, it works aggressively in multiple sites – extending from the new screen culture and mainstream media to the schools – to produce desires, needs and values as a form of second nature, internalized as a habit and common sense.[16]

It is crucial here to note that the effects of this dead zoning of public education in the US are deeply racialized. They echo, in perverse fashion, the ways in which that most of that nation's public and private sectors were essentially built during the Jim Crow era of legal and paralegal racial segregation and continue to reproduce racial injustice. Overlapping bureaucracies intentionally and unintentionally did all they could to stymie Black thriving.[17] These realities continue most egregiously in the racialized systems of civil warfare waged against racialized Americans through the systems of "mass incarceration" today, which likewise entangle criminalized subjects and their families in a web of bureaucratic terrors that, while allegedly neutral and color-blind, work again and again to strangulate specific populations.[18]

It goes almost without saying that students "educated" in such vengeful environments would be discouraged from cultivating the kind of thinking that might make recognizable the systemic and structural conditions of their deprivation, boredom, and oppression. It is a form of education that lends itself toward easy, individualized understandings of social problems and their potential solutions. It is a form of systemic pedagogical vengeance and, in its turn, tills the soil in which revenge politics might grow. This is not only true for the disadvantaged, largely racialized students whose schools are chronically underfunded, but also for the privileged, whose schooling is oriented to a desperate attempt to instill human capital and a competitive ethos to make youth ready to take their place and to help reproduce an unforgiving world.

I don't really care, do you?

Giroux does not take his application of Graeber's metaphor of the dead zone further, but much is revealed if one does. Graeber argues that dead zones of the imagination form within institutions of structural violence because, as with all forms of violence and coercion, obedience can be achieved by the powerful without the need to really understand, let alone sympathize with, the oppressed. While some forms of power do require the oppressor to study and try and get in the mind of the oppressed, violence is simply the exercise or threat of coercive force and is usually marked by a near-complete disinterest on the part of the oppressor. While the oppressed must typically learn to study and understand the oppressor to navigate the world the oppressor has created, and to avoid harm, the oppressor is rarely required to undertake what Graeber calls this "interpretive labor" of a kind of sympathetic imagination – indeed, it is often a liability.

Such an asymmetry is perhaps easiest to see in situations of obscene and obtuse power imbalances, such as when slavers can't even be bothered to understand the origins or languages of their slaves and obscenely dehumanize them so as to render any interpretive labor unnecessary: if they are less than human, why even try and understand them? But Graeber surprises us by arguing that violence's ability to obviate the need for interpretive labor

> becomes most salient when the violence itself is least visible, in fact, where acts of spectacular physical violence are least likely to occur. These are situations of what I've referred to as structural violence, on the assumption that systematic inequalities backed up by the

threat of force can be treated as forms of violence in themselves. For this reason, situations of structural violence invariably produce extreme lopsided structures of imaginative identification.

In other words, institutions of structural violence produce situations in which those institutions, like for instance neoliberal public schooling, become massive, uncaring, disinterested structures that increasingly and unceasingly reduce those over whom they have power to dehumanized statistics to be managed on the basis of raw efficiency. The dead zone of the imagination, then, also exists at the very core of the institution itself, the kind of dull banality that reduces the complexity of the social world to a series of sub-routines. In other words, interpretive labor is reduced to an absolute minimum. Meanwhile, subjects of those institutions, such as students and teachers in neoliberalized public schools, are tasked with tuning their interpretive labor to devising methods of survival, care, entrepreneurship or revenge within the institution. To connect this discussion to the terms I have been introducing in this book, dead zones of the imagination are both the means and the effects of revenge capitalism, a form of structural and systemic violence that appears to be retribution for unknown infraction, expressed against whole populations not out of personal malice (though that can play a role) but through the banality of stupid systems. Revenge here is the character, not the intention, of capitalism in its neoliberal, financialized valence which relentlessly seeks to recode social life and institutions to better accommodate its imperatives of accumulation.

III. THE DEAD ZONES OF FINANCIALIZATION

The world of global finance is changing so rapidly that it is constantly churning up new metaphors for hitherto unimaginable maneuvers. Here, too, the metaphor of the dead zone has a place. It is typically used by those specializing in foreign currency exchange (ForEx) markets to describe a daily lull in trading volumes (and therefore price volatility) that make for sluggish potential for profit. This "dead zone" occurs around 11am in New York as European markets begin to close and before Asian markets open.[19] Thanks to the digital integration of global markets, these overlap periods present many lucrative opportunities for methods including various forms of arbitrage (the taking-advantage of momentary price differentials between two markets), many techniques that are now almost completely automated and executed by algorithmically-driven supercomputers.[20]

These opportunities have grown exponentially since the 1970s thanks to a number of factors, including the global digital integration of financial markets, new mathematical models developed to price and manipulate risk, the neoliberal pressure to deregulate national currency transactions aimed at "liberalizing" international trade and promoting global investment, and the emergence of a range of new financial players: banks and companies that operate in multiple countries and have need for access to foreign currencies. These include large firms and even national treasuries seeking to trade in foreign currencies to hedge their own operations, massive institutional investors like pension funds looking to make the trade in national currencies part of their diverse portfolios, shark-like hedge funds eager to make a quick buck, even entrepreneurial online day-traders and hobbyists who essentially use global currency markets as a kind of thinking-man's casino (and not to mention the companies and scams that prey on them).[21]

As numerous scholars and critics have noted, the ForEx trade, while often extremely profitable for some (typically large institutional investors employing powerful algorithms), it does, on the whole, produce practically nothing of value and is profoundly structurally violent.[22] For one, they can and often do wreak havoc on the price of national currencies which are subject to massive speculation, with dramatically more disastrous consequences for poorer nations.[23] Forty years into a neoliberal revolution which forced global market integration onto almost all nations and many are almost completely reliant on foreign trade for basic staples like food, medicine and electricity, the relative prices of which can be drastically affected by the speculative trade of those nations' currencies. For this reason, the fickle foreign exchange markets have a tremendous disciplinary power over national governments who, just as they fear the power of international bond markets to punish non-neoliberal policy, also fear that any government (or even social movement) activity seen to jeopardize the rule of corporate power and transnational finance (for instance, re-regulating foreign currency exchange) will lead to a sharp drop in the value of the national currency, with grievous humanitarian implications.[24]

An empire of indifference

For this reason, already over a decade ago, social scientists of finance Brian LiPuma and Benjamin Lee described these financial operations as a kind of mass, distributed global structural violence.[25] This framing echoed that of theorists, journalists, and activists from the Global South, who identified the global financial apparatus as the latest form of imperialism, this time deceptively detached from any particular occupier or colonizer.[26] For LiPuma and Lee, global financial markets and especially derivatives markets have a structurally violent impact all around the world, but mask that violence and dilute responsibility for it among many competing market players. When foreign currency speculation leads to the drastic devaluation of a poor nation's currency, meaning the skyrocketing of prices for imported grains or bottled water, or the cancellation of government-funded primary health programs, people suffer and die.[27] But no individual is responsible: all those who divested themselves of the currency were simply following the market whose currents they helped to create but over which they had no real control, and of whose overarching impacts most functionaries are hardly even aware.

The kind of mute, stupefying banality that Graeber associates with the dead zone of the imagination inherent to bureaucracy here reaches a kind of climax, especially when we consider that most of the individual agents of these nightmares are not even human: they are robots designed and unleashed by humans, humans who barely understand how the robots even work.[28]

It is tempting to see global finance as a kind of massive, opaque, unanswerable bureaucracy. Without wishing to downplay the very real leviathan-like and crony-capitalist power of a small number of financial players (major international investment banks, private equity funds, hedge funds, and asset management firms), finance and financialization is driven forward by structural rivalry between multiple competing interests.[29] More crucially for our purposes, it both foments and depends on a profound transformation of all participating social subjects and institutions, not just the "big fish."

I and others have insisted that we must see the processes of digitalized financialization as more than just the growing power and influence of the financial sector over the global economy, over firms and even over governments. Financialization achieves, sustains, and grows this power by recalibrating social institutions and social life so as to both reach expansively around the globe, and deep into the social fabric.[30]

Financialization, then, depends on and foments a transformation in all sorts of social actors toward a logic of speculation and preemption. It is not simply that we learn the proto-authoritarian values of competitiveness, distrust, and obedience; we are habituated to calibrate our imaginations toward a financialized form of survival. Dead zones form when this financialized behavior, either by financial professionals or the rest of us, rushes into a zone, a process, or a sphere of life with catastrophic, vengeful results no one individual necessarily intends, predicts, or wants.

IV. ACTUALLY EXISTING DEAD ZONES

Urban dead zones

The potency of the allegory of the dead zone first struck me in considering the tendencies known (often somewhat deceptively) as gentrification: the process by which lower-income, often oppressed and racialized populations are slowly but surely cleansed from neighborhoods to make way for more affluent residents.[31] Many have insisted that we link this process to financialization and, in particular, the way that transnational flows of capital are eager to invest in urban real estate speculation.[32] It is also vital to recognize these processes as continuations of longer histories of colonial dispossession and what Marxist theorists term "enclosure."[33] Communities struggle for generations to transform a neighborhood and create physical and cultural infrastructures that foster life in common; these forms of social cohesion, neighborhood vitality, and cultural vibrancy are often precisely what then attracts investors eager to capitalize on them through property acquisition, the raising of rents, the tactical use of policing, and other mechanisms.

The result is often that, as companies and speculators buy up housing stock or replace the built environment with more lucrative infrastructure, and as wealthier inhabitants move in, the rich cultural, social, and human ecosystem that "added value" to the neighborhood in the first place is gradually replaced or put under fatal stress. What often emerges is a kind of socio-cultural dead zone, emblematized by the whole neighborhoods of global cities like London, New York, San Francisco, Sydney, and Vancouver that are favored by absentee owners who use their property largely as a vehicle for speculation or as a stable offshore place to park their money.[34] Even when the new, richer neighbors actually live in the area the trend is for businesses to cater to their more affluent fancies, leading to the apocryphal high street full of expensive shoe stores, luxury pet-care retailers, and cafés whose artisanal brews cost the equivalent of the hourly on minimum wage. As Sarah Shulman notes in her analysis of the gentrification of New York's Lower East Side, what is lost is precisely the cultures of solidarity, ingenuity, and creativity formed within the collective experience of marginalization and oppression expressed in urban space.[35]

Once again, the metaphor of the dead zone is revealing, not only because it names what results from this process, but also part of the mechanisms of the process itself. Aquatic dead zones, recall, are created not because toxins kill everything and not because of a scarcity of nutrition, but because of its synthetic overabundance. The example of the gentrifying neighborhood offers a fine example of how digitized, financialized global capital introduces a kind of vindictive wealth or overabundance into urban ecologies, a kind of nutrition that promotes the growth of opportunistic life forms, in this case housing speculators large and small. Like the algae who opportunistically feed on the runoff of synthetic fertilizers from intensive (market-oriented) agriculture, the speculators and newcomers to gentrifying neighborhoods end up starving for light the very ecosystem that drew them in in the first place, leaving behind a dead zone.

The phenomenon we know of as gentrification is not simply the fault of insufferable trust-fund enabled hipsters or shadowy foreign speculators. It is in large part driven by the way that financialized capitalism has stripped many people of various forms of security and stability and encouraged the purchase of and speculation on private property as a means to hedge life in a world of unforeseeable risks. In many countries the neoliberal period has seen a raft of policies aimed at encouraging middle class people to invest in housing markets as a means to secure their wealth in real estate, the better to suffer the slings and arrows of the merciless new economy.[36] This is true too on a global scale, where international housing speculators seek to use cosmopolitan global cities as safe places to park their wealth or use as collateral. But on a deeper level, the process of urban property speculation is driven, at least in part, by the relatively innocent quotidian actions of financialized subjects whose activities, in aggregate, end up deadzoning the very urban systems on which they seek to capitalize.[37]

Of dead zones and sacrifice zones: the man camp

Dead zones are different from but connected to what some have termed sacrifice zones or wastelands of global racial capitalism. While both topographies are exploited and ravaged by the pathologies of speculative capital, sacrifice zones and wastelands are destroyed either by systematic disinvestment or the introduction of toxins: they are starved or poisoned.[38] By contrast, dead zones are created by an influx of too much destructive nutrition, a kind of overfeeding that creates its own monsters. Yet the two logics do often work in tandem, and the process of "dead zoning" (opening a space to an influx of speculative wealth) can lead to a wasteland or a sacrifice zone, as in an aquatic system where a dead zone might persist for decades, even centuries after the influx of synthetic nutrition, thanks to the way the process has destroyed the complex web of life and created a perpetual deoxygenated zone where new life can't thrive.

An example of a dead zone that is also a sacrifice zone might be the "man camps" that are a seemingly necessary feature of extractive projects the world over, where imported specialized mining labor is brought in to "remote" areas and accommodated, often for months or years at a time, in company-provided temporary housing.[39] The vast majority of these workers are men working in an industry not especially known for its commitments to challenging patriarchal notions, expectations, and performances of masculinity.[40] Sociologists and geographers have studied the ways in which the presence of these "man camps" dramatically increase the level of risk and incidences of harm to local populations, notably women and girls, including increases in the prevalence and danger of sex work and increased rates of sexual assault.[41] More generally, the presence of these man camps and the markets they create (for goods and services, including recreational drugs and sexual services) has dramatic effects on local populations not only in terms of transforming the social and labor character of the place but also leading to the recalibration of the often impoverished local economy toward providing for the camp. For instance, many traditional, subsistence, and community-centered economic practices (hunting, foraging, farming, craft-making) are abandoned or marginalized as local individuals seek to provide goods or services for the man camp, in part to be able to gain enough money to pay for the influx of imported goods at inflated prices.[42]

The arrival of a man camp, for many such communities, represents the influx of a kind of vindictive wealth, a eutrophication. But the sociological and communal impacts can often be characterized as a kind of slow death, a socio-cultural asphyxiation as those traditional practices and relationships of survival and provisioning atrophy. Extractive industries are, by definition, temporary. When the resource being exploited runs out, or when it proves no longer profitable to continue the exploitation, the man camp is shuttered and the local community is left with a radically transformed economic and social landscape: a wasteland or sacrifice zone which has ceased to be of use to the circuits of global capitalism.

This form of patriarchal extractivism has long and deep roots that stretch back to the very intertwined origins of capitalism and colonialism, emblematized by the invasion and conquest of the Americas where sexual assault and misogynistic violence were key weapons used to seize Indigenous lands, and enslave or exploit Indigenous labor.[43] Yet the speed and ease with which extractive projects today are now initiated, operated, and relocated is an affordance of digitalized financialization.[44] The transformation of a landscape into an extractive dead zone is determined and resourced a world away, on stock markets and in the office towers of global metropoles. The financial risk and reward is decomposed and recomposed thousands of times as shares in and debts of the mining companies in question, as well as their subcontractors and clients, are traded, a massive, unanswerable, decentralized bureaucracy. Here, as ever, risk is calculated and assessed purely in terms of the speculative consequences for profitability, not for the affected population whose fate is rendered completely invisible.[45] Structural violence is enabled and exacerbated by the competitive technocratic field and, frequently, managed largely by computers. Its harms and ecological impacts are barely registered.

IV. INTERNAL DEAD ZONES

To those over the age of 25, streaking refers to the prank of running through a public or televised space, most famously a sports field, naked, usually as a mischievous prank but occasionally for political purposes to draw attention to a certain cause.

But for most under 25 it has a completely different meaning. For them, streaking names the practice of a sustained daily interaction with another person on the popular social media network Snapchat, famous for pioneering the feature of deleting public posts and private messages after 24 hours.[46] Over the past several years, Snapchat rose (and fell) as one of the most popular platforms among young people because of this feature which means that, unlike Facebook, one can cultivate online social interactions without worrying that it is leaving a kind of eternal archive that might come back to haunt one, or that might be found by parents, teachers, and so on. However, Snapchat's coded ephemerality of messages sacrifices one of the more attractive features of social networking apps for many young users: any yardstick by which to measure and compare the number and intensity of social bonds. Young users not only want to communicate, they also want to be seen to be communicating by others, and to feel validated in some way for communicating, as do we all.

Enter streaking: when one communicates on Snapchat in any way with another person for three consecutive days, a small flame icon appears next to that interlocutor's name in one's list of contacts, along with a tally which increases for every day of uninterrupted contact. The content of the contact is unimportant, so long as each of the two parties sends some reciprocal content at least once every 24 hours: it could be a digital novel, a nude image, or a confession of a deep secret, but equally and more commonly it could simply be an emoji, a random meaningless photo, or even just the word "streak" or the letters STRK. As the uninterrupted duration of the streak increases, Snapchat's algorithm rewards the two users with special icons that appear next to one another's names.

According to young people interviewed by various news outlets beginning in 2017, when the trend of streaking was extremely popular, the goal was to streak with many individuals, which speaks to many mutually rewarding relationships.[47] Young people would often publicly post screenshots of their Snapchat contact lists lit up with streak icons and daily tallies as evidence of their diverse and intensive social activity. Recall that these messages may be almost completely empty. What makes for a successful streak is simply the rigorous daily regularity of contact of any kind, no matter how vacuous. And what affords users social prestige and a sense of accomplishment is to be streaking with many different people, preferably (other) people with prestige in their social circles.

On one level, this is nothing new. It is no secret that adolescents are eager to experiment with relationships and are highly attuned to, even obsessed with, the games of social status. What is, perhaps, new is that digitized, financialized capitalism has developed a suite of profit-oriented efforts to hack into this inclination and monetize it, of which Snapchat is one particularly lucky (for its investors) example. And in their competitive efforts to outmaneuver one another and better hack into adolescent psycho-social networks these "start-up" companies cut closer to the proverbial bone, not simply supplementing but helping to transform the very field of activity they are operating on in ways that are profoundly unsettling.[48]

The killer app

In other research I have made a similar argument about the way the Pokémon brand was engineered to "hack" into the complex world of children's imaginative play, not so much to supplant children's natural creative inclinations (which include breaking rules and inventing new meanings to toys and games), but to supplement them.[49] I argued that the Pokémon brand offered diverse commodities (especially video games and trading cards) as a resources for children's imaginative agency. In this way, the brand was itself the product of financialization (driven by the parent corporation Nintendo's desire for market share and, ultimately, returns for investors) but also helped to inadvertently teach children to better participate in that system. I argued that financialization is, in part, characterized by the recalibration of our imaginations and the excitement of our agency toward participation in speculative capitalism.

The case of Snapchat is similar. The news about the popularity of streaking broke, not coincidentally, in the run-up to its parent company's initial public offering (IPO), during which time it was being hyped by the firm's public relations department and by the investment banks that were managing the IPO as the killer app that would unseat Facebook. While Facebook remains the world's largest social media company by users, its growth in new users has slowed dramatically and use by younger users has dropped precipitously. Many young people think of Facebook as a quasi-professionalized and highly boring "adult" sphere, yesterday's news.[50] The flocking of youth to Snapchat around 2015/2016 made headlines in the tech world, in part because it surprised even the app's designers, who were unprepared for the influx.[51]

As can happen in Silicon Valley, new staff and a more mature management structure were brought on board who charted a pathway for the company toward the IPO. In the tech sector, an IPO is a particularly important event because it means that many of the workers who had built the platform could sell their stock in the company, with which they had essentially been being paid while building it. Snapchat to date has never, as a company, made money. In fact it *loses* millions of dollars a year.[52] Its advertising revenues are minimal, as are its sale of data. The firm exists, ultimately, to attract users, produce its own hype, and drive up its own share prices. Like so many social media apps and digital platform start-ups, Snap's business plan was ultimately to find venture capitalists (VCs) to fund it for a span of years in which it could lose millions of dollars building a platform. The hope here was to develop a platform that so thoroughly stitched itself into the lives of millions of users that it became, like Facebook, both totally banal and functionally necessary for modern social life.[53] Once some threshold is reached, it is speculated, the firm will be able to monetize either the attention of its users, sold off by the millisecond to advertisers, or the personal and behavioral data those users shed as part of using the app.[54] Meanwhile, at some point the promise of that eventual moment of triumph is enough to entice a few risk-taking VCs and, later, enough investors when the company goes public.

Snapchat has not revealed in public the story behind the development of the streaking feature, though if recent revelations about Silicon Valley are any indication it is likely that it was proposed, workshopped, and designed by a cadre of user-interface engineers who are voraciously studying methods for hacking the human brain.[55] Inspired and modeled on the forms of engineering that were first developed for creating notoriously addictive slot machines, these technologists are keen researchers of the dopamine and opioid-receptor reward systems in the brain, as well as the craving of the human animal for recognition, affirmation, connection, and validation.[56] The rewarding of dedicated users who send daily potentially meaningless messages with equally meaningless icons appears to be calibrated to trigger, on a literally molecular level, the psycho-social-chemical components of the relational human mind, as if to replace the dense ecosystem of a social forest with individually fabricated trees. Whether or not this was the intent or process by which Snapchat's engineers and executives developed the streaking functionality of their app, it certainly helped build the kind of hype so essential to the firms' weird and equally meaningless business plan, which appears to be: generate a quickly growing set of seemingly-addicted users desperate to use the app constantly, even to the point of generating a scandal, all the better to rope in new investors and sustain the unsustainable microeconomics of the firm.[57] Just as Snapchat's IPO was coming online, news outlets began running sensationalist stories about the desperate and absurd lengths to which young people would go to sustain their streaks: stealing one another's phones when their own were confiscated or broken, refusing to go on family vacations lest they jeopardize their access in some remote location, even suicidal ideation when long-standing streaks were sundered or when young users could not find enough fellow participants to streak with because they were unpopular.[58]

Infinite scroll

Snapchat's popularity is waning, but its influence lives on, notably in the incorporation of ephemeral, self-deleting posting in Facebook and Instagram "stories." In any case it represents an example of the financialized model of digital technology's development today. The evidence is still scant on the long-term psychological impacts of this kind of financialized technocapitalist neurohacking, though both early indications and common sense would lead us to believe that it is negative if not catastrophic.[59] James Bridle, for instance, goes so far as to introduce the metaphor of a new dark age to discuss the potential and ongoing sociological consequences.[60]

For my purposes I want to introduce the metaphor of the dead zone to describe, simultaneously, several aspects of what Geert Lovink calls "platform nihilism": the particular disposition of the subject of corporatized social media. "Welcome to the New Normal," he writes, "Social media is reformatting our interior lives. As platform and individual become inseparable, social networking becomes identical with the 'social' itself ... Forward-looking confidence has been shattered – the seasonality of hype reduced to a flatline future."[61] Asking us to consider how social media platforms function ideologically Lovink points to the way their rules and dispositions become an a self-evident common sense that shapes subjects/users.[62] It's not that the sociality that social media platforms fosters is "false", but it is nihilistic: it is created by and for a form of capitalism that endlessly speculates on how to take advantage of our most minute, intimate, and even biochemical responses and inclinations, and it does so with no overarching goal or agenda beyond the imperative for competitive profit-seeking. The sum result, Lovink argues, is a kind of apathetic exhaustion from constant micro-overstimulation: social media, and the product that they sell (the attention of the sensing subject), are "sad by design."[63]

In the first place, the dead zone seems to describe the phenomenological experience of being trapped in the attention-harvesting algorithmic loops of social media, the proverbial "infinite scroll" where minutes, hours, and days elapse as we swipe through our newsfeeds. The metaphor of the dead zone here is not only poetic in terms of the kind of "dead time" and feeling of torpor that grips us, which would seem to be the result of the way social media essentially re-habituate the brain to a constant low-level waveform cycle of endogenous dopamine production.[64] It also, I think, reveals that social media information is, for the most part, a kind of vindictive nutrition, a synthetic overabundance that triggers a set of ecologically destructive feedback loops. In this case, the ecology is the mind itself, by which I mean that ineffable network of brain, body, and social environment. And the metaphor of the dead zone seems to describe the social environment of Snapchat, which are full of communication but devoid of meaning: teenagers are obsessed with perpetuating their streaks even if the content of the messages themselves are all but completely empty.

The dead zone is, then, not just an external process of global capitalism; it is also something implanted and growing within the subjects of that system. It emerges within us, as it grows in various spheres of human activity, precisely through the way financialized capitalism forecloses the future and encourages each of us to assist in this task by internalizing its imperatives and axioms.

Senselessness and insensibility

In his haunting and disturbing short book *Heroes: Mass Murder and Suicide* Italian theorist Franco "Bifo" Berardi links a new form of nihilism to the confluence of financial power and digital media in an era he characterizes as semio-capitalism.[65] Here, global finance has radically and catastrophically deterrititorialized and reterritorialized social life, transforming the world into a huge casino where various jurisdictions (nation-states, regions, ecologies) are simply different rooms within which a global super-elite throws the dice. Berardi also notes, as I have above, that financialization both drives forward and relies upon the transformation of each and every one of us into a speculative subject, something he links to another crucial dimension of the transition toward semio-capitalism: the movement of cognitive labor to the center of the capitalist economy. With the rise of the service sector and the importance of the fields of technology, management, logistics, and research and development, it's not simply that more and more workers use their minds more than their bodies to make a living; it's also that all workers are tasked with mobilizing their cognitive and social competencies to survive and compete in increasingly austere times.[66] For the most privileged workers this may take the form of endless freelancing to sell one's creative and imaginative powers in an increasingly precarious economy. For the poorest workers and those denied even the opportunity for their own exploitation this can take the form of the monetization of their attention, or simply the downloading of all sorts of forms of care from the welfare state and society at large onto the individual. Digitally-integrated finance capital drives this process and benefits from it, in ways we have seen throughout this chapter.

For Berardi, the transformation of ever more spheres of life into venues for financialized speculation and competition, the torqueing of the imagination toward financial ends, dovetails with the process of desensitization I have, in the last section, been associating with the internalized dead zone germane to an age of digital overstimulation. The two come together in the monetization of "attention," as for instance in the case of Snapchat. Berardi argues that

> Sensibility itself is at stake, here. Sensibility is the faculty that allows human beings to understand those signs that are not verbalized, and that cannot be reduced to words. Sensibility (and sensitivity, which is the physical, erotic face of the non-verbal ability to understand and to exchange meaning) is the interpersonal film that makes possible the empathic perception of the other. Empathy (the ability to feel the pleasure and the sorrow of the other as part of our pleasure and sorrow) is not a natural emotion, but rather a psychological condition that is cultivated and refined, and which, in the absence of such cultivation, can wither and disappear.[67]

In the terms I have introduced, an internal dead zone takes shape in precisely the delicate part of the ecosystem where subjectivity meets politics. A kind of exhaustion sets in beneath the overstimulation. There is, Berardi argues, a crucial parallel and feedback loop between this nihilism at the core of the financialized subject and the moral nihilism at the core of the system. In contrast to the "hermeneutic nihilism" of bygone eras, which is concerned largely with the philosophical skepticism of the subject toward the claims truth and justice of the social order, which could have liberating and also reactionary outcomes, today's is a form of "annihilating nihilism" that "actively produces nihil as its effect." He continues that while "hermeneutic nihilism originated from the realization that the world is not a place in which an ontological essence is embodied, or a moral truth is revealed, but the place where meaning is continually created by the conscious activity of men [sic]." Conversely,

> annihilating nihilism actively destroys the shared values (both moral values and economic values) produced in the past by human production and democratic political regulation, in order to affirm the primacy of the abstract force of money. Annihilating nihilism is a peculiar phenomenon – the product of financial capitalism. In the sphere of financial capitalism, destroying concrete wealth is the easiest way to accumulate abstract value.[68]

This is a nihilism, a dead zone in my terms, at the core of the system and also instilled in the subject, the apogee of which, for Berardi, are the spectacularly violent suicide-murders and mass shooting incidents so prevalent in the US but also on the rise around the world. For Berardi, these heinous acts are the result of

> the establishment of a kingdom of nihilism and the suicidal drive that is permeating contemporary culture, together with a phenomenology of panic, aggression and resultant violence. This is the point of view from which I'm looking at mass murder, focusing in particular on the spectacular implications of these acts of killing, and on their suicidal dimension … I see them as the heroes of an age of nihilism and spectacular stupidity: the age of financial capitalism.[69]

In other words, rather than (as so many do) retreating into explanations for these monumental acts of terror in terms of mental derangement or even gun control, Berardi asks us to see these nihilistic killers as bloodcurdling champions of a nihilistically destructive system of which we are all a part, one that relies on a constant process of both stimulation and numbing.

V. THE ONTOLOGICAL DEAD ZONE

There is a blemish or lacunae in Berardi's otherwise brilliant and deeply perceptive book: all the mass shooters he analyzes, and almost all mass shooters around the world, are men, and most of them explicitly or implicitly espouse misogynistic and anti-feminist ideology.[70]

The connection between "mass shooting" and misogyny has been addressed with great care and thoughtfulness elsewhere, analyses that date back to the case of the anti-feminist massacre of 14 female students by a man at Montreal's École Polytechnique in 1989.[71] For my purposes I want to take this observation as a jumping off point for my analysis of the dead zone.

As early as the 1950s (arguably earlier), feminist theorists have sought to understand the persistence of patriarchy as sustained by the ongoing and often violent construction binary gender system in which, regardless of the underlying bodily sex (which itself would rightly come under critical scrutiny), certain traits and values were ascribed to normative notions of men and women, masculinity and femininity.[72] In patriarchal capitalist, colonial and white-supremacist "modernity," masculinity claimed for itself virtues of reason, intelligence, strength, creativity, order, law, and progress, casting women as the precise opposite.[73] Indeed, it was only by first naturalizing a gender binary and then by naturalizing women as the abject "other" within it that a coherent notion of men and masculinity could be sustained.[74] This naturalization occurred to justify and normalize an economic and social relationship of women's patriarchal subordination and the pathologization and erasure of those who did not or could not conform to the binary. It also dovetailed and was intertwined, as we'll see in a moment, with a ruling class, white-supremacist and patriarchal worldview that exalted rich white "able-bodied" men as the paragons of human achievement and aligned women, racialized "others," workers, the "disabled" and other "others" as fit only to serve or be obliterated.[75]

For our purposes, what this analysis reveals is that there are no necessary or essential qualities of men or masculinity that lead to patriarchy: these qualities are produced discursively, materially, and historically. Further, the category of masculinity (and femininity) are ultimately arbitrary and hollow and thus only held in place by convention: convention backed by violence or the threat of violence, usually structural violence. Thus, at the core of hegemonic masculinity is a kind of dead zone.[76] It's not simply that it is devoid of life, it's also that it is bleached of content because of a kind of overinvestment of vindictive wealth. In this case, the wealth are those privileges, freedoms, and material benefits that accrue to men in a patriarchal society.

Vitally, for many radical feminists, the goal is not simply to devalorize masculinity and valorize femininity but to fundamentally challenge the entire paradigm; it is not to reverse the binary but to abolish it.[77] In the work of many radical feminist writers then and today, this horizon is not only the liberation of women and non-binary people, it is even and also the liberation of those who, today, "enjoy" the toxic benefits, privileges, and freedoms offered to those who are able to perform masculinity and be taken for men.[78] The more recent discourse of "toxic masculinity," which essentially refers to the ill-effects of this performance not only on society at large but on men themselves, points in this direction: if masculinity as such is not an essential set of traits but an imaginary construct held in place by the material and symbolic degradation of "others," then not only do those (men) who benefit from it bear the weight of a huge moral burden for the subjugation of over half of humanity, they are also themselves trapped in a kind of competitive performance from which they can never escape.[79] Those who are told they ought to or must be men are constantly and necessarily failing to live up to the impossible ideal. For many feminist theorists, it is precisely this inherent, constant failure that leads masculinity to be so violent.[80]

The dialectics of the dead zone

There is a long line of criticism that arguably begins with Marx's inversion of Hegel, that seeks to place in the hands of oppressed peoples and groups a narrative of subversive ontological valorization amidst conditions of exploitation, abjection, and cultural annihilation.[81] In Marx, this is vernacularized in his naming of capital as a vampire and its ruling class as parasites.[82] In Marx's day and today we are constantly subjected to a dominant public discourse that fathoms the bourgeoisie as "job creators," "innovators," "pioneers," and, indeed, the saviors not only of the economy but of humanity itself.

More generally, the elevation of capitalists or members of their class to the most prestigious positions in the arts or government solidifies the illusion that they represent the cream of humanity. It's not just that the rest of us must work to enable them to pursue their noble and lofty goals, it's also that we are dependent on them, that anything good or whole or real about us is dependent on them and their intentional or unintentional

:

largesse. Something that set Marxism apart in the nineteenth century is that it purported to marshal one of the bourgeoisie's own prized tools, science, to demonstrate that the bourgeoisie were, themselves, little more than parasites. For all their individual creativity the system that enriched and empowered this tiny minority was actually the enemy of progress because it delimited the freedom and potential of the vast majority of workers. In fact, the bourgeoisie were, in a fundamental way, as a class, dead inside, vampires dependent on the lifeblood of living labor. The bourgeoisie has no actual ontological reality except for its dependency on the proletariat: the core of capitalism itself is a dead zone.

This radical dialectical reversal has been central to other movements of liberation. Though we may reject Marx's pretensions of science as well as his arguably narrow, Eurocentric, and sexist definition of the "working class," I think we should retain this wisdom. For instance, it informed and continues to inform generations of anti-colonial thinkers. Frantz Fanon, for one, explored the ways that the material and socio-cultural dependency of the colonizer on the colonized, the fact that the colonizer could neither survive nor have any sense of identity or community without their continued brutal subjugation of the colonized, led to a kind of vicious half-life.[83]

Edward Said likewise introduced a framework for thinking about the way the entities known as "Europe" or "the West" or even "Christendom" were not based on any positive definition or internal coherence, but, rather, developed against the backdrop of imperialism in the so-called Orient.[84] Here, imperialism both depended on and enabled European scholars, artists, commentators, and specialists to define whole diverse regions as unified "races" or "peoples" – as a unified "other" – and thereby to provide a kind of false or at least vastly over-simplistic definition of the coherent "self."[85] Of course, as all these critics note, the dead zone at the core of the colonial worldview is accompanied by a kind of frantic violence as the oppressor seeks to fill the vacant gap and is also, underneath it all, pathologically resentful and vengeful toward those subjugated populations on whom he depends, both materially and ontologically.[86]

Such analyses dovetail with and are informed by the field of critical whiteness studies too, which has taught us about the historic flexibility and perennial vindictive violence of the category of whiteness whose definition and criteria for inclusion change to adapt to the white-supremacist capitalist power structures.[87] Here, whiteness is an abstraction that demands the creation of other, more abject abstractions, notably as numerous thinkers from the Black radical tradition inform us, the abstraction of Blackness born of the transatlantic slave trade, whereby the diverse populations of Africa were melded into a single dehumanized population who, throughout white-supremacist capitalist modernity and still today, would be made to stand in for the ultimate Other for the notions of civilization, ability, progress, uplift, intelligence, and reason that whiteness falsely monopolized.[88]

In all these cases a similar thesis emerges: the oppressors, exploiters, and colonizers who depend on the labor of subjugated populations define themselves as a group, and normalize and legitimate their rule, by creating a unified and hegemonic notion of their Other and through this process of othering, which is not merely cultural but also material, thereby define themselves. Indeed, they not only define themselves, they define the reigning constellation of moral values, which they associate with themselves and which, thanks to their domination of cultural and educational institutions, they monopolize. Yet they are organized around a dead zone.

Revenge

It is in this context that, once again, the dialectics of revenge come into focus. The dreamlike unity and identity of the powerful is based on a negation of the Other, a dream that is contradicted by lived experience, by differences within that unity and by the inevitability of human diversity. The identity of the powerful depends on the exclusion, expulsion, and projection of certain condemned behaviors, traits, and characteristics onto the Other, but this identity is always already in ontological crisis, crisis that not only demands a response but produces a kind of vengefulness within the imaginary of the powerful. The Other is blamed for the failures of the system of their oppression and the fundamental inconsistencies and contradictions of its rule.[89] Vengeance, masquerading as justice, is a common feature across the interlaced field of power: vengeance not for any particular infraction of offense the oppressed may have committed but, rather, for the existential agony of the system itself, and of its beneficiaries. Patriarchal violence, public lynchings or witch trials, pogroms against migrants or "outsiders," or the slow social torture of colonial occupation are extreme but predictable forms of systemic and structural revenge. But so too are the cruel jokes, the arrogant slights, the aggrieved insolence, and the casualized negation of the Other.

Meanwhile, as we have seen in Chapter 1, in all these cases, these actions are undertaken in the shadow of a fear, sometimes stated sometimes implied, of the nihilistic vengefulness attributed to the Other, which demands that the Other be controlled, that preemptive action be taken. The Other is cast as unable to appreciate the benevolence of the oppressor or control their vengeful spirits. Men must be warned of vindictive women; masters must be warned of vengeful servants; colonial elites share tales of the bloodthirsty, envious masses. One can never be too careful. The boot can never be removed from their neck … for their own good.

If this sort of phobic dead zone is always at the heart of power, how is it connected to the dead zone as a particular archetype of financialized capitalism? I would hazard the following: today, many of the systems of power discussed in this section find their expression in the economic realm as it saturates social life. Despite the claims of financial inclusion discussed in Chapter 3, vast disparities remain globally and within Northern nations along the lines of race and gender. Still, the persona and ethos of the financier, the risk-taking, self-maximizing individual, is promoted as the only realistic and safe approach to a world without guarantees, made up of similarly competitive, risk-taking self-maximizers.

The surplussed

A keen observer of this trend, Annie McClanahan, has recently noted that one limitation of the theory that financialization makes everyone into a speculative subject is that it fails to recognize the millions of subjects, perhaps the majority of the globe, who will never have assets to leverage and whose participation in the economy is largely meaningless.[90] These surplussed populations are those whose labor time is cheapened to such a degree that it is hardly worth exploiting, who are compelled to live in a kind of temporal dead zone.[91] As I noted in this book's introduction, I have elected to use the term "surplussed" in order to recognize that this is a process imposed upon people, not an inherent quality. Such an awareness also sensitizes us to the many ways people and polities resist surplussing.[92]

Yet even these populations are beset by exhortations to embrace a competitive and speculative ethos, for instance through the micro-credit schemes or "investor"-oriented shifts to public education. We might also look to the realm of popular culture, such as rags-to-riches reality television where secret talents, invested in obscurity, get their payoff, or where corporate-selected hip hop synchronizes the self-organization of the oppressed in "gangs" with the rhythms of corporate success. We might also even read revanchist nationalism as a kind of mistaken fury over the alleged "theft" of the invested wealth of the nation by migrants and outsiders. It is less a fear of losing some distinct and unifying primordial culture or ethnic unity and more a kind of shareholder activism against the nations' political leadership ("senior management team") who appears to be letting kindhearted foolishness get in the way of a fiduciary duty to ruthlessly pursue the greatest market return.

What then unifies the semi-mythological political community of risk-taking financiers of the self whose unintended but inevitable impacts are the growth of dead zones? A revanchist resentment against all those perceived to be avoiding embracing self-responsibility, to be looking for a "hand out" from the state, who appear to be cynically leveraging some specious claim to systemic harm to gain some unfair advantage at the expense of the world of hard-working investors. It is characterized by a loathing of the surplussed and a fear of becoming surplussed.[93] As Daniel Martinez HoSang and Joseph E. Lownes illustrate in the American context, this shift toward what they frame as a neoliberal castigation of "parasitism" is a "transposition" of "racial scripts" once reserved for the defamation of Black and other racialized people onto a much broader swath of actors now deemed morally, culturally, and even genetically inadequate and a source of risk to those who are cast by the reactionary imagination as the hard-working risk-takers.[94]

At the very core of the investor ethos at the core of financialization is a dead zone because it is predicated on a kind of obscuration of its own ontological truth: the investor-self imagines that its wealth, success, and autonomy comes (or could someday come, if they compete well enough) from individual competition, self-maximization, perseverance, and intelligence. In fact, their (longed-for) wealth and security is merely the unfairly distributed (and unfairly wrought) wealth of the society of which they are a part, but whose implications and responsibilities they loathe. In other words, the investor, whether real or imagined, is a taker who resentfully thinks themselves a giver.

As in the case of the dead zone at the core of the other systems of power and identity we have discussed, this hateful but oblique dependency produces vengeful affects. The *jouissance* of discursive and political attacks on social welfare systems and mechanisms of wealth redistribution, and on those who appear to depend on them including the impoverished, the elderly, the disabled, and even the young, emerges from this dead zone, as too does the driving and abiding fear of a kind of vengeance from society at large, perhaps in the form of taxation or other alleged limits to "freedom."

In other words, like all subjecthoods of power, the investor-self, which has now been sold not only to the privileged but to all of us as the necessary and logical ethos to cultivate in a cutthroat age, is animated by an internal dead zone. It's not only that its claims to a positive, durable ontology are false. This compulsory but illusory ethos is perpetually in crisis because of its underlying material conditions. While it valorizes ruthless independence, competition, and self-maximization, we all ultimately rely on a complex social fabric of interdependence, cooperation, and mutuality, even if we imagine otherwise. The investor-self is a parasite that believes itself the host, and so loathes the host it believes is the parasite.

VI. CONCLUSION

In King's *The Dead Zone*, Johnny awakens from his coma in the wrong time. Five years of profound economic, social, and political change have passed in what seemed like, for him, a brief nap. He is in exile from history, in a kind of temporal dead zone, as it were. And yet, it is precisely the dead zone that gives rise to his powers and his responsibilities. Because of his powers and insight, it appears that Johnny alone can witness Stillton's rise to power as the slow normalized march of fascism, an impression verified when the two shake hands and Johnny sees a vision of the apocalyptic future Stillton will bring to pass.

In a sense, Johnny's vocation or calling in the film is to avenge a crime against the future itself, rather than an infraction in the past.

Like Johnny, today it feels like we have all overslept, perhaps from injury, perhaps from carelessness. And like Johnny we have all shaken hands with the death of our world, though in our case, while perhaps there are more than enough fascists to go around, the villain I have in mind is more intimate: the countless pressures and exhortations we all face to participate in a financialized system of inequality that is dead zoning the planet and our lives.

It is from the dead zone that Johnny's visions arise: the damaged area of his brain. The dead zone also refers to the feeling of numbness when the visions grip him, and also the illegible, confusing, frustrating, tantalizing opacity of the visions at precisely the point where Johnny's own actions might change the future. When Johnny shakes hands with Stillton, the narrative turns as Johnny struggles with the responsibility to prevent a future only he can foresee. The struggle is of self-doubt (can he trust his powers?) and moral (can he justify murder in the name of preventing a catastrophe he feels is certain to occur?). King even leaves us to wonder if Johnny's vision and actions are genuine or if they are the hallucinatory product of the fatal tumor growing in the dead zone in his brain.

To my mind, Johnny's predicament is a fitting though ambiguous allegory for our own political conundrums in our age of dead zones and deadzoning. Yet who are we to assassinate, exactly? Where is the literal or proverbial lynchpin which, if removed, will prevent doom? I am not averse to identifying the particular people that have caused or benefited from the current nightmare. But one of the qualities of our age, which makes any sense of avenging perplexing, is this way we have each and all been made to be partially complicit in the reproduction of a system that is destroying us; indeed, the means of survival we have been given typically directly contribute to the apocalypse we are inheriting – this is the very meaning of our dead zone.

Within this context, we, like Johnny, have a vague and terrifying vision of the dead zoned future. We are yet are haunted by the sense we might act to change it, yet the means and mechanisms to do so are opaque to us: they are in a kind of collective dead zone.

Johnny's final act of attempting to assassinate Stillton fails but also succeeds. He acts to avenge a future that deserves to exist, and to avenge the heinous destruction Stillton will unleash. But while he does succeed in causing the end of Stillton's rise to power, he does so in a way he could not predict. Though Johnny doesn't intend it, in causing Stillton to use a baby as a human shield, Stillton reveals, in an undeniable way, his truly monstrous nature, leading to a kind of collective political awakening of his otherwise charmed followers.

We have had more than enough revelations about the monstrous nature of the system and its functionaries. King's conjecture that such heartless cowardice might sink a politician's career seems, today, optimistic to say the least. That aspect of us trapped in the dead zone is primed to accept, even in a strange way celebrate, the very worst.

But Johnny's ability to enter into the dead zone, to activate his clairvoyant powers, depends on physical contact, skin-to-skin. If we are to envision some future beyond the dead zone, it will come from contact, not in any romantic sense, but simply from the ways in which our relationships, forms of affinity, and methods of mutual aid, which will become more and more important as capitalism abandons so many more of us, help us to understand our powers to create a new and different world together.

Conclusion

Revenge fantasy or avenging imaginary?

Revenge capitalism, as I have sought to define it throughout this book, is a dimension of capitalist accumulation at its intersections with other systems of power wherein it appears to take needless, warrantless, and ultimately self-destructive vengeance on humans and other forms of life. I have argued that it names both a general tendency within capitalism throughout its history as well as a valence of the particular period in which we live, since roughly the mid-1970s, coterminous with neoliberalism, financialization, and capitalist globalization. My appending of the adjective "revenge" to capitalism does not seek to offer a categorical or definitional qualifier but, rather, to encourage us to orient our imagination to the vindictive qualities capitalism exhibits. I have sought to demonstrate the fruits of such an orientation in the chapters of this book. These chapters have been written as different windows onto the same multidimensional phenomenon, rather than as stages in a unified argument. As a result, this conclusion can't be summative. It is, rather, geared toward making one final distinction that has been hinted at throughout the forgoing pages, a distinction between revenge fantasy and an avenging imaginary.

In my reading, revenge capitalism is not primarily motivated and perpetuated by anger, bitterness, resentment, or rage, though it may give rise to these sentiments. The vengeful dimension of capital is a reflection of its inherent structural tendencies and contradictions. Importantly it is a system not orchestrated by a total monarch, an oligarchy, or a conspiracy but, rather, by the sum of the contradictory actions of innumerable competitive capitalist actors.[1] While sometimes these capitalist actors conspire or work in explicit and intentional concert (in cartels, in secret or not-so-secret societies, in industry blocks, corporatist states, and so on), such collusion can imperil the fundamental dynamic of capitalist accumulation: the necessity of intercapitalist competition. This competition drives each capitalist actor to ever-greater excess in search for profit (and, more abstractly, a share or surplus value) and ultimately drives the reduction of wages, the enclosure of the commons, the desolation of the earth, the proliferation of inter-imperial rivalry, and war, and the surplussing of populations.[2] Capitalism can act vengefully even if operated by angels.

This tendency is exacerbated in an age of neoliberal, global capitalist accumulation. This is a moment when capitalist accumulation has vested itself in the hypermobility of capital around the globe, allowing it to play nation-states against one another in the name of attracting or retaining investment and forestalling economic ruin. It also drives the transformation of every social actor into a partial capitalist agent, a kind of universalized complicity and victimhood, though with radically different opportunities and consequences.[3] Ours is a moment when capitalism has developed powerful new ways to avoid, capture, undermine, or reconfigure in its own interests most forms of social and governmental regulation.[4] The universal imperative toward the hyper-capitalist dispositions of entrepreneurialism, competition, and private accumulation is offered as the individualized remedy to the world of paranoid precariousness that capitalism is, itself, creating. From the false freedom of the "gig economy" to the sabotaged charity of subprime and microfinance loans, capitalism's contemporary logic is to, in a profoundly destructive way, make each and every human into not only a source of exploitable labor power but a small-time agent of capitalist accumulation.[5] That most of us will fail is irrelevant: we will be told our failure is our own fault, or sold a fantasy that our failure is the result of Others who cheated in the game (migrants, minorities, "special interests").

Capitalism, of course, has no desires, no sentiments, and no dreams, but as the sum of the actions of its parts- actions motivated by its structural demands for competition unto death- it comes to *appear* as a system of reckless vengeance on those whom it depends. Meanwhile, its pervasive imperative toward competition, and the social, ecological and political chaos this competition unleashes (see Chapter 5), tills the psycho-social soil in which the seeds of revenge politics germinate.

In bringing the notion of revenge into proximity with the system of capitalism, then, I have sought to do four things:

1   I wish to account for the seemingly irrational and vindictive patterns of capitalist accumulation today, which are destroying the life support systems of the planet, immiserating and indebting most of us, surplussing an ever increasing number of humans, and unleashing the specters of political revenge: war, fascism, fundamentalism, and economic sadism.

2   I have argued that revenge is not only, as we have been led to believe, a timeless human frailty but also (and more importantly) something that is defined differently, and for particular ideological purposes, in each historical and social context. If this is so, then there is something important at stake in how we define revenge, an important struggle over its meaning. My effort in these pages has been, in the face of the overwhelming sentimentality and opprobrium attached to liberal capitalism's preferred myths of revenge, to suggest that revenge can be used to describe the operation of interlocking systems of oppression and exploitation, specifically capitalism. Against the idea that revenge is a timeless monster of human nature that has been banished by the knights of reason to the political hinterland (to rogue states, ganglands, prisons, or slums), I have sought to argue that revenge is at work in the very heart of the allegedly hyper-rational system.

3   In accounting for capitalism as a system of revenge I hope to have contributed to efforts to bring into focus how this system's vitality and longevity is in no small part due to the way it operates both at the level of brutal economic reason and also through fantasy, affect, and sociality. In the forgoing chapters of this book I hope to have offered a demonstration of these contradictory and non-linear relationships.

4   Throughout this book I have also attempted to map the ways that capitalism has always been fundamentally and inexorably entangled with racism, (hetero-)sexism, patriarchy, colonialism, imperialism, and ableism, that these systems interlock and reinforce one another, and that part of this interlocking and reinforcement operates through a vengeful logic.

In this conclusion, then, I want to return to these entanglements one final time in the name of offering a warning about the rise of revenge fantasy and by sketching the outlines of ways to think about fomenting an anti-capitalist avenging imaginary.

PART 1: REVENGE FANTASY

Cognitive scientists and psychologists admit that, in spite of the fact we live in a society that generally condemns revenge, and one where acts of premeditated revenge (as opposed to immediate reaction) are relatively rare, revenge fantasy is extremely common.[6] We have all felt it, this desire to retribute a hurt, or act upon a nursed jealousy, worried to a pearl in the imagination.[7] Revenge fantasies are remarkably common among children and adolescents.[8] One might even argue that vengefulness is a formative experience in human development and that a great deal about any civilization can be understood from the ways in which it shapes young people's notions of what kinds of revenge are acceptable and unacceptable, honorable and dishonorable.[9] For Nietzsche, modern civilization itself is based on the sublimation and subterfuge of revenge.[10] On the surface, revenge is castigated as morally reprehensible and bestial, a key narrative by which "man" is shaped into a domesticated "moral animal." At the same time, it is precisely the authors of this moralism, those enfranchised by the structures of power to define and protect public virtue- (clergy, judges, kings etc), that are the most secretly vengeful, based on a loathing of the weakness of those whom they dominate. Meanwhile, the oppressed find their toothless satisfaction in resentful dreams of revenge which are never consummated, including the fantasy that God or some other supernatural power will, in this world or in the afterlife, take revenge on behalf of the wronged. For Nietzsche, there is bad faith on all sides: the powerful preach forgiveness to mask their own vindictive power; the oppressed ascent to their own powerlessness for fear of their own power, and make do with resentment.

This, perhaps, explains why revenge fantasy is so common when actual acts of revenge are so relatively rare. As George Orwell cunningly observed (as noted in this book's preface), "there is no such thing as revenge. Revenge is an act which you want to commit when you are powerless and because you are powerless: as soon as the sense of impotence is removed, the desire evaporates also."[11] In other words, a revenge fantasy is one that sustains the soul in a situation of injustice and powerlessness. It's a scrap fire that keeps warm a broken heart.

James Baldwin takes us deeper: "Revenge is a human dream." Upon its successful culmination

> there is no way of conveying to the corpse the reasons you have made him one – you have the corpse, and you are, thereafter, at the mercy of a fact which missed the truth, which means that the corpse has you.[12]

The revenge fantasy is fixated on and haunted by not the act of retribution but precisely the moment *after* revenge is exacted, and yet in this moment both the avenger and their nemesis are not the subjects they were at the time of the original injury, nor in the long interregnum between that injury and its retribution in which the "human dream" of revenge works itself around the wounded heart. In the actual moment of revenge, the balance of power, and the subjects of it, are radically transformed: the hated tormentor, when finally in the power of the ascendant avenger, is no longer a giant but a worm. Even if they are not actually dead, in this moment when revenge is finally possible the nemesis is already a corpse, robbed of precisely that loathed and envied power which made the tormentor capable of causing injury in the first place, and that allowed the pain and shame of that injury to implant itself deep in the soul of the would-be avenger.

Hamlet's interregnum

Hence the apocryphal tales of the avenger who chooses not to take revenge at the last moment and walks away. In many narratives, both fictional and real, we learn that, in precisely this moment, when revenge is in hand, the avenger realizes that to take the final act, as Baldwin notes, would be to consign oneself forever to the grip of that corpse: to risk being forever the thing you have become through your revenge fantasy. Better to let the fantasy and the nemesis go and to live another life, or die a different death. Or perhaps it is better still not to take the final act and, instead, retain the endlessly unfulfilled fantasy around which we have built our sense of self. In Slavoj Žižek's Lacanian reading, to which we will return in a moment, fantasy is always thus: fantasy is not something that slithers out from the darkest recesses of the authentic soul but, rather, something we are constantly generating to help us make sense of our place in the social order.[13] We fantasize about something we can't have (or don't have the courage to take), be it a lusted-after relationship or a yearned-for revenge, precisely so we can explain our own inaction and helplessness to ourselves. In other words, we create ourselves and find our way in the world in the abeyance between fantasy and actualization, Hamlet's interregnum, we might call it.

In that famous play it is already clear from the very first scene (long before it is finally spoken aloud, in the final scene of the first act) that the ghost of Hamlet's father has returned to charge his son to avenge his murder and usurpation at the hands of his brother (Hamlet's uncle). The entire (brilliant) play occurs in the interregnum as Hamlet dwells in the realm of fantasy, generating endless prevaricating schemes and plots to take revenge, but which function to endlessly forestall his action. Eventually, Laertes, kin of Hamlet's hapless victims (Laertes' sister Ophelia and father Polonius) returns to actually take revenge on Hamlet, which sets off a chain reaction of revenge events that leave almost the entire cast dead in the final scene. Hamlet's constant plotting, fantasizing, philosopizing about revenge are undertaken precisely so he can exonerate himself from taking it.

Thus, revenge fantasy, as distinct from the act of revenge, is often a means of maintaining oneself within an intolerable or contradictory situation. It is not only the sweetness of the fantasy itself which becomes sustaining. In the nursing of the grudge, in the calculation and recalculation of the debt, we come to understand ourselves within otherwise intolerable and inscrutable contradictions and forestall a painful transformation. But in contradiction to the Nietzschean approach, which might encourage us to imagine that the oppressed and powerless dream of revenge as a resentful compensatory fantasy to help justify their cowardly inaction, I would suggest that sometimes, oftentimes, it is all one has.[14] If one is denied the opportunity to exercise the radical imagination, which is to say to come together with others across difference, and discover the shared source of oppression, if one is forbidden from devising, based on the transversal experience of that pain, a vision for a world without the pain, then revenge fantasy may ironically be the only way to maintain one's humanity in a situation of relentless dehumanization. To dream of revenge is, in part, to hold fast to the knowledge that what you love has value in a world where it is made worthless. (It is the height of arrogance to condemn fantasies of revenge without asking how their bearers are structurally or explicitly prohibited from (or made cynical toward) more capacious dreams of collective liberation.) For so many, a dream of revenge is all they have, though often that revenge is framed in ways that, if achieved, will reproduce the dominant order and economy, with perhaps slightly different winners and losers. Indeed, to fall prey to the moral blackmail that forbids us to think *with* revenge is to fail to recognize how widespread its fantasies are.

It is to the way in which collective revenge fantasies form, and the ways in which they are (dangerously) mobilized and manipulated, to which we will now turn.

The smell of urine

In the introductory pages of the German philosopher Ernst Bloch's magisterial three volume *Principles of Hope*, written from exile in 1941, is a revelatory reflection on the way in which the Nazi regime was able to foment and cultivate collective revenge fantasy. Echoing Nietzsche, Bloch writes that "revenge is sweet when merely imagined, but also shabby. Most men are too cowardly to do evil, too weak to do good; the evil that they cannot, or cannot yet do, they enjoy in advance in the dream of revenge."[15] But Bloch quickly distinguishes his notion of revenge as a phenomenon that emerges in specific ways under capitalism, focusing on the particularly vindictive politics of the petit bourgeoisie: small business owners, professionals, minor bureaucrats, and others who serve the capitalist class but do not have a meaningful stake in the means of production and almost no real power over the system they serve and from which they seek to benefit. They, as a class, were among the Nazis' earliest and most ardent supporters, who have

> traditionally been fond of the fist clenched in the pocket; this fist characteristically thumps the wrong man, since it prefers to lash out in the direction of least resistance ... The Nazi dream of revenge is also subjectively bottled up, not rebellious; it is blind, not revolutionary rage.

There is, he argues, a kind of displacement, in which the castigated moral turpitude and economic parasitism of the racialized other, bombastically trumpeted in the pages of petit-bourgeois tabloids, is, in fact, an expression of perverse self-loathing:

> Just as, with its revenge, [the middle class] does not hate exploitation but only the fact that it is not itself an exploiter, so virtue does not hate the slothful bed of the rich, but only the fact that it has not become its own and its alone.

Hence, the immediate impulse to set oneself up in place of the detested person one has now eliminated "after an act of retribution which, in the supposedly detested fraud, merely replaces the subject which is practicing it." Here, revenge fantasy is a dream of the usurpation of the blood-soaked throne, not its destruction.

> The malicious and brutal aspect of this, the repulsiveness of this kind of wish, as pervasive as the smell of urine, has always characterized the mob. This mob can be bought, is absurdly dangerous, and consequently it can be blinded and used by those who have the means and who have a real vested interest in the fascist pogroms. The instigator... of course, is big business, but the raving petit bourgeois was the astonishing, the horribly seducible manifestation of this essence. From it emerged the terror, which is the poison ... that has nowhere near been fully excreted. His wishes for revenge are rotten and blind; God help us, when they are stirred up. Fortunately though, the mob is equally faithless; it is also quite happy to put its clenched fist back into its pocket when crime is no longer allowed a free night on the town by those at the top.

For Bloch, then, revenge is shaped by political-economic circumstance and class position. The petit-bourgeois of the 1920s were among the most susceptible to the Nazis' revanchist narrative against Jews, Communists, Social Democrats, and others whom they blamed for stabbing the German military in the back and causing the loss of World War One, for signing the humiliating and socially destructive Paris armistice with its massive unpayable debts that led to so much social agony in the Weimar Period, and for, more generally, betraying the imperial promise of a united German racial empire.

In this context it is easy enough to see how, in moments of profound social agony and dislocation, collective revenge fantasy can be a profoundly powerful force in the hands of revanchist political entities. Yet this, I would suggest, is no less the case under what I am terming revenge capitalism. Revenge fantasy provides a set of shared coordinates by which individuals can make sense of their experience within conditions of crisis and contradiction that otherwise defy the imagination. Here, like Bloch, I want to focus not on the revenge fantasies of the most oppressed and exploited (which I will return to in the next section), nor of the truly powerful, but of those intermediaries who are invested in the reproduction of the capitalist system but also, at the same time, oppressed, exploited, or at the very least alienated by it.[16]

The revenge fantasies of this class are shaped by a pivotal contradiction: on the one hand, this class (by virtue of their ideological and material investment in the system) is generally attached to conventional notions that hold revenge to be a retrograde, sinful, loathsome, and bestial sentiment that, while once it ruled human affairs, has been banished thanks to the liberal rule of law and the rise of indifferent markets that reward hard work and sacrifice. On the other hand, this class experiences increasing insecurity, precariousness, and indebtedness thanks to revenge capitalism, to such an extent that, while they may still identify with the normative comforts, aspirations and values of the middle class, its accompanying economic security is becoming functionally impossible for many. It is in this contradiction that today's revenge politics are bred.

The veils of revenge (and forgiveness) fantasy

We will return in a moment to summarize how these revenge politics appear in the political sphere, but it is important first to trace the way in which these collective revenge fantasies are generated and profited by in the wider cultural sphere, which will better reveal their contradictions.

To do so, I will borrow (and somewhat simplify) three aspects of a seven-part schema of the ideological role of fantasy identified by Slavoj Žižek in his influential essay "The Seven Veils of Fantasy" in which he applies a Lacanian frame.[17] As noted earlier, within this psychoanalytic frame, fantasy does not emerge from some impenetrable primordial depth of the human psyche but, rather, is actively and continually produced by the subject as they seek to make coherent sense of their own experience of a world that is otherwise fragmentary and chaotic. Far from being subversive (no matter how perverse), these fabricated fantasies are in fact the means to find and ground ourselves within a given symbolic order. Žižek's effort is to show that ideology emerges from collective fantasies by which we create a falsely unified and misleading understanding of the world and power within it. For Žižek, the key to the success of this ideological function is not that it offers a rigid set of narratives that we must each adopt but, rather, a flexible set of resources by which each of us comes to imagine that we, autonomously and knowingly, and realistically understand our world, yet do so in such a way that we end up acquiescing to and reproducing the status quo. He identifies seven such "veils," though I will briefly explore three with reference to the way revenge is imagined through popular recent products of the cultural industries.

Like Foucault's Victorians, who in seeking to never speak of sex spoke of little else, so too do we, a society that generally but relentlessly pathologizes revenge, obsess over it in our cinematic, literary, and cultural fantasies.[18] This is much thanks to contemporary cultural industries whose business-models seem to increasingly be fixated on hooking viewers to "binge-worthy" serial content or filmic franchises that are reassuringly familiar, recycling the same tropes again and again (e.g., superhero films, Star Wars, Quentin Tarantino). Here, a simplified, Manichean presentation of revenge, which we are led to imagine we understand so well, is a key narrative technology, a reliable character motivation, and recurring plot device that not only perpetuates an endless cycle of new releases but also typically offers an alibi for gratuitous titillating violence or cheap melodrama. Revenge culture is driven by the financialized imperatives of the entertainment industry but also by the desires of audiences habituated by revenge capitalism.

The transcendental schema

In Žižek's account, we attach ourselves to a fantasy not because we desire this or that forbidden thing, but because having that fantasy, being beholden to that fantasy and its ever forestalled or deferred fulfillment, grounds a worldview. It becomes the anchor of a transcendental schema: a set of coordinates in which other aspects of life make sense. We might think here of the phenomenal popularity of HBO's fantasy epic eight-season *Game of Thrones*, by some estimates the most popular and profitable televisual spectacle of all time, whose narrative was mostly intertwined stories of revenge between warring elite families.[19] This collective revenge fantasy ultimately has one overarching political lesson from which there are two preferred interpretations. The setting is a primordial medieval world where revenge rules, which encourages us to accept a transcendental schema wherein revenge is the true "reality" of human affairs. The optimistic reading is to thank God we, today, have the benefit of the rule of law and capitalism's "gentle commerce" to save us from ourselves, without which we would descend "back" into vengeful chaos; the pessimistic reading is that nothing has changed and revenge is an eternal aspect of human nature, driven by the inexorable lust for power. Accordingly, today's political-economic order is merely *Game of Thrones*-style revenge by other means, now disguised by the niceties and pleasantries of statecraft and economic reason. Yet this is a false choice, as both perspectives ultimately take the present order as natural necessity and make sense of its contradictions in terms of a dismal view of human nature, a view shaped precisely by the revenge capitalism which it now justifies.

One can observe the tension between these two perspectives at play in the political sphere in many countries today in the false choice between, on the one hand, the so-called neoliberal "globalists," who advocate the expansion of *Pax Capitalis* and the rule of law through international institutionalism, and, on the other, the reactionary and neoconservative Nationalists, who cynically market themselves as protectors of the people in a hostile and unforgiving world (a world they are, of course, helping make more hostile and unforgiving). As with all fantasies, this one functions to both (a) mystify the *actual* origins of the contradictions (i.e., revenge capitalism) and (b) make it seem the false option it produces (globalism versus nationalism) is inevitable, falsely painting each pole as representative of a complete and coherent moral schema. In fact, they are rivals in a secret conspiracy where both agree and insist that only two options are possible. Hence the growing loathing between revanchist liberals and revanchist conservatives, who come to see one another as profoundly evil.

Intersubjectivity

For Žižek, one's fantasy is not actually what one truly wants, that which, if acquired, would fulfil one completely. Such complete fulfillment is impossible. Rather, one's fantasies are always the fantasy of the Other. What we want is what we imagine that others want us to want. As social animals, what we really desire is acceptance, esteem, and companionship, a place in a community of inscrutable others. We seek to imagine ourselves as worthy of these by aligning our desires with what we imagine we *ought* to want. But in many cases the things we tell ourselves we want actually perpetuate our participation in a system that is destructive to us or to others. The classic example here is the way so many of us are taught to seek acceptance by performing the heteronormative desires expected of us and participating in their social institutions, which not only foreclose other possibilities for intimacy, relationships, and kinship outside this frame, but help to reproduce the heteronormative order.

I would suggest that this observation can help us understand the flip side of revenge fantasy: the fetishization of forgiveness and reconcilophelia that I have noted at several points in this book. We are infatuated with such representations, among them blockbuster films, about figures like Dr. Martin Luther King Jr. (*Selma*) and Nelson Mandela (*Invictus*) whose hyperbolized acts of political forgiveness, when isolated from the broader arc of struggle of which they were a part, implicitly contribute to legitimating the reigning moral order. Conversely, we are also treated to innumerable terrible but predictable scenes where, near the climax of, many films, the villain spurns forgiveness so as to reassure us of their inherent evil (for instance Kylo Ren in *Star Wars: The Force Awakens*, who is offered his father's forgiveness for essentially being a Nazi warlord and responds with murder).

There is nothing on the face of it that is objectionable about forgiveness and reconciliation, except that as a structure of collective fantasy it serves at least two ideological functions. In the first case, it participates in the Manichean demonization of revenge which casts the vengeful Other as inherently pathological. Any and all who refuse the imparative to forgive are cast as monsters. Indeed their pathological vengefulness is usually displayed to us to justify their extrajudicial execution and preemptive precautionary vengeance. Hence, for instance, the ability of many liberals to countenance the vengeful drone assassinations, "enhanced interrogation" (torture) and "collateral damage" of the so-called War on Terror:[20] "these vengeful monsters would not accept our forgiveness, even if we offered it, so why bother." Meanwhile, of course, the fetish of forgiveness coheres a political community around the avoidance of a guilty consciousness. We are obsessed with fantasies of reconciliation because, while we cannot look directly at the violence we have enacted or caused through our (largely unavoidable) blackmailed participation in revenge capitalism, we sense a reckoning is coming. The manifold injustices and inequalities, the disposability of human life are hidden in plain sight. We hope that those whom we have participated in wronging will be as forgiving as we would like to imagine we, ourselves, would be.

Narrative occlusion of antagonism

Fantasy, for Žižek, is always calibrated around a sense of loss in whose wake we have become who we are. In the case of the individual, we imagine that if only we had not lost or been denied that which we desire, we would be well, whole, and happy. In actuality, we retroactively create the perfect object (person or experience) we allegedly lost or are denied in order to explain to ourselves why we are unwell, inconsistent, and unhappy. The fiction of loss is used to construct a coherent narrative of how we came to be the way we are, but such a narrative usually veils an actual engagement with reality and brackets out the causes that are unacceptable to our worldview. In the case of collective revenge fantasy, we can observe the way that we are obsessed with representations of economies of revenge: violent prisons, gangland slums, mafia heterotopias, or lawless failed states where revenge rules. The extremely popular serial *Breaking Bad* is an example in which a mild-mannered white New Mexico public school chemistry teacher, trying to pay for his cancer treatment, becomes a drug dealer and is plunged into a revenge-driven predominantly racialized (Latinx) underworld.[21] While most such narratives completely bracket out the socio-economic factors of revenge capitalism that lead to such violence, *Breaking Bad* at least makes gestures toward the kinds of slow and structural violence that might contextualize such a world. These include the violence of what Harsha Walia calls border imperialism: the separation of people from land and community, the militarized enforcement of frontiers, sexual violence, formal and informal labor exploitation, ecological despoliation, and racism, all in the name of capitalist accumulation and the assuaging of its contradictions.[22] Yet the narrative remains one where revenge is isolated within a tit-for-tat world of abject gangster para-justice, which conveniently forgets the context of a broader system of legalized structural revenge.

From revenge culture to revenge politics

In unfolding these three examples, I hope to have demonstrated the dominant or hegemonic way in which mediatized fantasies of revenge (and forgiveness) are deployed as a means to capitalize on the contradictions inherent to revenge capitalism, a system within which revenge is everywhere in the fabric of the system and yet, at the same time, foreclosed as an acceptable fantasy by their reigning moral order that such a system (re)produces and on which it depends. In the above examples I have focused on the ways in which the culture industry in particular gives expression to and also foments collective revenge (and forgiveness) fantasies. Though deeply ideological, these fantasies have no explicit political intentions but rather seek to earn profit for large media corporations by at once rehearsing and agitating dominant social mores around revenge. Its ideological function is not to cohere subjects around a political movement but, rather, to give resources to subjects who are seeking to make sense of their place in a system of violent contradictions such that they can continue to participate and compete in it, and thereby help reproduce it as well. What is offered in each is a fantasy of revenge (or forgiveness) that gives it safe, non-transformative expression.

But what of the explicitly political mobilization of revenge fantasy? My argument is that we cannot understand the particular rise of contemporary revenge politics without connecting them to both revenge capitalism (the mystified major force behind ongoing violence, oppression, and alienation) and also the revenge fantasies that revenge capitalism produces. Today, these fantasies offer the scaffolding for revanchist political narratives of betrayed generosity (the spurned forgiver, stabbed in the back by the evil revenger), of the decontextualized Manichean villain (the pathologically and unintelligibly vengeful monster Other who must be destroyed), and of the fantasy of collective loss (of national virility, of innocence, of purity, of social cohesion).

It is valuable here to return to Bloch's historically materialist account of the susceptibility of the petit-bourgeois to the siren's song of Nazi revenge politics. Here, the political revenge fantasy emerges at precisely the cusp of economic and moral instability. This class's relative privilege (when compared to the proletariat and poor) and relative powerlessness (when compared to the actual bourgeoisie, who own the means of production, or to the residual aristocracy). In a moment of economic crisis the petit-bourgeoisie are caught between wanting to defend their imperiled privilege (and the mythic order in which that privilege is legitimate and well-deserved) and their sense of powerlessness. Because it is both ideologically and materially invested in capitalism and its notions of justice and fair play, the petit-bourgeoisis cannot admit that its agony and alienation stem from the structures of the reigning capitalist order. These insecurities must, therefore, be blamed on convenient others (Jews, Communists, etc.). The fist clenched in the pocket strikes the wrong target.

An age of vengeance

Yet what is perhaps different and important about our own age of financialized neoliberalism is the trend toward the stealthy re-proletarianization of the petit-bourgeoisis and the bourgeois-ification of the proletariat. The condition of being relatively privileged but powerless, of having a stake in the system but no means to control one's fate within it, is now felt to be a much wider experience. On the one hand, the middle class in almost every jurisdiction is functionally shrinking: in spite of individuals increasingly identifying with the middle class, it is becoming harder and harder to maintain the hallmarks of middle class social reproduction: housing, education, stable employment, health services, employment benefits, etc.[23] This is largely because of stagnating wages, the undermining of the redistributive powers of the state, lower union density, increasingly precarious work, and cutbacks to government services and regulations on employers.[24] At the same that many who identified as middle class are no longer able to maintain that material reality, a new wave of neoliberal ideology has encouraged all workers (not just professionals and business owners) to see themselves as petty bourgeois entrepreneurs. The rise of the gig economy, where menial and highly-exploited service workers are sold the lie that their own oppression is an opportunity for entrepreneurial flexibility, freedom, and opportunity, is only the latest and most egregious example.[25] Over the last 40 years, the neoliberal attack on state provisioning has advanced through selling the idea that everyone is an entrepreneur, competing in a hostile world of opportunities and risks.[26]

This is the most fertile contradiction for the rise of revenge politics. While it may be true that the super-oppressed and surplussed of revenge capitalism have better justification for a politics of revenge than do those who feel their foothold on privilege constantly slipping, it is the latter who are the most dangerous today.[27] Yet this danger typically expresses itself, as we have seen, in the demotic actualization of revenge fantasy in the form of support for hyper-reactionary governments. While it is important to account for the differences in the reactionary and authoritarian turn in formal democracies including the United States, the United Kingdom, Turkey, India, and Brazil, numerous commentators have noted the importance in each case of the reactionary middle class who, in a moment of generalized secular stagnation, fear the loss of those privileges to which they have become accustomed.[28]

PART 2: TOWARD AN AVENGING IMAGINARY

At risk of disappointing the reader who surely by now is holding back demoralization in the hopes of a triumphant conclusion, in the remaining pages I can only offer some hints as to what an avenging imaginary might be that could, without falling prey to the lure of reconcilophelia, rise to the challenge of our moment and contribute to the kind of revolutionary movements we would need to capsize and replace revenge capitalism. I have opted to decline the urge to be prescriptive in this book. I have also opted, for the most part, to avoid a common temptation to conclude with a celebration of contemporary social movements, though I am inspired by many and believe that collective mobilization is the only way to change the world. Rather, I have opted to take wisdom from a set of authors who, while (like all of us) caught up in revenge capitalism, theorize from the perspective of communities most targeted by its vengefulness, notably radical Indigenous thinkers from the territories currently colonized by Canada and Black feminist thinkers struggling within, against, and beyond the confines of a white-supremacist United States. If, as I have argued, revenge politics thrives in the tension between relative privilege and functional powerlessness, the authors I rely on below ground their analysis of resentment, anger, and solidarity in the experiences of intersectional Black, Indigenous, and queer positionalities which have been systematically disempowered and have access to few if any privileges within revenge capitalism. Indeed, in the forgoing pages I have illustrated how the very historical and ongoing possibility of revenge capitalism has made all of these categories the target of both systemic vengeance and the sadistic violence that system breeds. In these authors' visions, then, we can find clues as to what it would mean to avenge not only the effects of revenge capitalism in the present, but also those ancestors whose dreams of freedom, plenty, and peace were thwarted, and further those future generations who, if revenge capitalism is allowed to persist, may have no desirable future at all to inherit.

First, some general notes on the distinction I am trying to draw between an avenging imaginary and revenge fantasy, one that is subtle but undeniable: the Avengers, after all, are a team of superheroes; the Revengers would be supervillains. No less an authority on the English language than Dr. Samuel Johnson, author of one of the most authoritative early dictionaries, instructs that "revenge is an act of passion; vengeance of justice. Injuries are revenged; crimes are avenged."[29]

As I have argued throughout this book, whereas revenge envisions the revisiting of a harm or a debt on its author in the same or a similar form in which it was issued, avenging strives to abolish the order or economy of power that licensed, authorized, or enabled that violence in the first place. An avenging imaginary is not satisfied to turn the tables but seeks to overturn them. An avenging imaginary does not simply dream of redistributing the winners and losers, the debtors and the creditors, the oppressors and the oppressed, but yearns to abolish the very foundations of the moral, political, and economic order on which those injustices are erected. In the most basic terms, an avenging imaginary dreams of revenge against a *system*, not (only) its agents and beneficiaries. Whereas revenge fantasies are often fixated on Others who come to stand in for systems, an avenging imaginary is informed by a complex understanding of the way individuals are made to (or choose to) become replaceable operatives within such systems. Whereas revenge fantasy speaks to an isolated fixation, an avenging imaginary emerges from and helps to reproduce sustained collective action.

The uses of anger

This refusal to be mollified or to let go of the desire for revenge in a situation of ongoing violence has also been explored by foundational thinkers of Black feminist thought.

bell hooks's *Killing Rage: Ending Racism* begins with a revenge fantasy of murdering a well-meaning but ultimately cowardly white male passenger seated beside the theorist on a plane after both had witnessed the humiliating treatment of hooks' Black friend at the hands of airline staff, an altercation that had come on the heels of a series of similar incidents throughout the day.[30] The encounter, though seemingly innocuous, provided hooks with an impetus to reflect on the importance, misunderstanding, and castigation of Black vengefulness. "A black person unashamed of her rage, using it as a catalyst to develop critical consciousness, to come to full decolonized self-actualization, [has] no real place in the existing social structure," hooks writes.

Reflecting on her upbringing in the US South amidst incessant racist degradation and violence, hooks details how survival depended on the repression of Black rage, based on an awareness of how fear of Black vengeance animated the white-supremacist worldview, and how, even after she moved North and entered university, the prohibition on her anger as a Black woman was palpable. She observes the way that this rage, then, turns toward other Black people in horrific forms of normalized lateral violence or inward in the form of addiction and self-destruction.

hooks continues that rage must be seen as a crucial element of struggle. "As long as Black rage continues to be represented as always and only evil and destructive, we lack a vision of militancy that is necessary for transformative revolutionary action." Indeed, for hooks, rage is a crucial element of building a transformative form of solidarity.

> Many of my peers seem to feel no rage or believe it has no place. They see themselves as estranged from angry black youth. Sharing rage connects those of us who are older and more experienced with younger black and non-black folks who are seeking ways to be self-actualized, self-determined, who are eager to participate in anti-racist struggle. Renewed, organized black liberation struggle cannot happen if we remain unable to tap collective black rage. Progressive black activists must show how we take that rage and move it beyond fruitless scapegoating of any group, linking it instead to a passion for freedom and justice that illuminates, heals, and makes redemptive struggle possible.

In the absence of an honest accounting for vengefulness and rage, solidarity is not possible, and a vision for a society beyond it is stymied. For hooks, accepting rage as a grounds for theory, solidarity, and organizing invites a vision of what it would actually mean to dismantle the system whose violences generate that rage.

Audre Lorde's pivotal "The Uses of Anger" is similarly inspired by the experience of being told or having it implied that Black women's anger is unacceptable or counter-productive.[31]

"Anger is a source of empowerment we must not fear to tap for energy rather than guilt," she writes,

> When we turn from anger we turn from insight, saying we will accept only the designs already known, those deadly and safely familiar. I have tried to learn my anger's usefulness to me, as well as its limitations ... We cannot allow our fear of anger to deflect us nor to seduce us into settling for anything less than the hard work of excavating honesty.[32]

> My response to racism is anger. I have lived with that anger, on that anger, beneath that anger, on top of that anger, ignoring that anger, feeding upon that anger, learning to use that anger before it laid my visions to waste, for most of my life. Once I did it in silence, afraid of the weight of that anger. My fear of that anger taught me nothing. Your fear of that anger will teach you nothing. [A]nger expressed and translated into action in the service of our vision and our future

is a liberating and strengthening act of clarification … Anger is loaded with information and energy.[33]

Sarah Ahmed writes of this passage:

> Here, anger is constructed in different ways: as a response to the injustice of racism; as a vision of the future; as a translation of pain into knowledge; and as being loaded with information and energy. Crucially, anger is not simply defined in relationship to a part, but opening up to the future … being against something is also being for something, but something that has yet to be articulated or is not yet.[34]

Yet as Ahmed points out, Lorde is explaining that the feminist project of anger implies "an interpretation of that which one is against, whereby associations and connections are made between the object of anger and broader patterns or structures."[35] It is not a pathological, vengeful fixation on the object that caused pain but a means of collaborative sense-making, renaming, and the cultivation of a vision of a world beyond the present.

In response to fears that Black women's anger might alienate white feminists, Lorde concludes:

> I have suckled the wolf's lip of anger and I have used it for illumination, laughter, protection, fire in places where there was no light, no food, no sisters, no quarter. We are not goddesses or matriarchs or edifices of divine forgiveness; we are not fiery fingers of judgment or instruments of flagellation; we are women always forced back upon our woman's power. We have learned to use anger as we have used the dead flesh of animals; and bruised, battered, and changing, we have survived and grown and, in Angela Wilson's words, we *are* moving on. With or without uncolored women. We use whatever we have fought for, including anger, to help define and fashion a world where all our sisters can grow, where our children can love, and where the power of touching and meeting another woman's difference and wonder will eventually transcend the need for destruction.[36]

Both hooks and Lorde offer powerful visions of rage and anger that avoid the imperative toward either revenge or forgiveness but, rather, call for a transformative affective relationality and honesty about the experience of oppression. This rage and anger is then capable of generating the kind of solidarity that can have some hope of coalescing the kind of grassroots power that might actually ground revolutionary movements. To the extent anger and rage are banished or shamed because they make us uncomfortable, these powerful forces either turn inward or lead to divisions based not on strategy or vision, but on comfort, usually the comfort of those whose lived experience means they are immune from the direct social violence that leads to the fury in the first place.

The foreclosure of forgiveness

Yellowknives Dene theorist Glen Coulthard productively takes up the Fanonian category of resentment in his analysis of the imperative toward reconciliation in settler colonial states like Canada in the contemporary period. In contrast to political theorists who (in the Nietzschean tradition) see resentment as the disempowering and stagnant spite of the powerless, Coulthard is interested in the way that the refusal to be reconciled, to give up vengefulness, can become a grounds for radical Indigenous resurgence which is not satisfied to simply find its place within capitalist multiculturalism. The insistence by the state on an agenda of reconciliation is predicated on the notion that settler colonialism is a matter of past atrocities which can be memorialized and forgiven and as such it necessarily must occlude its ongoing realities, such as those cataloged in Chapter 2.

In such a context:

> state-sanctioned approaches to reconciliation must ideologically manufacture such a transition [from a violent colonial past to a peaceful multicultural present] by allocating the abuses of settler colonization to the dustbins of history, and/or purposely disentangle processes of reconciliation from questions of settler-coloniality as such... Reconciliation takes on a temporal character as the individual and collective process of overcoming the subsequent *legacy* of past abuse, not the abusive colonial structure itself. And what are we to make of those who refuse to forgive and/or reconcile in these situations? They are typically cast as being saddled by the damaging psychological residue of this legacy, of which anger and resentment are frequently highlighted.[37]

For Coulthard, reckoning with resentment is an important step toward developing a radical honesty about the ongoing reality of settler colonial violence and dispossession, as well as the sentiments it generates. Such a reckoning can become the means by which communities can rid themselves of the kind of colonized self-loathing of which the moralizing bestialization of revenge fantasy is a part.

For Coulthard, then, resentment and vengefulness are not impotent fantasies but vital means to craft and calibrate political strategies that operate outside of the logic of the dominant order, that envision decolonized futures that are irreconcilable with the settler colonial capitalist future. Revenge here might be said to operate as an ethics of generative refusal toward a system.

Like Coulthard, Unangax̂ theorist Eve Tuck is interested in what it would mean to reject the politics of reconciliation and normative "social justice" in a context of ongoing settler colonialism. For Tuck, writing with K. Wayne Yang, these efforts are stymied by the refusal of the colonial settler state to actually return the land which it has stolen, on which autonomous Indigenous life might be possible.[38] In the absence of such an (impossible, under capitalism) rematriation, efforts at reconciliation, even at solidarity, typically end up reproducing "settler moves to innocence": they function primarily to help non-Indigenous settlers (who benefit from the land's theft) reposition themselves as morally virtuous and worthy of remaining with almost no change to the conditions of Indigenous people.

In contrast, Tuck is interested in what it might mean to accept the calling to monstrously refuse such self-serving, non-transformative forms of reconciliation, and recognize oneself and one's task as a future ghost: one who is fated, under the current colonial order, to a premature death. Writing with C. Ree, Tuck dwells with the politics of such vengefulness directly:

> Settler colonialism is the management of those who have been made killable, once and future ghosts – those that had been destroyed, but also those that are generated in every generation... Haunting... is the relentless remembering and reminding that will not be appeased by settler society's assurances of innocence and reconciliation... Haunting doesn't hope to change people's perceptions, nor does it hope for reconciliation. Haunting lies precisely in its refusal to stop. Alien (to settlers) and generative for (ghosts), this refusal to stop is its own form of resolving. For ghosts, the haunting is the resolving, it is not what needs to be resolved … Haunting is the cost of subjugation. It is the price paid for violence, for genocide … Erasure and defacement concoct ghosts; I don't want to haunt you, but I will.[39]

The ghost's revenge, then, is one of relentless presence, of a refusal to be exorcized, dispelled or mollified. It is to retain a fidelity to vengeance in the face of the imperative to reconcile.

> Over our lifetimes, you and I have been told in many different ways that we should try to right wrongs, and certainly never wrong wrongs. Revenge is wronging wrongs, a form of double-wronging. You, like me, have been guided/good-girled away from considering revenge as a strategy of justice. To even consider revenge might be deemed dangerous, mercenary, terrorizing. At the same time, righting wrongs is so rare. Justice is so fleeting. And there are crimes that are too wrong to right... Wronging wrongs, so reviled in a waking life, seems to be the work of nightmares and hauntings and all the stuff that comes after opportunities to right wrongs and write wrongs have been exhausted. Unreadable and irrational, wronging wrongs is the work of now and future ghosts and monsters, the supply of which is ever-growing.[40]

Tuck and Ree offer us no easy solutions but, rather, leave us with a generative kind of riddle: how are we to find the means of radical social transformation "after opportunities to right wrongs and write wrongs have been exhausted?" To my mind, dwelling with this riddle is the key to cultivating an avenging imaginary.

Abolition and the negation of the negation

The notion of wronging wrongs resonates with an abolitionist vision that recognizes the ways in which multiple systems of power are entangled and that seeks to generate a transversal understanding of social transformation through what, at least in the eyes of the powerful, seem like destructive ends, in order that new possibilities might grow.[41] The abolitionist approach embraces the need for the negation of the negation: the abolition of those systems and institutions that currently negate life, possibility, and flourishing. Such a negation of a negation can only appear, in the cosmology of the powerful, as a phantom or a monster. As Tuck and Ree note,

> to the (purported)(would-be) hero, revenge is monstrous, heard but not seen, insatiable, blind with desire, the Cyclops robbed of her eye. To the self-designated hero, revenge hails a specter of something best forgotten, a ghost from a criminal past. To the monster, revenge is oxygen.[42]

Such an abolitionist perspective draws on the theories of "abolition democracy" developed by W. E. B. DuBois in his study of Black-led efforts to create a truly just and equal republic in the US South after the Civil War and Emancipation, efforts which were stymied, undermined, and viciously targeted by white-supremacist revanchism in ways that continue to resonate in today's political climate (see Chapter 2).[43] For Angela Davis, abolition democracy remains the goal, one that challenges us to understand that a commitment to true democratic life would necessarily demand the abolition of multiple mutually reinforcing social institutions of power, privilege, and oppression.[44] It would, for instance, understand that formal political democracy is impossible without economic equality or at least freedom from poverty, or that civil liberties for some are meaningless when they are systematically denied to others, explicitly or implicitly, on the basis of race. Focusing on the ways in which white supremacy and capitalism are reproduced through the contemporary prison system in the US (which, as we observed in Chapter 1, is integral to revenge capitalism), Davis and other abolitionist thinkers challenge us to recognize a number of things: first, how deeply enmeshed the prison is in multiple other aspects of these systems (including policing, ghettoization, the cheapening of Black labor, the management of surplussed populations, the subsidizing of white rural prison-hosting communities, the subversion of voting rights, the control over and exploitation of women's reproductive labor, and the power of public scapegoating).[45] Second, how if we desire to abolish prisons (as indeed we should), we must turn our attention to what would replace them or, more accurately, how the social needs that the prison now falsely claims to meet could be met otherwise. These needs might include how to care for, contain, or punish those in our communities who use violence or exploit others, how to meet people's needs so they do not turn toward (often harmful) activities that are today criminalized, or how to generate common safety beyond the disciplinary violence of policing. Further still, such an abolitionist approach begs the question of how we might start building and operating alternative institutions such that their functioning example might reveal the parasitical obsolescence of dominant institutions.[46]

Thus the negation of the negation is not purely destructive, though it may be framed that way by the powerful. It is generative of new institutions, relationships, solidarities, and modes of life, but these are largely invisible, ghostly, or monstrous in the eyes of the powerful.

The avenging imaginary and the radical imagination

Fundamentally, what distinguishes an avenging imaginary from the realm of revenge fantasy, or what can elevate and coalesce individual revenge fantasies into a collective avenging imaginary, is the radical imagination. As I have explored at length with Alex Khasnabish, the radical imagination is a term often cited but rarely defined.[47] In general terms, it speaks to the capacity to envision radically different worlds, to dream of a fundamentally different society. It is distinguished from reactionary thought (which can also have a radical analysis) in that, rather than anchoring itself to essentialist ideas of the natural or God-given order of the world fixated on the purity of race, gender roles, or social hierarchies, the radical imagination embraces the limitless possibility of the power of the imagination as a social force. Whereas reactionary thought (largely of the far-right, but occasionally claiming to represent a project of liberation) nostalgically fixates on this loss of purity and concocts a revenge politics around regaining it through purification, the radical imagination begins from the recognition of the power and indeterminacy of our cooperative potential.[48]

We have developed our notion of the radical imagination based in part on the work of philosopher Cornelius Castoriadis for whom "radical" refers to the deep "roots" of the imagination in social life.[49] For Castoriadis, the imagination is not just an individual quality of mind but a social substance out of which we fashion the social institutions through which we cooperate: not only materialized institutions like schools, factories, and borders but also immaterial institutions like the expectations around gender roles, social ranks, and forms of honor and esteem. Society is a constant collaborative work of the imagination to produce and reproduce such social institutions. Our imaginations, in turn, are shaped by these institutions as well. In this sense, the imagination is intimately and dialectically connected to how we cooperate and distribute the fruits of that cooperation. Under situations of coercion, the imagination operates heteronomously: we imagine that social institutions are eternal, necessary, and natural. For Castoriadis, the goal is to recognize and take collective responsibility for the cooperative creative power of the imagination, the project of autonomy.[50] The radical imagination is a kind of subterranean, tectonic force which, like volcanic magma, erupts in molten form and hardens into institutions that we take for permanent, only for them to be swept away or covered over by new eruptions of the radical imagination.[51]

Castoriadis's concept is invaluable because it centers the imagination as a pivotal force in the ongoing reconstruction of social reality. In other work, I have sought to more clearly link this to the way in which capitalism appears as a system of power that seeks to command, conscript, and contain social cooperation, and therefore also the imagination.[52]

As Robin D. G. Kelley observes in his study of the Black radical imagination, to the extent we are able to envision other, less violent orders of social cooperation, we rely on moments of friction and dialog.[53] It is through collective struggles against power that the radical imagination is awakened, and it thrives in debates, discussions, tensions, and disagreements rather than in unanimity. Kelley tracks the ways in which revolutionary Black visions of liberation in America and more broadly in the African diaspora resonated between philosophers, artists, musicians, activists, religious leaders, athletes, and visionaries. More profoundly, Kelley illustrates the importance of intergenerational links between struggles as well.

Informed by this approach to the radical imagination, we could make the following observations about the avenging imaginary:

1   The avenging imaginary is not simply a privately nursed grudge or an individual flight of fancy; it is an abolitionist vision cultivated in the collective experience of refusal of a revenge system.
2   Though the finding of common cause and the sharing of pain and rage is a vital aspect of allowing revenge fantasy to cohere into an avenging imaginary, such an imaginary is a matter of not only *fellow feeling* but *common practice*. This practice can take the form of acts of refusal, rebellion, and destruction. But it can also take the form of new modes of cooperation, care, and creation. These practices are undertaken literally *in spite* of a system that is seeking to revenge itself upon us.
3   An avenging imaginary is rooted in the reckless determination and relentless insistence that what you love has value within a system that renders it worthless, disposable, and surplus. Maybe it's your life, your kin, your ancestors, or the earth. Insisting on the value of what or whom you love is an ongoing act of revolutionary refusal and creation.
4   An avenging imaginary holds individuals to account for the part they play in revenge systems of oppression, exploitation, and agony, but recognizes that these systems themselves must be abolished. It refuses to reconcile itself with these systems. It may forgive individuals, recognizing that these systems force all of us into some

degree of complicity, but it does not forgive these systems.

5   An avenging imaginary surpasses the revenge fantasy of a short-sharp revolutionary break with the past and, while not giving up on the importance of the destruction of revenge systems, insists on experimenting with and building new institutions, forms of cooperation, and modes of care in the present, forms which actively deprive revenge systems of resources and allow people to survive outside their blackmail, while at the same time setting the stage for the society to come.

6   An avenging imaginary takes Benjamin's caution (parsed in Chapter 1) to heart. In his reading, the anti-capitalist struggle is one that dreams of answering an intergenerational call. For this reason, he argues that, in Marx's work, the proletariat "appears as the last enslaved class, as the avenger that completes the task of liberation in the name of generations of the downtrodden." Thus it is not enough (indeed, it is dangerous) to focus triumphantly on struggle as the "redeemer of future generations." To do so would be to cut "the sinews of [our] greatest strength" by making us "forget both [our] hatred and... spirit of sacrifice, for both are nourished by the image of enslaved ancestors rather than that of liberated grandchildren." There is, we must remember, "a secret agreement between past generations and the present one. Our coming was expected on earth. Like every generation that preceded us, we have been endowed with a weak Messianic power, a power to which the past has a claim. That claim cannot be settled cheaply."

Coda

11 Theses on revenge capitalism

1   Revenge is the reckless determination that what you love has value in a world where it is rendered worthless.
2   When you live in someone else's utopia, all you have left is revenge.
3   Oppression is held in place by the preemptive revenge of the powerful, justified as a precaution against the fantasized vengeance of the oppressed.
4   Capitalism claims to have banished revenge to its borderlands; in fact, revenge is at its core and is revealed most clearly in its moments of crisis.
5   Whereas all systems of oppression take vengeance against those whom they oppress, capitalism is unique in that the vengeance emerges from the contradictions of the system itself, without any necessary malice or hatred. Revenge is the outcome, not the motive.
6   The revenge politics to which revenge systems give rise often take mistaken targets, in part because these systems mask their own vengeance as economic necessity, peaceful justice, or human nature.
7   The history and present of revenge capitalism cannot be disentangled from other vengeful systems, including patriarchal gender terrorism, genocidal colonial brutality, and slavery.
8   The easy condemnation of revenge is usually the narcissism of the privileged. Revenge is not a dark cloud on the horizon, it is already upon us. Condemning it is futile. The task is to foment an avenging imaginary for revolutionary transformation.
9   The authors and beneficiaries of revenge capitalism have names and addresses. But they are also all completely replaceable. Revenge capitalism's success rests in its ability to conscript all of us to its reproduction, in one way or another.
10 Sometimes, a revenge fantasy is all you have. But while a revenge fantasy dreams of payback in the same coin in which the pain was issued, an avenging imaginary dreams of the abolition of that (moral, political) economy.

11 The task before us is to avenge the future of peace, care, abundance, connection, and thriving that we are owed, but that revenge capitalism denies us, as well as to avenge all those who have died and continue to die, fast or slow, to reproduce this system.

Postscript

After the pandemic – against the vindictive normal

Strikes across the frontier and strikes for higher wage
Planet lurches to the right as ideologies engage
Suddenly it's repression, moratorium on rights
What did they think the politics of panic would invite?
Person in the street shrugs "Security comes first"
But the trouble with normal is it always gets worse
                    Bruce Cockburn, "The Trouble with Normal"

The arrival of the COVID-19 pandemic in early 2020, unfolding around the world as I write these words, will likely be remembered as an epochal shift. In this extended winter, as borders close, as lockdowns and quarantines multiply, as people succumb and recover, there is a strong sense that, when the spring finally arrives we will awaken in a drastically changed landscape.

Those of us now in isolation, in spite of our fear and frustrations, in spite of our grief (for those who have died or may die, for the life we once lived, for the future we once hoped for), there is also a sense we are cocooned, transforming, waiting, dreaming. True: Terrors stalk the global landscape, notably the way the virus (or our countermeasures) will endanger those among us whom we, as a society, have already abandoned or devalued. So many of us are already disposable. So many of us are only learning it now, too late. Then there is the dangerous blurring of the line between humanitarian and authoritarian measures. There is the geopolitical weaponization of the pandemic.

But when the Spring comes, as it must, when we emerge from hibernation, it might be a time of profound global struggle against both the drive to "return to normal" (the same normal that set the stage for this tragedy) and the "new normal" which might be even worse. Let us prepare as best we can, for we have a world to win.

THE COMING REVENGE OF THE NEW NORMAL

I imagine that struggles to come will be defined by either the desperate drive to "return to normal," or a great refusal of that normal. But this is no manichean melodrama.

On the one hand, there will be those who seek to return us to the order of global revenge capitalism to which we had become accustomed: a nihilistic system of global accumulation that appears to be taking a needless, warrantless vengeance on so many of us, though without any one individual intending any particular malice, and one which breeds the worst kind of revenge politics.

Of course, we should expect the demand that we return to the vindictive normal from the beneficiaries of that system (the wealthy, the political elite) who have everything to gain from business as usual. But we should also expect it from millions of those oppressed, exploited, and alienated by that system, whose lives have been reduced to slow death under it. After months of chaos, isolation and fear, the desire to return to normal, even if normal is an abusive system, may be extremely strong. The stage is set for this desire to be accompanied by a frantic revanchism. Will we want someone to blame, especially those of us who lose loved ones? Must there be blood, figurative or literal?: a baptism by fire so that the old order (which, of course, created the conditions of austerity and inequality that made this plague so devastating) can be reborn in purified form.

Of course, things will never be "normal" again: some of us, the privileged and wealthy, may be afforded the illusion, but this illusion is likely to be carried on the backs of the vast majority who will work harder, longer and for less, suffer greater risks and fewer rewards. The debts of the pandemic, literal and figurative, will have to be repaid.

On the other hand (or maybe at the same time), we can also expect that, among the powerful and among the rest of us, there will be calls to reject the "return to normal," but in order to embrace something *even worse*. It is likely that the chaos and deaths of the pandemic will be blamed on too much democracy, liberalism, and empathy. Now that states are flexing their muscles and taking full command of society, there will be many who do not want the sleeve to be rolled back down. We may yet see, in this crisis, the use of repressive force on civilians (as it is already being used on migrants and incarcerated people), and I fear that it will be seen by many as justified, a human sacrifice to feed the Gods of fear.

In the wake of the pandemic we can be sure that fascists and reactionaries will seek to mobilize tropes of (racial, national, economic) purity, purification, parasitism, and pollution to impose their long-festering dreams on reality. The vengeful romance of the border, now more politicized than ever, will haunt all of us in the years to come. The "new" authoritarians, whether they emphasize the totalitarian state or the totalitarian market (or both), will insist that we all recognize we now live (have always lived) in a ruthless, competitive world and must take measures to wall ourselves in and cast out the undesirable. Other times, authoritarianism may come by stealth, cloaked in the rhetoric of science, liberalism, and the common good.

Meanwhile, there will almost certainly be efforts by those vastly enriched and empowered in the last decades, notably in the intertwined technology and financial sectors, to leverage their influence and resources, as well as the weakness and disarray of traditional institutions, to lead the reorganization of society along neo-technocratic lines. They will continue to generously offer the services of their powerful and integrated surveillance, logistics, financial, and data empires to "optimize" social and political life. This corporate dystopia can wear a human face: basic income, hypervigilance for new epidemics, personalized medicine. Already they arrive, bearing gifts to help us in this emergency: tracking disease vectors, banning disinformation, offering states help with data and population management. Underneath the mask will be the reorganization of society to better conform to the hyper-capitalist meta-algorithm which, though driven by capitalist contradictions, will essentially be neofeudal for most of us: a world of data and risk management where only a small handful enjoy the benefits. We will be told it is for our own good.

OUR AVENGING REFUSAL

Against all these fateful outcomes there will be those among us who refuse to return to normal, or to embrace the "new normal," those of us who know that "the trouble with normal is it only gets worse."

Already, in the state of emergency that the crisis has unleashed, we are seeing extraordinary measures emerge that reveal that much of the neoliberal regime's claims to necessity and austerity were transparent lies. The God-like market has fallen, again. In different places a variety of measures are being introduced that would have been unimaginable even weeks ago. These have included the suspension of rents and mortgages, the free provision of public transit, the deployment of basic incomes, a hiatus in debt payments, the commandeering of privatized hospitals and other once-public infrastructure for the public good, the liberation of incarcerated people, and governments compelling private industries to reorient production to common needs. We hear news of significant numbers of people refusing to work, taking wildcat labor action, and demanding their right to live in radical ways. In some places, the underhoused are seizing vacant homes.

We are discovering, against the upside-down capitalist value paradigm which has enriched the few at the expense of the many, whose labour is truly valuable: care, service, and frontline public sector workers. There has been a proliferation of grassroots radical demands for policies of care and solidarity not only as emergency measures, but in perpetuity. Right-wing and capitalist think-tanks are panicking, fearful that half a century of careful ideological work to convince us of the necessity of neoliberalism (the transformation of our very souls) will be dispelled in the coming weeks and months. The sweet taste of freedom--real, interdependent freedom, not the lonely freedom of the market--lingers on the palate like a long-forgotten memory, but quickly turns bitter when its nectar is withdrawn. If we do not defend these material and spiritual gains, capitalism will come for its revenge.

Meanwhile, the quarantined and semi-isolated are discovering, using digital tools, new ways to mobilize to provide care and mutual aid to those in our communities in need. We are slowly recovering our lost powers of life in common, hidden in plain sight, our secret inheritance. We are learning again to become a cooperative species, shedding the claustrophobic skin of *homo oeconomicus*. In the suspension of a capitalist order of competition, distrust, and endless, pointless hustle, our ingenuity and compassion are returning like birds to the smog-free sky.

When the Spring arrives, the struggle will be to preserve, enhance, network, and organize this ingenuity and compassion to demand no return to normal and no new normal. Around the world there has, over the past few years, been an unprecedented level of mobilization and organization of movements against revenge capitalism, sometimes around electoral candidates (eg. Corbyn in the UK, Sanders in the US) but also around grassroots campaigns: strikes against necro-neoliberalism in France, anti-authoritarianism in Hong Kong, anti-corruption in Lebanon and Iraq, anti-austerity in Chile, feminism in Mexico, struggles against gentrification and urban cleansing in cities around the world, migrant solidarity in Europe, Indigenous struggles in Canada, the climate struggle everywhere.

These pre-2020 struggles, important in their own right, will, I think, be remembered as the training grounds for a generation to whom now falls the burden of one of those turning points of history. We have learned how to bring a capitalist economy to its knees through non-violent protest in the face of overwhelming, technologically augmented oppression. We are learning how to become ungovernable by either states or markets. Equally importantly, we have learned new ways to care for one another without waiting for the state or for authorities. We are rediscovering the power of mutual aid and solidarity. We are learning how to communicate and cooperate anew. We have learned how to organize and to respond quickly, how to make collective decisions and to take responsibility for our fate.

Like the heroes of all good epics, we are not ready, our training was not completed, yet fate will not wait. Like all true heroes, we must make do with what we have: one another and nothing else.

As the world closes its eyes for this strange, dreamlike quarantine (save of course for those frontline health, service and care workers who, in the service of humanity, cannot rest, or those who have no safe place to dream), we must make ready for the waking. We are on the cusp of a great refusal of a return to normal and of a new normal, a vengeful normalcy that brought us this catastrophe and that will only lead to more catastrophe. In the weeks to come, it will be time to mourn and to dream, to prepare, to learn, and to connect as best we can.

When the isolation is over, we will awaken to a world where competing regimes of vindictive normalization will be at war with one another, a time of profound danger and opportunity. It will be a time to rise and to look one another in the eye.

Max Haiven
London, March 2020

> History says, Don't hope
> on this side of the grave.
> But then, once in a lifetime
> the longed for tidal wave
> of justice can rise up,
> and hope and history rhyme.
> So hope for a great sea-change
> on the far side of revenge.
> Believe that a further shore
> is reachable from here.
> Believe in miracles
> and cures and healing wells.

Seamus Heaney, from *The Cure at Troy: Sophocles' Philoctetes*
(London, Faber & Faber, 2018)

Notes

PREFACE

1 George Orwell, "Revenge Is Sour," in *Fifty Essays* (1945), http://gutenberg. net.au/ebooks03/0300011h.html#part31

2 See Max Haiven, "The Colonial Secrets of Canada's Most Racist City," *ROAR Magazine*, February 13, 2019, https://roarmag.org/essays/ colonial-secrets-canadas-racist-city/

3 See Tanya Talaga, *Seven Fallen Feathers: Racism, Death, and Hard Truths in a Northern City* (Toronto: House of Anansi Press, 2017). I would also highly recommend the award-winning "Thunder Bay" podcast on the city produced by Ryan McMahon and the team at Canadaland, available at https://www.canadalandshow.com/shows/thunder-bay/

4 Ivory Tuesday, "Anonymous Stories of 'Sousveillance' from the Thunder Bay Moccasin Telegram" (MA Creative Project, Social Justice Studies, Lakehead University, 2019).

5 Leanne Betasamosake Simpson, *As We Have Always Done: Indigenous Freedom through Radical Resistance*, Indigenous Americas (Minneapolis, MN: University of Minnesota Press, 2017).

6 Max Haiven and Alex Khasnabish, *The Radical Imagination: Social Movement Research in the Age of Austerity* (London and New York, NY: Zed Books, 2014); On the Radical Politics of the Indigenous Story, see Aman Sium and Eric Ritskes, "Speaking Truth to Power: Indigenous Storytelling as an Act of Living Resistance," *Decolonization: Indigeneity, Education & Society* 2, no. 1 (2013): I–X.

7 Thomas King, *The Truth about Stories* (Toronto: House of Anansi, 2003).

INTRODUCTION

1 C. L. R. James, *The Black Jacobins: Toussaint L'Ouverture and the San Domingo Revolution*, 2nd edition (New York, NY: Vintage, 1989), 88–89.

2 Eve Tuck and C. Ree, "A Glossary of Haunting," in *Handbook of Autoethnography*, ed. Stacy Holman Jones, Tony E. Adams, and Carolyn Ellis, (London and New York, NY: Routledge, 2013), 644.

3 Naomi Klein, *This Changes Everything: Capitalism vs. the Climate* (New York, NY: Knopf, 2015).

4 Shannon Hall, "Exxon Knew about Climate Change Almost 40 Years Ago," *Scientific American*, October 26, 2019, https://www.scientificamerican.com/ article/exxon-knew-about-climate-change-almost-40-years-ago/.

5   Rob Law, "I Have Felt Hopelessness over Climate Change. Here Is
    How We Move Past the Immense Grief," *The Guardian*, May 9, 2019,
    https://www.theguardian.com/commentisfree/2019/may/09/i-have-
    felt-hopelessness-over-climate-change-here-is-how-we-move-past-
    the-immense-grief.

6   Dan Bulley, Jenny Edkins, and Nadine El-Enany, eds., *After Grenfell:
    Violence, Resistance and Response* (London and New York, NY: Pluto,
    2019).

7   Gilbert Achcar, *The Clash of Barbarisms: The Making of the New World
    Disorder*, Updated and expanded ed (Boulder, CO: Paradigm Publishers,
    2006); Arlie Russell Hochschild, *Strangers in Their Own Land: Anger
    and Mourning on the American Right* (New York, NY: New Press, 2016);
    Jeff McCausland, "Enemies Foreign and Domestic: Inside the U.S.
    Military's White Supremacy Problem," *NBC News*, May 25, 2019, https://
    www.nbcnews.com/think/opinion/inside-u-s-military-s-battle-white-
    supremacy-far-right-ncna1010221; Mohammad-Mahmoud Mohamedou, *A
    Theory of ISIS: Political Violence and the Transformation of the Global Order*
    (London: Pluto Press, 2018); Mike King, "Aggrieved Whiteness: White
    Identity Politics and Modern American Racial Formation," *Abolition: A
    Journal of Insurgent Politics* 1 (May 5, 2017), https://abolitionjournal.org/
    aggrieved-whiteness-white-identity-politics-and-modern-american-racial-
    formation/.

8   For a more sophisticated approach to this question, see Hannah Arendt,
    "On Forgiveness," in *The Human Condition* (Chicago, IL: University of
    Chicago Press, 1958), 238–43.

9   Later in the book I will dwell more on the uniquely human quality of
    revenge, but for a fascinating study of the retaliation of other animals, see
    Jason Hribal, *Fear of the Animal Planet: The Hidden History of Animal
    Resistance* (Oakland, CA and Edinburgh: AK Press, 2011).

10 On this, see Margaret Atwood, *Payback: Debt and the Shadow Side of
    Wealth* (Toronto: Anansi, 2008).

11 Sara Ahmed, *The Promise of Happiness* (Durham, NC and London: Duke
    University Press, 2010).

12 On the way systems are held in place by sadism, but then give rise to an
    excess of violence, see Ella Myers, "Beyond the Wages of Whiteness: Du
    Bois on the Irrationality of Antiblack Racism," *Items: Insights from the
    Social Sciences*, March 21, 2017, https://items.ssrc.org/reading-racial-
    conflict/beyond-the-wages-of-whiteness-du-bois-on-the-irrationality-of-
    antiblack-racism/

13 See Harry Cleaver, *Reading Capital Politically* (Edinburgh and San
    Francisco, CA: AK Press, 2000); Massimo de Angelis, *The Beginning of
    History: Value Struggles and Global Capitalism* (London and Ann Arbor,
    MI: Pluto, 2007).

14 I will explore this myth in more detail in future chapters, but for a very
    compelling articulation, see Steven Pinker, *The Better Angels of Our Nature:
    Why Violence Has Declined* (New York, NY: Penguin, 2012).

15 On the reproduction of the frontier as a horizon of the violence of accumulations, see Raj Patel and Jason W. Moore, *The History of the World in Seven Cheap Things* (Berkeley, CA: University of California Press, 2017).

16 See, for instance, Daniel HoSang and Joseph E. Lowndes, *Producers, Parasites, Patriots: Race and the New Right-Wing Politics of Precarity* (Minneapolis, MN: University Of Minnesota Press, 2019).

17 See Mark Fisher, *Capitalist Realism: Is There No Alternative?* (London: Zero Books, 2009). See also Mark Fisher, "Exiting the Vampire Castle," *OpenDemocracy.* November 24, 2013. https://www.opendemocracy.net/en/opendemocracyuk/exiting-vampire-castle/. While I differ from Fisher on a number of points, many of the tendencies he identifies here that I am associating with revenge politics within social justice and liberation movements echo my personal experience and my ethnographic observations, the fruits of which can be found in Max Haiven and Alex Khasnabish, *The Radical Imagination: Social Movement Research in the Age of Austerity* (London and New York, NY: Zed Books, 2014).

18 "Global Study on Homicide: Gender-Related Killing of Women and Girls," (Vienna: United Nations Office on Drugs and Crime, 2019), https://www.unodc.org/documents/data-and-analysis/gsh/Booklet_5.pdf

19 "A National Epidemic: Fatal Anti-Transgender Violence in the United States" (Washington, DC: The Human Rights Campaign Foundation, 2019), https://assets2.hrc.org/files/assets/resources/Anti-TransViolenceReport2019.pdf

20 Maria Mies, *Patriarchy and Accumulation on a World Scale: Women in the International Division of Labour* (London: Zed Books, 1986); Nancy Fraser, *Fortunes of Feminism: From State-Managed Capitalism to Neoliberal Crisis* (London and New York, NY: Verso, 2013).

21 Verónica Gago, "Is There a War 'on' the Body of Women?: Finance, Territory, and Violence," *Viewpoint Magazine*, March 7, 2018, https://www.viewpointmag.com/2018/03/07/war-body-women-finance-territory-violence/; Silvia Federici, *Witches, Witch-Hunting, and Women* (Oakland, CA: PM Press, 2018); Sayak Valencia, *Gore Capitalism*, trans. John Pluecker (Los Angeles, CA: Semiotext(e), 2018).

22 Sara R. Farris, "Social Reproduction, Surplus Populations and the Role of Migrant Women," *Viewpoint Magazine*, November 1, 2015, https://www.viewpointmag.com/2015/11/01/social-reproduction-and-surplus-populations/.

23 See Debbie Ging and Eugenia Siapera, eds., *Gender Hate Online: Understanding the New Anti-Feminism*, (Switzerland: Palgrave MacMillan, 2019).

24 For a scholarly articulation of this cosmology, see the essays in Gerald Schneider and Nils Petter Gleditsch, eds., *Assessing the Capitalist Peace* (London: Routledge, 2013).

25 Some have made entire careers of making this argument. See for instance, Ann H. Coulter, *Demonic: How the Liberal Mob Is Endangering America* (New York, NY: Crown Forum, 2012). While Coulter is an extreme example, we might for instance think about the work done by the term "vindictive protectiveness" in Greg Lukianoff, and Jonathan Haidt's

extremely influential "The Coddling of the American Mind," *The Atlantic*, September 2015, https://www.theatlantic.com/magazine/archive/2015/09/the-coddling-of-the-american-mind/399356/. The phrase was intended to suggest that the bastion of liberalism, the university, has been betrayed from within by vengeful barbarians (students), oversensitive and censorious towards class content and speech that makes them uncomfortable.

26 Cedric J. Robinson, *Black Marxism: The Making of the Black Radical Tradition*, 2nd ed (Chapel Hill, NC: University of North Carolina Press, 2000); Valencia, *Gore Capitalism*; Jackie Wang, *Carceral Capitalism* (Los Angeles, CA: Semiotext(e), 2018); David Harvey, *A Brief History of Neoliberalism* (Oxford: Oxford University Press, 2005); Max Haiven, *Cultures of Financialization: Fictitious Capital in Popular Culture and Everyday Life* (London and New York, NY: Palgrave Macmillan, 2014); Shoshana Zuboff, *The Age of Surveillance Capitalism* (New York, NY: Public Affairs, 2019); Yann Moulier Boutang, *Cognitive Capitalism*, trans. Ed Emery (Cambridge and Malden, MA: Polity Press, 2011); Laurent De Sutter, *Narcocapitalism: Life in the Age of Anaesthesia*, trans. Barnaby Norman, (Cambridge and Madford, MA: Polity Press, 2017); Michael Hardt and Antonio Negri, *Empire* (Cambridge, MA: Harvard University Press, 2000); Andrea Fumagalli, "Twenty Theses on Contemporary Capitalism (Cognitive Biocapitalism)," *Angelaki* 16, no. 3 (September 1, 2011): 7–17, https://doi.org/10.1080/0969725X.2011.626555; Susan Lettow, "Biocapitalism," *Krisis: Journal for Contemporary Philosophy* 2 (2018), https://krisis.eu/biocapitalism/

27 Andrew Ross, *Creditocracy* (New York, NY: OR Books, 2014).

28 Miranda Joseph, *Debt to Society: Accounting for Life under Capitalism* (Minneapolis, MN: University of Minnesota Press, 2014).

29 Éric Toussaint, *The Debt System: A History of Sovereign Debts and Their Repudiation* (Chicago, IL: Haymarket, 2019).

30 Robert Aldrich, "Apologies, Restitutions, and Compensation: Making Reparations for Colonialism," in *The Oxford Handbook of the Ends of Empire*, ed. Martin Thomas and Andrew Thompson (Oxford: Oxford University Press, 2018), 696–732, https://doi.org/10.1093/oxfordhb/9780198713197.013.39; Robin D.G. Kelley, "'A Day of Reckoning': Dreams of Reparations," in *Freedom Dreams: The Black Radical Imagination* (Boston, MA: Beacon, 2002), 110–34.

31 Domenico Losurdo, *Liberalism: A Counter-History*, trans. Gregory Elliott (London and New York, NY: Verso, 2014); Lisa Lowe, *The Intimacies of Four Continents.* (Durham, NC: Duke University Press, 2015).

32 See Bue Rübner Hansen, "Surplus Population, Social Reproduction, and the Problem of Class Formation," *Viewpoint Magazine*, October 31, 2015, https://www.viewpointmag.com/2015/10/31/surplus-population-social-reproduction-and-the-problem-of-class-formation/; Sara R. Farris, "Social Reproduction, Surplus Populations and the Role of Migrant Women," *Viewpoint Magazine*, November 1, 2015, https://www.viewpointmag.com/2015/11/01/social-reproduction-and-surplus-populations/

33 David Neilson and Thomas Stubbs, "Relative Surplus Population and Uneven Development in the Neoliberal Era: Theory and Empirical Application," *Capital & Class* 35, no. 3 (October 2011): 435–53, https://doi. org/10.1177/0309816811418952; Michael McIntyre, "Race, Surplus Population and the Marxist Theory of Imperialism," *Antipode* 43, no. 5 (September 2011): 1489–1515, https://doi.org/10.1111/j.1467-8330.2011.00898.x

34 Prem Kumar Rajaram, "Refugees as Surplus Population: Race, Migration and Capitalist Value Regimes," *New Political Economy* 23, no. 5 (September 2018): 627–39; "Misery and Debt: On the Logic and History of Surplus Populations and Surplus Capital," *Endnotes* 2 (2010), https://endnotes.org. uk/issues/2/en/endnotes-misery-and-debt

35 Siyaves Azeri, "Surplus-Population and the Political Economy of Fear," *Critical Sociology*, November 10, 2017; Joshua Clover, *Riot. Strike. Riot: The New Era of Uprisings* (London and New York, NY: Verso, 2016).

36 Zygmunt Bauman, *Wasted Lives: Modernity and Its Outcasts* (Oxford and Malden, MA: Polity, 2004); Jackie Wang, *Carceral Capitalism* (Los Angeles, CA: Semiotext(e), 2018).

37 Peter Linebaugh, *The Magna Carta Manifesto: Liberties and Commons for All* (Berkeley, CA: University of California Press, 2009).

38 David A. Chang, "Enclosures of Land and Sovereignty: The Allotment of American Indian Lands," *Radical History Review* 2011, no. 109 (December 2011): 108–19, https://doi.org/10.1215/01636545-2010-018; Peter Linebaugh, *Stop, Thief!: The Commons, Enclosures, and Resistance* (Oakland, CA: PM Press, 2014); The Midnight Notes Collective, "New Enclosures," in *Subverting the Present, Imagining the Future: Insurrection, Movement, & Commons*, ed. Werner Bonefeld (New York, NY: Autonomedia, 2009), 13–26; Raj Patel and Jason W. Moore, *The History of the World in Seven Cheap Things* (Berkeley, CA: University of California Press, 2017).

39 Max Haiven, "Commons as Actuality, Ethos and Horizon," in *Edcational Commons in Theory and Practice*, ed. Alex Means, Graham Slater, and Derek Ford (London and New York, NY: Palgrave MacMillan, 2017), 23–37.

40 Max Haiven, *Cultures of Financialization: Fictitious Capital in Popular Culture and Everyday Life* (London and New York, NY: Palgrave Macmillan, 2014).

41 Carole Cadwalladr, "Fresh Cambridge Analytica Leak 'Shows Global Manipulation Is out of Control,'" *The Observer*, January 4, 2020, https:// www.theguardian.com/uk-news/2020/jan/04/cambridge-analytica-data-leak-global-election-manipulation

42 Nick Srnicek, *Platform Capitalism* (Cambridge and Malden, MA: Polity Press, 2017).

43 Franco "Bifo" Berardi, *Precarious Rhapsody: Semiocapitalism and the Pathologies of the Post-Alpha Generation* (New York, NY: Autonomedia, 2009).

44 Nick Dyer-Witheford, *Cyber-Proletariat: Global Labour in the Digital Vortex* (London and New York: Pluto, 2015).

45 Geert Lovink, *Sad by Design: On Platform Nihilism*, (London and New York: Pluto 2019).

46 Kyle Chayka, "The Empty Promises of Marie Kondo and the Craze for Minimalism," *The Guardian*, January 3, 2020, https://www.theguardian.com/lifeandstyle/2020/jan/03/empty-promises-marie-kondo-craze-for-minimalism; Ronald E Purser, *McMindfulness: How Mindfulness Became the New Capitalist Spirituality* (London: Zero Books,2019); Cassie Thornton, "Feminist Economics Yoga," *Public Seminar*, July 26, 2018, https://publicseminar.org/2018/07/feminist-economics-yoga/

47 Chris Hedges, "Onward, Christian Fascists," *Salon.com*, January 3, 2020, https://www.salon.com/2020/01/03/onward-christian-fascists_partner/; Mohamedou, *A Theory of ISIS*; Arundhati Roy, "India: Intimations of an Ending," *The Nation*, November 22, 2019, https://www.thenation.com/article/arundhati-roy-assam-modi/; Achin Vanaik, *The Rise of Hindu Authoritarianism: Secular Claims, Communal Realities* (London and New York, NY: Verso, 2017).

48 Frantz Fanon, *Black Skin, White Masks*, trans. Richard Philcox, New ed. (New York: Grove, 2008); Frantz Fanon, *The Wretched of the Earth* (New York, NY: Grove, 1963); Friedrich Wilhelm Nietzsche, *On the Genealogy of Morals: A Polemic*, ed. Robert C. Holub, Trans. Michael A. Scarpitti (New York, NY: Penguin, 2013).

49 Glen Coulthard, *Red Skin, White Masks: Rejecting the Colonial Politics of Recognition* (Minneapolis, MN and London: University of Minnesota Press, 2014), 110.

50 Sara Ahmed, *The Promise of Happiness* (Durham, NC and London: Duke University Press, 2010); Sara Ahmed, *The Cultural Politics of Emotion* (London and New York, NY: Routledge, 2004); Lauren Berlant, *Cruel Optimism* (Durham, NC and London: Duke University Press, 2011); Ann Cvetkovich, *Depression: A Public Feeling* (Durham, NC: Duke University Press, 2012); Elizabeth Stephens, "Bad Feelings: An Affective Genealogy of Feminism," *Australian Feminist Studies* 30, no. 85 (July 2015): 273–82, https://doi.org/10.1080/08164649.2015.1113907

51 Lauren Berlant, *Cruel Optimism*; William Davies, *Happiness Industry – How the Government and Big Business Sold Us Well-Being* (London and New York: Verso, 2015); Barbara Ehrenreich, *Bright-Sided: How Positive Thinking Is Undermining America*, 2010; Purser, *McMindfulness*.

52 Clover, *Riot. Strike. Riot.*

53 Fanon, *Black Skin, White Masks*; Saidiya Hartman, *Scenes of Subjection: Terror, Slavery, and Self-Making in Nineteenth-Century America* (Oxford and New York, NY: Oxford University Press, 1997); Jasbir K. Puar, *The Right to Maim: Debility, Capacity, Disability*, (Durham, NC: Duke University Press, 2017).

54 Chantal Mouffe, *Agonistics: Thinking the World Politically* (London and New York, NY: Verso, 2013); Ernesto Laclau and Chantal Mouffe, *Hegemony and Socialist Strategy: Towards a Radical Democratic Politics*, 2nd ed. (London and New York, NY: Verso, 2001).

55 Gilbert Achcar, *The Clash of Barbarisms: The Making of the New World Disorder*, Updated and expanded ed (Boulder, CO: Paradigm Publishers, 2006); Arjun Appadurai, *Fear of Small Numbers: An Essay on the Geography*

of Anger, Public Planet Books (Durham, NC: Duke University Press, 2006); Henry A. Giroux, *American Nightmare: Facing the Challenge of Fascism* (San Francisco, CA: City Lights, 2018); Imogen Tyler and Tom Slater, "Rethinking the Sociology of Stigma," *The Sociological Review* 66, no. 4 (June 2018): 721–43, https://doi.org/10.1177/0038026118777425

56 John B. Judis, *The Populist Explosion: How the Great Recession Transformed American and European Politics* (New York, NY: Columbia Global Reports, 2016); Pankaj Mishra, *Age of Anger: A History of the Present*, (London: Penguin, 2018).

57 Valencia, *Gore Capitalism*; Wang, *Carceral Capitalism*.

1. TOWARD A MATERIALIST THEORY OF REVENGE

1 Francis Bacon, "On Revenge," https://www.commonlit.org/texts/on-revenge

2 Mauro Scalercio, "Dominating Nature and Colonialism. Francis Bacon's View of Europe and the New World," *History of European Ideas* 44, no. 8 (2018): 1076–91.

3 Carolyn Merchant, "The Scientific Revolution and The Death of Nature." *Isis* 97 (2006): 513–33.

4 Silvia Federici, *Caliban and the Witch: Women, Capitalism and Primitive Accumulation* (New York, NY: Autonomedia, 2005); Maria Mies, *Patriarchy and Accumulation on a World Scale: Women in the International Division of Labour* (London: Zed Books, 1986).

5 Vandana Shiva, *Monocultures of the Mind: Perspectives on Biodiversity and Biotechnology* (London: Zed Books, 1993). On the centrality of empiricism and the scientific method to the development of political economy, as well as the politics thereof, see Michael Perelman, *The Invention of Capitalism: Classical Political Economy and the Secret History of Primitive Accumulation* (Durham, NC and London: Duke University Press, 2000).

6 Thomas Hobbes, *Leviathan* (London: Penguin, 1985); Adam Smith, "Of the Unsocial Passions," In *Theory of Moral Sentiments*, http://knarf.english.upenn.edu/Smith/tms123.html, (1759). Locke is most explicit: "If the king shall shew an hatred... [and] sets himself against the body of the commonwealth, whereof he is the head, and shall, with intolerable ill usage, cruelly tyrannize over the whole, or a considerable part of the people, in this case the people have a right to resist and defend themselves from injury: but it must be with this caution, that they only defend themselves, but do not attack their prince: they may repair the damages received, but must not for any provocation exceed the bounds of due reverence and respect. They may repulse the present attempt, but must not revenge past violences: for it is natural for us to defend life and limb, but that an inferior should punish a superior, is against nature. The mischief which is designed them, the people may prevent before it be done; but when it is done, they must not revenge it on the king, though author of the villainy." (John Locke, "Of the Dissolution of Government," in *Second Treatise of Civil Government* (1690).

Marxist Internet Archive. https://www.marxists.org/reference/subject/politics/locke/ch19.htm)

7   Harry Cleaver, *Reading Capital Politically* (Edinburgh and San Francisco, CA: AK Press, 2000).

8   Friedrick Engels, *The Condition of the Working Class in England* (London: Penguin Books, 1987).

9   Friedrich Engels, "The Program of the Blanquist Fugitives from the Paris Commune," *Der Volksstaat*, June 26, 1874, https://www.marxists.org/archive/marx/works/1874/06/26.htm

10 Karl Marx and V. I. Lenin, *The Civil War in France and the Paris Commune* (New York, NY: International, 1993).

11 Nick Robins, *The Corporation That Changed the World: How the East India Company Shaped the Modern Multinational*, 2nd ed. (London: Pluto Press, 2012), 162–67.

12 Kevin Anderson, *Marx at the Margins: On Nationalism, Ethnicity, and Non-Western Societies*, 2nd ed. (Chicago, IL: The University of Chicago Press, 2016), 37–41.

13 Karl Marx, "The Indian Revolt," *New York Tribune*, September 16, 1857, https://www.marxists.org/archive/marx/works/1857/09/16.htm

14 Aimé Césaire, *Discourse on Colonialism*, Trans. Joan Pinkham (New York, NY and London: Monthly Review, 1972); C. L. R. James, *The Black Jacobins: Toussaint L'Ouverture and the San Domingo Revolution*, 2nd ed. (New York, NY: Vintage, 1989).

15 See Robins, *The Company That Changed the World*.

16 Karl Marx, "A Bourgeois Document," *Neue Rheinische Zeitung*, January 4, 1849, https://www.marxists.org/archive/marx/works/1849/01/04.htm

17 C. L. R. James, *The Black Jacobins: Toussaint L'Ouverture and the San Domingo Revolution*, 2nd ed. (New York, NY: Vintage, 1989).

18 See Peter James Hudson, *Bankers and Empire: How Wall Street Colonized the Caribbean* (Chicago, IL: The University of Chicago Press, 2017), especially Chapter 3.

19 Jerome Roos, *Why Not Default?: The Political Economy of Sovereign Debt*, Princeton NJ and London: Princeton University Press, 2018); Éric Toussaint, *The Debt System: A History of Sovereign Debts and Their Repudiation*, Chicago, IL: Haymarket, 2019).

20 See Robbins, *The Corporation that Changed the World*.

21 Éric Toussaint, *The Debt System*.

22 Lisa Lowe, *The Intimacies of Four Continents* (Durham, NC: Duke University Press, 2015).

23 K-Sue Park, "Money, Mortgages, and the Conquest of America: Money, Mortgages, and the Conquest of America," *Law & Social Inquiry* 41, no. 4 (2016): 1006–35.

24 See Saidiya Hartman, *Scenes of Subjection: Terror, Slavery, and Self-Making in Nineteenth-Century America* (Oxford and New York, NY: Oxford University Press, 1997).

25 Paul Avrich, *The Haymarket Tragedy, Volume 2* (Princeton NJ: Princeton University Press, 1984), 189–90.

26 Joyce L. Kornbluh, ed., *Rebel Voices: An IWW Anthology* (Oakland, CA: PM Press, 2011), 29.

27 Hayley C. Cuccinello, "'Game Of Thrones' Season 6 Costs $10 Million Per Episode, Has Biggest Battle Scene Ever," *Forbes*, April 22, 2016, https://www.forbes.com/sites/hayleycuccinello/2016/04/22/game-of-thrones-season-6-costs-10-million-per-episode-has-biggest-battle-scene-ever/

28 S. Clarke Hulse, "Wresting the Alphabet: Oratory and Action in 'Titus Andronicus.'" *Criticism* 21, 2 (1979): 106–18.

29 Cited in Kenji Yoshino, "Revenge as Revenant: Titus Andronicus and the Rule of Law," *Yale Journal of Law & the Humanities* 21, 2 (2009): 203–25.

30 See Jonathan Dollimore, *Radical Tragedy: Religion, Ideology, and Power in the Drama of Shakespeare and His Contemporaries*, 3rd ed. (Durham NC: Duke University Press, 2004).

31 See Henry A. Giroux and Grace Pollock, *The Mouse That Roared: Disney and the End of Innocence*, 2nd ed. (Lanham, MD: Rowman & Littlefield Publishers, 2010).

32 Ishaan Tharoor, "Why the West's Far-Right – and Trump Supporters – Are Still Obsessed with an Ancient Battle," *The Washington Post*. November 7, 2016, https://www.washingtonpost.com/news/worldviews/wp/2016/11/07/why-the-wests-far-right-and-trump-supporters-are-still-obsessed-with-an-ancient-battle/

33 Joshua Green, "Steve Bannon: This Man Is the Most Dangerous Political Operative in America," *Bloomberg*, October 8, 2015, https://www.bloomberg.com/politics/graphics/2015-steve-bannon/; Ann Hornaday, "You Can Learn a Lot about Steve Bannon by Watching the Films He Made," *The Washington Post*, February 2, 2017, https://www.washingtonpost.com/lifestyle/style/you-can-learn-a-lot-about-steve-bannon-by-watching-the-films-he-made/2017/02/02/6eaa2688-e8b2-11e6-b82f-687d6e6a3e7c_story.html; Michael Wolff, "Ringside With Steve Bannon," *The Hollywood Reporter*, November 18, 2016, http://www.hollywoodreporter.com/news/steve-bannon-trump-tower-interview-trumps-strategist-plots-new-political-movement-948747

34 William L. Shirer, *The Rise and Fall of the Third Reich: A History of Nazi Germany*, 50th anniversary ed. (New York, NY: Simon & Schuster, 2011).

35 Dan O'Sullivan, "Vengeance Is Mine," *Jacobin*, November 2016, http://jacobinmag.com/2016/11/donald-trump-election-hillary-clinton-election-night-inequality-republicans-trumpism

36 Matea Gold, "GOP Mega-Donors Robert and Rebekah Mercer Stand by Trump," *The Washington Post*, October 8, 2016, https://www.washingtonpost.com/news/post-politics/wp/2016/10/08/gop-mega-donors-robert-and-rebekah-mercer-stand-by-trump/

37 Adrienne Massanari, "#Gamergate and The Fappening: How Reddit's Algorithm, Governance, and Culture Support Toxic Technocultures," *New Media & Society* 19, no. 3 (2017): 329–46. https://doi.org/10.1177/1461444815608807

38 Silvia Federici, *Caliban and the Witch: Women, Capitalism and Primitive Accumulation* (New York, NY: Autonomedia, 2005).

39 Chandra Talpade Mohanty, *Feminism without Borders: Decolonizing Theory, Practicing Solidarity* (Durham, NC and London: Duke University Press, 2003).

40 Frantz Fanon, *Black Skin, White Masks*. Trans. Richard Philcox, New ed. (New York, NY: Grove, 2008).

41 Andrea Smith, *Conquest: Sexual Violence and American Indian Genocide* (Cambridge MA: South End Press, 2005); Lee Maracle, *I Am Woman: A Native Perspective on Sociology and Feminism* (Vancouver: Press Gang Publishers, 1996); Joyce A. Green ed. *Making Space for Indigenous Feminism* (Halifax, NS: Fernwood, 2007); Sarah Hunt, "Representing Colonial Violence: Trafficking, Sex Work, and the Violence of Law," *Atlantis* 37, 2 (2016): 25–39; Joanne Barker, ed., *Critically Sovereign: Indigenous Gender, Sexuality, and Feminist Studies* (Durham, NC: Duke University Press, 2017).

42 Ann Stoler, *Race and the Education of Desire: Foucault's History of Sexuality and the Colonial Order of Things* (Durham, NC, and London: Duke University Press, 1995).

43 Lisa Nakamura, "The Unwanted Labour of Social Media: Women of Colour Call out Culture as Venture Community Management," *New Formations* 86 (2015), /https://lnakamur.files.wordpress.com/2011/01/unwanted-labor-of-social-media-nakamura1.pdf; Lisa Nakamura, "Racism, Sexism, and Gaming's Cruel Optimism," in *Gaming Representation: Race, Gender, and Sexuality in Video Games*, ed. Jennifer Malkowski and Trea Andrea M. Russworm (Bloomington, IN: Indiana University Press, 2017).

44 On this genre, and feminist critics' diverse responses to it, see, Carol J. Clover, *Men, Women, and Chain Saws: Gender in the Modern Horror Film*, Princeton classics ed. (Princeton, NJ: Princeton University Press, 2015); Alexandra Heller-Nicholas, *Rape-Revenge Films: A Critical Study* (Jefferson, NC: McFarland, 2011); Sarah Projansky, *Watching Rape: Film and Television in Postfeminist Culture* (New York, NY: New York University Press, 2001); Jacinda Read, *The New Avengers: Feminism, Femininity, and the Rape-Revenge Cycle* (Manchester and New York, NY: Manchester University Press, 2000).

45 "National Intimate Partner and Sexual Violence Survey" (Atlanta, GA: National Center for Injury Prevention and Control, Centers for Disease Control and Prevention, 2011); "Global Study on Homicide: Gender-Related Killing of Women and Girls" (Vienna: United Nations Office on Drugs and Crime, 2019), https://www.unodc.org/documents/data-and-analysis/gsh/Booklet_5.pdf

46 See Debbie Ging and Eugenia Siapera, eds., *Gender Hate Online: Understanding the New Anti-Feminism* (London: Palgrave MacMillan, 2019).

47 Leigh Claire La Berge, "The Men Who Make the Killings: American Psycho, Financial Masculinity, and 1980s Financial Print Culture," *Studies in American Fiction* 37, no. 2 (2010): 273–96.

48 See Ging and Siapera, *Gender Hate Online: Understanding the New Anti-Feminism*. (Switzerland: Palgrave MacMillan, 2019).

49 "Global Study on Homicide: Gender-Related Killing of Women and Girls" (Vienna: United Nations Office on Drugs and Crime, 2019), https://www.unodc.org/documents/data-and-analysis/gsh/Booklet_5.pdf

50 Walter Benjamin, "Theses on the Philosophy of History," in *Illuminations*, ed. Hannah Arendt (New York, NY: Schocken, 1969), 253–64.

51 Franco Berardi, "Bifo," "After the European Union," *Verso Books Blog*, March 16, 2017, http://www.versobooks.com/blogs/3129-after-the-european-union

52 Neil Smith, *The New Urban Frontier: Gentrification and the Revanchist City* (London and New York, NY: Routledge, 1996).

53 David Harvey, *Rebel Cities: From the Right to the City to the Urban Revolution* (London and New York, NY: Verso, 2012).

54 Ruth Wilson Gilmore, *Golden Gulag: Prisons, Surplus, Crisis, and Opposition in Globalizing California*, (Berkeley, CA: University of California Press, 2007).

55 Samuel Stein, *Capital City: Gentrification and the Real Estate State* (London and New York, NY: Verso, 2019).

56 Robert Nichols, for one, has fruitfully problematizes and complicates these Marxist notions of the temporalities of accumulation – Robert Nichols, "Disaggregating Primitive Accumulation," *Radical Philosophy* 194 (2015): 18–28.

57 Giovanni Arrighi, *The Long Twentieth Century: Money, Power, and the Origins of Our Times* (London and New York, NY: Verso, 1994); Fredric Jameson, "Culture and Finance Capital," *Critical Inquiry* 24, 1 (1997): 246–65.

58 Costas Lapavitsas, *Profiting Without Producing: How Finance Exploits Us All* (London and New York, NY: Verso, 2013).

59 Max Haiven, "Finance as Capital's Imagination?: Reimagining Value and Culture in an Age of Fictitious Capital and Crisis," *Social Text*, 108 (2011): 93–124.

60 David Harvey, *The Limits to Capital*, 2nd ed. (London and New York, NY: Verso, 2006).

61 Keeanga-Yamahtta Taylor, *Race for Profit: How Banks and the Real Estate Industry Undermined Black Homeownership* (Chapel Hill, NC: University of North Carolina Press, 2019).

62 James Baldwin, *The Devil Finds Work: An Essay* (New York, NY: Vintage International, 2011), 39–46; George Yancy, "Noam Chomsky on the Roots of American Racism," *The New York Times*, March 18, 2015, https://opinionator.blogs.nytimes.com/2015/03/18/noam-chomsky-on-the-roots-of-american-racism/

63 Michelle Alexander, *The New Jim Crow: Mass Incarceration in the Age of Colorblindness* (New York, NY: The New Press, 2010); Angela Davis, *Abolition Democracy: Beyond Empire, Prisons and Torture* (New York, NY: Seven Stories, 2005); Ruth Wilson Gilmore, *Golden Gulag*, 2007.

64 Saidiya Hartman, *Scenes of Subjection*, 1997.

65 Theodore W. Allen, *The Invention of the White Race* (London: Verso, 1994); David R. Roediger, *The Wages of Whiteness: Race and the Making of the American Working Class*, 2nd ed. (London and New York, NY: Verso, 1999).

66 Loïc Wacquant, "Class, Race and Hyperincarceration in Revanchist America," *Socialism and Democracy* 28, 3 (2014): 35–56.
67 Jackie Wang, *Carceral Capitalism* (Los Angeles, CA: Semiotext(e), 2018).
68 Elsewhere I have taken up Derrida's concept of the crypt in this fashion in more depth. See Max Haiven, *Art after Money, Money after Art: Creative Strategies Against Financialization* (London and New York: Pluto, 2018).
69 Aimé Césaire, *Discourse on Colonialism*, Trans. Joan Pinkham (New York, NY and London: Monthly Review, 1972).
70 Naomi Klein, *No Is Not Enough* (Chicago, IL: Haymarket, 2017).
71 Simon Childs, "The Far-Right International," *New Internationalist*, March 28, 2019, https://newint.org/features/2019/02/11/far-right-international; Kevin Sullivan, "A Nationalist Abroad: Stephen Bannon Evangelizes Trump-Style Politics across Europe," *Washington Post*, September 25, 2018, https://www.washingtonpost.com/politics/a-nationalist-abroad-stephen-bannon-evangelizes-trump-style-politics-across-europe/2018/09/25/4f47d046-code-11e8-be77-516336a26305_story.html
72 Shuja Haider, "The Darkness at the End of the Tunnel: Artificial Intelligence and Neoreaction," *Viewpoint Magazine*, March 28, 2017, https://www.viewpointmag.com/2017/03/28/the-darkness-at-the-end-of-the-tunnel-artificial-intelligence-and-neoreaction/
73 Karl Marx, *Capital I: A Critique of Political Economy*, Trans. Ben Fowkes (New York, NY: Penguin, 1992), Chapter 31.
74 Michael Denning, "Wageless Life," *New Left Review* 66 (2010): 79–97.
75 See David McNally, *Monsters of the Market: Zombies, Vampires, and Global Capitalism* (Chicago, IL: Haymarket, 2012).
76 Luxemburg, Rosa, *The Accumulation of Capital*, Translated by Agnes Schwarzschild (London and New York, NY: Routledge, 2003).
77 David Brooks, "The Strange Persistence of Guilt," *The New York Times*, March 31, 2017, https://www.nytimes.com/2017/03/31/opinion/the-strange-persistence-of-guilt.html
78 Frantz Fanon, *The Wretched of the Earth* (New York, NY: Grove, 1963).
79 Glen Coulthard, *Red Skin, White Masks: Rejecting the Colonial Politics of Recognition* (Minneapolis, MN, and London: University of Minnesota Press, 2014).
80 Ward Churchill, *Pacifism as Pathology* (Edinburgh, Scotland, Oakland, CA: AK Press, 2007); Peter Gelderloos, *How Nonviolence Protects the State* (Cambridge, MA: South End Press, 2007).
81 Talat Ahmed, *Mohandas Gandhi: India's Non-Violent Revolutionary?* (London and New York, NY: Pluto, 2016); Martin Luther King, *The Radical King*, ed. Cornel West (Boston, MA: Beacon, 2016); Danny Schechter, *Madiba A to Z: The Many Faces of Nelson Mandela* (New York, NY: Seven Stories Press, 2013).
82 Jacques Derrida, "On Forgiveness," in *On Cosmopolitanism and Forgiveness*, Trans. Michael Hughs (London and New York, NY: Routledge, 2001), 25–60.
83 James Baldwin, *The Devil Finds Work: An Essay* (New York, NY: Vintage International, 2011), 44.

SHYLOCK'S VINDICATION, OR VENICE'S BONDS?

1   For a brilliant analysis of the inherent violence of contracts and their integral importance to patriarchy, capitalism and global racial ordering, see Angela Mitropoulos, *Contract & Contagion: From Biopolitics to Oikonomia* (Brooklyn, NY: Minor Compositions, 2012), http://www.minorcompositions.info/?p=482

2   On such exaltation, see Sunera Thobani, *Exalted Subjects: Studies in the Making of Race and Nation in Canada* (Toronto: University of Toronto Press, 2007).

3   See Michael Asch, *On Being Here to Stay: Treaties and Aboriginal Rights in Canada* (Toronto: University of Toronto Press, 2014).

4   John Gross, *Shylock: A Legend and Its Legacy* (New York, NY: Simon & Schuster, 1994).

5   See, for instance, Albert Memmi, *The Colonizer and the Colonized* (London: Earthscan, 2003).

6   bell hooks, *Killing Rage: Ending Racism* (New York, NY: Henry Holt, 1996).

7   See Arun Kundnani, *The Muslims Are Coming! Islamophobia, Extremism, and the Domestic War on Terror* (London and New York, NY: Verso, 2014).

2. THE WORK OF ART IN AN AGE OF UNPAYABLE DEBTS

1   Thomas Sankara, "A United Front Against Debt (1987)," *Viewpoint Magazine* (blog), February 1, 2018, https://www.viewpointmag.com/2018/02/01/united-front-debt-1987/

2   Vanessa Pérez-Rosario, "Unpayable Debt: Capital, Violence, and the New Global Economy: An Interview with Frances Negrón-Muntaner," *Small Axe* (blog), June 18, 2018, http://smallaxe.net/sxlive/unpayable-debt-capital-violence-and-new-global-economy-interview-frances-negron-muntaner

3   David Graeber, *Debt: The First 5000 Years* (New York, NY: Melville House, 2011); Gustav Peebles, "The Anthropology of Credit and Debt," *Annual Review of Anthropology* 39, 1 (2010): 225–40, https://doi.org/10.1146/annurev-anthro-090109-133856; William Pietz, "The Spirit of Civilization: Blood Sacrifice and Monetary Debt," *RES: Anthropology and Aesthetics* 28 (1995): 23–38.

4   Margaret Atwood, *Payback: Debt and the Shadow Side of Wealth* (Toronto: Anansi, 2008).

5   Graeber, *Debt: The First 5000 Years.*

6   See for instance Steven Pinker, *The Better Angels of Our Nature: Why Violence Has Declined* (New York, NY: Penguin, 2012).

7   Friedrich Wilhelm Nietzsche, *On the Genealogy of Morality*, ed. Keith Ansell-Pearson, trans. Carol Diethe (Cambridge and New York, NY: Cambridge University Press, 2007).

8 Eve Tuck and C. Ree, "A Glossary of Haunting," in *Handbook of Autoethnography*, ed. Stacy Holman Jones, Tony E. Adams, and Carolyn Ellis, (Walnut Creek, CA: Left Coast Press, 2013), 639–57.

9 Max Haiven, *Art After Money, Money After Art: Creative Strategies Against Financialization* (London: Pluto, 2018).

10 Leigh Claire La Berge, *Wages Against Artwork: Socially Engaged Art and the Decommodification of Labor* (Durham, NC and London: Duke University Press, 2019); Suhail Malik and Andrea Phillips, "Tainted Love: Art's Ethos and Capitalization," in *Contemporary Art and Its Commercial Markets: A Report on Current Conditions and Future Scenarios*, ed. Maria Lind and Olav Velthuis (Berlin: Sternberg, 2012), 209–40; Marina Vishmidt, "Notes on Speculation as a Mode of Production in Art and Capital," in *Joy Forever: The Political Economy of Social Creativity*, ed. Michał Kozłowski et al. (London: Mayfly, 2015), 47–64.

11 Phil Hubbard, *The Battle for the High Street: Retail Gentrification, Class and Disgust* (London, United Kingdom: Palgrave Macmillan, 2017); Geoffrey De Verteuil, "Immigration and Gentrification," in *Handbook of Gentrification Studies*, ed. Loretta Lees and Martin Phillips (2018), 428–43.

12 David Harvey, *Rebel Cities: From the Right to the City to the Urban Revolution* (London and New York, NY: Verso, 2012); Samuel Stein, *Capital City: Gentrification and the Real Estate State* (London and New York, NY: Verso, 2019).

13 Stevphen Shukaitis, "Art Strikes and the Metropolitan Factory," in *Joy Forever: The Political Economy of Social Creativity*, ed. Michał Kozłowski et al. (London: Mayfly, 2015), 227–36.

14 Rob Aitken, "Capital at Its Fringes," *New Political Economy* 11, 4 (2006): 479–98; Joe Deville, *Lived Economies of Default: Consumer Credit, Debt Collection and the Capture of Affect* (London and New York, NY: Routledge, 2015); Paul Langley et al., "Indebted Life and Money Culture: Payday Lending in the United Kingdom," *Economy and Society* 48, 1 (January 2, 2019): 30–51.

15 Karl Marx and Friedrich Engels, *The Communist Manifesto*, trans. Len Findlay (Peterborough, ON: Broadview, 2004); Frederick Engels, *The Origin of the Family, Private Property and the State*, 1884, https://www.marxists.org/archive/marx/works/1884/origin-family/

16 Pierre Bourdieu, *The Logic of Practice* (Stanford, CA: Stanford University Press, 1990).

17 bell hooks, *Teaching to Transgress: Education as the Practice of Freedom* (London and New York, NY: Routledge, 1994); Henry A. Giroux, *Public Spaces, Private Lives: Beyond the Culture of Cynicism* (Lanham, MD: Rowman & Littlefield Publishers: Distributed by National Book Network, 2001); Jack Zipes, *Breaking the Magic Spell: Radical Theories of Folk and Fairy Tales*, Rev. and expanded ed. (Lexington, KY: University Press of Kentucky, 2002).

18 Benjamin R. Barber, *Consumed: How Markets Corrupt Children, Infantilize Adults, and Swallow Citizens Whole* (New York, NY: Norton,

2007); Beryl Langer, "Commodified Enchantment: Children and Consumer Capitalism," *Thesis Eleven* 69, 1 (2002): 67–81, https://doi.org/ 10.1177/0725513602069001005; Viviana A. Zelizer, *Pricing the Priceless Child: The Changing Social Value of Children* (Princeton, NJ: Princeton University Press, 1994).

19   Lee Edelman, *No Future: Queer Theory and the Death Drive* (Durham, NC and London: Duke University Press, 2004).

20   Zygmunt Bauman, *In Search of Politics* (Stanford, CA: Stanford University Press, 1999), 9–11.

21   La Berge, *Wages Against Artwork*.

22   Bea Cantillon et al., eds., *Children of Austerity: Impact of the Great Recession on Child Poverty in Rich Countries* (Oxford: United Nations Children's Fund and Oxford University Press, 2017).

23   Randy Martin, *Financialization of Daily Life* (Philadelphia, PA: Temple University Press, 2002); Caitlin Zaloom, *Indebted: How Families Make College Work at Any Cost* (Princeton, NJ and Oxford: Princeton University Press, 2019).

24   Lynn A. Karoly, ed., *Investing in Our Children: What We Know and Don't Know About the Costs and Benefits of Early Childhood Interventions* (Santa Monica, CA: Rand, 1998); Mark Wietecha, "The Case for Investing in Child Health as a Matter of Our Nation's Security, Economy and Well-Being," Children's Hospital Association, October 28, 2016, https://www. childrenshospitals.org/research-and-data/pediatric-data-and-trends/2016/ the-case-for-investment-in-child-health-as-a-matter-of-our-nations-security-economy-and-well-being

25   Rupert Jones, "One in Four UK Retirees Burdened by Unpaid Mortgage or Other Debts," *The Guardian*, February 17, 2017, https://www. theguardian.com/money/2017/feb/17/one-in-four-uk-retirees-burdened-by-unpaid-mortgage-or-other-debts

26   Ross, *Creditocracy* (New York: OR Books, 2015).

27   Max Haiven, "Can Pikachu Save Fannie Mae? Value, Finance and Imagination in the New Pokeconomy," *Cultural Studies* 26, 4 (2012): 516–41.

28   Graeber, *Debt: The First 5000 Years*.

29   Nancy Fraser, "Contradictions of Capital and Care," *New Left Review* 100 (2016): 99–117.

30   Laura Parker, "Kids Suing Governments about Climate: It's a Global Trend," *National Geographic*, June 26, 2019, https://www.nationalgeographic.com/ environment/2019/06/kids-suing-governments-about-climate-growing-trend/; John Schwartz, "Judges Give Both Sides a Grilling in Youth Climate Case Against the Government," *The New York Times*, June 4, 2019, https:// www.nytimes.com/2019/06/04/climate/climate-lawsuit-juliana.html

31   Bruna Fetter, "Documenta 14: What Can We Still Learn from Art?," *PORTO ARTE: Revista de Artes Visuais* 22, no. 37 (December 2017): 289, https://doi. org/10.22456/2179-8001.80137; Mary Anne Francis, "Documenta 14, Kassel 10 June–17 September 2017," *Journal of Visual Art Practice* 17, 1 (January 2, 2018): 126–28, https://doi.org/10.1080/14702029.2017.1366695

32 "'Parthenon of Books' Constructed from 100,000 Banned Books Rises at Nazi Book Burning Site in Germany," *ArchDaily*, July 10, 2017, http://www.archdaily.com/875525/parthenon-of-books-constructed-from-100000-banned-books-rises-at-nazi-book-burning-site-in-germany

33 Philip Larratt-Smith, "Marta Minujín in New York (Interview)," *Arte Al Día*, 2010, http://www.artealdia.com/International/Contents/Artists/Interview_-_Marta_Minujin

34 Victoria Verlichak, "Marta Minujín," *Art Nexus*, 2010, http://artnexus.com/Notice_View.aspx?DocumentID=21029

35 Jerome Roos, *Why Not Default?: The Political Economy of Sovereign Debt* (Princeton, NJ and London: Princeton University Press, 2018).

36 Georgios Papadopoulos, "Documenta 14 and the Question of Colonialism: Defending an Impossible Position Between Athens and Kassel," *Journal of Visual Art Practice*, October 21, 2019, 1–18, https://doi.org/10.1080/14702029.2019.1676996

37 Yanis Varoufakis, *Adults in the Room* (Farrar, Straus and Giroux, 2018).

38 Roos, *Why Not Default?*

39 Varoufakis, *Adults in the Room.*

40 Heiner Flassbeck and Costas Lapavitsas, *Against the Troika: Crisis and Austerity in the Eurozone* (London and New York, NY: Verso, 2015).

41 Varoufakis, *Adults in the Room.*

42 Roos, *Why Not Default?*

43 "Preliminary Report" (Athens: Truth Committee on Public Debt, 2015), http://cadtm.org/IMG/pdf/Report.pdf

44 Larry Elliott, "What was Good for Germany in 1953 is Good for Greece in 2015," *The Guardian*, July 6, 2015, http://www.theguardian.com/business/2015/jul/06/germany-1953-greece-2015-economic-marshall-plan-debt-relief

45 Bello, *Capitalism's Last Stand?: Deglobalization in the Age of Austerity* (London and New York: Pluto).

46 Flassbeck and Lapavitsas, *Against the Troika.*

47 Ndikumana and Boyce, *Africa's Odious Debts*; Toussaint, *The Debt System.*

48 Reece Jones, *Violent Borders: Refugees and the Right to Move* (London and New York, NY: Verso, 2017); Krystian Woznicki, *Fugitive Belonging* (Berlin: Diamond Paper, 2018).

49 Mark Bergfeld, "Germany: In the Eye of the Storm," in *Europe in Revolt*, ed. Catarina Príncipe and Bhaskar Sunkara (Chicago, IL: Haymarket Books, 2016), 115–27.

50 Mark Bergfeld, "Germany's Willkommenskultur: Trade Unions, Refugees and Labour Market Integration," *Global Labour Journal* 8, 1 (January 31, 2017), https://doi.org/10.15173/glj.v8i1.3131

51 "After 16 Refugees Drown, Greeks Rally Against EU-Turkey Swap Deal," *National Herald*, March 18, 2018, https://www.thenationalherald.com/194160/after-16-refugees-drown-greeks-rally-against-eu-turkey-swap-deal/

52 Patrick Wintour, "Germany's Refugee Response Not Guilt-Driven, Says Wolfgang Schäuble," *The Guardian*, March 4, 2016, http://www.theguardian.

com/world/2016/mar/04/germanys-refugee-response-not-guilt-driven-says-wolfgang-schauble

53 Burt Neuborne, "Holocaust Reparations Litigation: Lessons for the Slavery Reparations Movement," *New York University Annual Survey of American Law* 58 (2003): 615.

54 Yardena Schwartz, "Frauke Petry, the New Face of Germany's Anti-Immigrant Right, Talks to Tablet," *Tablet Magazine*, February 7, 2017, http://www.tabletmag.com/jewish-news-and-politics/224027/frauke-petry-tablet-interview; For an English equivalent, see Douglas Murray, *The Strange Death of Europe: Immigration, Identity, Islam*, Updated ed. (London and New York, NY: Bloomsbury, 2018).

55 Mohammad-Mahmoud Mohamedou, *A Theory of ISIS: Political Violence and the Transformation of the Global Order* (London and New York: Pluto Press, 2018).

56 Beverly Crawford, "It's the German Economy, Stupid! Economic Inequality, Not Immigration, Explains Far Right Rise in Germany," *The Berkeley Blog*, September 27, 2017, http://blogs.berkeley.edu/2017/09/27/its-the-german-economy-stupid-economic-inequality-not-immigration-explains-the-rise-of-the-far-right-in-germany/

57 Cas Mudde, "What the Stunning Success of AfD Means for Germany and Europe" *The Guardian*, September 24, 2017, https://www.theguardian.com/commentisfree/2017/sep/24/germany-elections-afd-europe-immigration-merkel-radical-right

58 Henri Neuendorf, "Germany's Far-Right Populist AfD Party Sues Documenta Over Financial Irregularities," *artnet News*, October 24, 2017, https://news.artnet.com/art-world/afd-documenta-lawsuit-1126277

59 Kate Müser, "Right-Wing AfD Politician Calls pro-Refugee Artwork 'disfiguring'" *DW*, August 17, 2017, http://www.dw.com/en/right-wing-afd-politician-calls-pro-refugee-artwork-disfiguring/a-40137498

60 "Documenta 14 Artists Pen Second Open Letter Defending Exhibition," *Art Forum*, December 1, 2017, https://www.artforum.com/news/documenta-14-artists-pen-second-open-letter-defending-exhibition-72702

61 Catherine Hickley, "Documenta Obelisk, Dismantled Last Week, to Remain in Kassel after All," The *Art Newspaper*, October 12, 2018, http://www.theartnewspaper.com/news/documenta-obelisk-dismantled-last-week-to-remain-in-kassel-after-all

62 For a systematic discussion of the similarities and differences, see Roos, *Why Not Default?*

63 Papadopoulos, "Documenta 14 and the Question of Colonialism."

64 See Haiven, *Art after Money, Money after Art: Creative Strategies Against Financialization.*

65 Jennifer Fisher and Jim Drobnick, "Nightsense," *Public* 23 (2012): 35–63.

66 Pierre Bélanger, ed., *Extraction Empire: Undermining the Systems, States, and Scales of Canada's Global Resource Empire, 2017–1217* (Cambridge, MA: MIT Press, 2018), 178–79.

67 Julie Nagam, "(Re)Mapping the Colonized Body: The Creative Interventions of Rebecca Belmore in the Cityscape," *American Indian Culture and Research Journal* 35, 4 (January 2011): 147–66, https://doi.org/10.17953/aicr.35.4.473083132022555l

68 Sylvia Van Kirk, *Many Tender Ties: Women in Fur-Trade Society, 1670–1870* (Norman, OK: University of Oklahoma Press, 1983).

69 Anishinaabe and Cree are Indigenous nations. Settler is a politicized term used to refer to non-Indigenous people, especially those of European ancestry.

70 Pow-wows are cultural gatherings that occur throughout Turtle Island (North America).

71 Sherene Razack, ed., *Race, Space, and the Law: Unmapping a White Settler Society* (Toronto: Between the Lines, 2002).

72 Haiven, "The Uses of Financial Literacy: Financialization, the Radical Imagination, and the Unpayable Debts of Settler-Colonialism" *Cultural Politics* (2017) 13 (3): 348–369.

73 Haiven, "The Uses of Financial Literacy".

74 Ian Baucom, *Specters of the Atlantic: Finance Capital, Slavery, and Philosophy of History* (Durham, NC: Duke University Press, 2005); Zenia Kish and Justin Leroy, "Bonded Life," *Cultural Studies* 29, 5–6 (September 2015): 630–51; Anita Rupprecht, "'Inherent Vice': Marine Insurance, Slave Ship Rebellion and the Law," *Race & Class* 57, 3 (2016): 31–44.

75 Brenna Bhandar, *Colonial Lives of Property: Law, Land and Racial Regimes of Ownership* (Durham, NC and London: Duke University Press, 2018); Rachel O'Reilly, "Dematerializations of the Land/Water Object," *E-Flux* 90 (2018), http://www.e-flux.com/journal/90/191918/dematerializations-of-the-land-water-object/; Park, "Money, Mortgages, and the Conquest of America."

76 Fran Schechter, "Belmore on Bay," *NOW Magazine*, September 30, 2009, https://nowtoronto.com/art/story.cfm%3Fcontent%3D171532; see also Kathryn Yuen, "Nuit Blanche: Illuminating the Spectacular and the Site-Specific," *Imaginations: Journal of Cross-Cultural Image Studies/Revue d'Études Interculturelle de l'Image* 7, no. 2 (2017).

77 Patrick Wolfe, "Settler Colonialism and the Elimination of the Native," *Journal of Genocide Research* 8, no. 4 (2006): 387–409.

78 Avery F. Gordon, *Ghostly Matters: Haunting and the Sociological Imagination*, New edition (Minneapolis, MN and London: University of Minnesota Press, 2008); Tuck and Ree, "A Glossary of Haunting,"

79 Alain Deneault and William Sacher, *Imperial Canada Inc.*, trans. Fred A. Reed and Robin Philpot (Vancouver: Talon, 2012); Todd Gordon and Jeffery R. Webber, *Blood of Extraction: Canadian Imperialism in Latin America*, (Halifax and Winnipeg: Fernwood, 2016).

80 Bélanger, *Extraction Empire*.

81 James Anaya, "The Situation of Indigenous Peoples in Canada," in *Report of the Special Rapporteur on the Rights of Indigenous Peoples*, A/HRC/27/52/Add.2, 2014, http://unsr.jamesanaya.org/country-reports/the-situation-of-indigenous-peoples-in-canada; "Out of Sight, Out of Mind: Gender,

Indigenous Rights, and Energy Development in Northeast British Columbia, Canada" (Amnesty International, 2016), https://www.amnesty.ca/outofsight; Insiya Mankani, "Canada Should Back Up Words With Action on Indigenous Rights," *Human Rights Watch*, June 21, 2019, https://www.hrw.org/news/2019/06/21/canada-should-back-words-action-indigenous-rights

82   Robert P. C. Joseph, *21 Things You May Not Know About the Indian Act: Helping Canadians Make Reconciliation with Indigenous Peoples a Reality* (Port Coquitlam, BC: Indigenous Relations Press, 2018).

83   "Honouring the Truth, Reconciling the Future: Final Report" (Ottawa: The Truth and Reconciliation Commission of Canada, 2015), http://www.trc.ca/websites/trcinstitution/File/2015/Honouring_the_Truth_Reconciling_for_the_Future_July_23_2015.pdf

84   Shiri Pasternak, "How Capitalism Will Save Colonialism: The Privatization of Reserve Lands in Canada" *Antipode* 47, 1 (2015): 179–96; Shiri Pasternak, "The Fiscal Body of Sovereignty: To 'Make Live' in Indian Country," *Settler Colonial Studies* 6, 4 (2016): 317–38.

85   Arthur Manuel and Ronald M. Derrickson, *Unsettling Canada: A National Wake-up Call* (Toronto: Between the Lines, 2015).

86   Isabel Altamirano-Jiménez, *Indigenous Encounters with Neoliberalism: Place, Women, and the Environment in Canada and Mexico*, 2013; Melanie Sommerville, "Naturalising Finance, Financialising Natives: Indigeneity, Race, and 'Responsible' Agricultural Investment in Canada," *Antipode*, 2018, https://doi.org/10.1111/anti.12395

87   Thomas Flanagan, André Le Dressay, and Christopher Alcantara, *Beyond the Indian Act: Restoring Aboriginal Property Rights* (Montréal; Ithaca, NY: McGill-Queen's University Press, 2010).

88   Glen Coulthard, *Red Skin, White Masks: Rejecting the Colonial Politics of Recognition* (Minneapolis, MN, and London: University of Minnesota Press, 2014); Audra Simpson, *Mohawk Interruptus: Political Life across the Borders of Settler States* (Durham, NC: Duke University Press, 2014); Wolfe, "Settler Colonialism and the Elimination of the Native."

89   Leanne Betasamosake Simpson, *As We Have Always Done: Indigenous Freedom through Radical Resistance* (Minneapolis, MN, and London: University of Minnesota Press, 2017).

90   Kathleen L. Ehrhardt, "Copper Working Technologies, Contexts of Use, and Social Complexity in the Eastern Woodlands of Native North America," *Journal of World Prehistory* 22, 3 (September 2009): 213.

91   Michelle Murphy, "Alterlife and Decolonial Chemical Relations," *Cultural Anthropology* 32, no. 4 (2017): 494–503.

92   Paula Chakravartty and Denise Ferreira da Silva, "Accumulation, Dispossession, and Debt: The Racial Logic of Global Capitalism – An Introduction," *American Quarterly* 64, no. 3 (2012): 361–85; Jackie Wang, *Carceral Capitalism* (Los Angeles, CA: Semiotext(e), 2018).

93   See also Alyosha Goldstein, "Finance and Foreclosure in the Colonial Present," *Radical History Review* 118 (2014): 42–63; Wang, *Carceral Capitalism*.

94 Haiven, "The Uses of Financial Literacy."

95 Daniel Paul, *We Were Not the Savages: Collision Between European and Native American Civilization* (Blackpoint, NS: Fernwood, 2006); Manuel and Derrickson, *Unsettling Canada.*

96 Deneault and Sacher, *Imperial Canada Inc.*; Anna Stanley, "Aligning Against Indigenous Jurisdiction: Worker Savings, Colonial Capital, and the Canada Infrastructure Bank," *Environment and Planning D: Society and Space* 37, 6 (December 2019): 1138–56, https://doi.org/10.1177/0263775819855404

97 Brenna Bhandar, "Possession, Occupation and Registration: Recombinant Ownership in the Settler Colony," *Settler Colonial Studies* 6, 2 (April 2, 2016): 119–32, https://doi.org/10.1080/2201473X.2015.1024366

98 Gloria Galloway, "First Nations Leaders Want to Rethink Residential Schools Agreement," *The Globe and Mail*, May 9, 2016, https://www.theglobeandmail.com/news/politics/first-nations-leaders-want-to-rethink-residential-schools-agreement/article29948063/

99 Haiven, "The Uses of Financial Literacy".

100 Coulthard, *Red Skin, White Masks.*

101 Marc-André Cossette, "Fix First Nations Child Welfare System Now, Says Cindy Blackstock," *CBC*, December 2, 2017, http://www.cbc.ca/news/politics/blackstock-philpott-children-welfare-1.4420658

102 Shiri Pasternak, *Grounded Authority: The Algonquins of Barriere Lake Against the State* (Minneapolis, MN: University of Minnesota Press, 2017).

103 Adam J. Barker, "'A Direct Act of Resurgence, a Direct Act of Sovereignty': Reflections on Idle No More, Indigenous Activism, and Canadian Settler Colonialism," *Globalizations* 12, no. 1 (January 2015): 43–65; Joanne Barker, ed., *Critically Sovereign: Indigenous Gender, Sexuality, and Feminist Studies* (Durham, NC: Duke University Press, 2017); Leanne Betasamosake Simpson, *As We Have Always Done: Indigenous Freedom through Radical Resistance* (Minneapolis, MN: University of Minnesota Press, 2017).

104 Graeber, *Debt: The First 5000 Years.*

105 Max Haiven, *Crises of Imagination, Crises of Power: Capitalism, Creativity and the Commons* (London and New York, NY: Zed, 2014).

106 Saidiya Hartman, *Scenes of Subjection: Terror, Slavery, and Self-Making in Nineteenth-Century America* (Oxford and New York, NY: Oxford University Press, 1997).

107 W. E. B. Du Bois, *Black Reconstruction in America, 1860–1880* (New York, NY: The Free Press, 1998).

108 Hartman, *Scenes of Subjection*, 126.

109 Hartman, *Scenes of Subjection*, 140.

110 Hartman, *Scenes of Subjection*, 129.

111 Hartman, *Scenes of Subjection*, 131.

112 Hartman, *Scenes of Subjection*, 131–32.

113 Hartman, *Scenes of Subjection*, 131–32.

114 Coates, "The Case for Reparations"; see also Ama Biney, "What Should Reparations for Slavery Entail?," *Pambazuka*, December 15, 2016, https://www.pambazuka.org/pan-africanism/what-should-reparations-slavery-

entail; Robin D.G. Kelly, "'A Day of Reckoning': *Dreams of Reparations*," in *Freedom Dreams: The Black Radical Imagination* (Boston, MA: Beacon, 2002).

115 See also Keeanga-Yamahtta Taylor, *Race for Profit: How Banks and the Real Estate Industry Undermined Black Homeownership* (Chapel Hill, NC: University of North Carolina Press, 2019).

116 Chakravartty and da Silva, "Accumulation, Dispossession, and Debt."

117 Hartman, *Scenes of Subjection*, 368.

118 Hartman, *Scenes of Subjection*, 370–71.

AHAB'S COIN, OR MOBY DICK'S CURRENCIES?

1 C. L. R. James, *Mariners, Renegades, and Castaways: The Story of Herman Melville and the World We Live In* (Hanover, NH: University Press of New England, 1952).

2 Michel Foucault, "Of Other Spaces," trans. Jay Miskowiec, *Diacritics* 16, no. 1 (1986): 22–27, https://doi.org/10.2307/464648

3 Marcus Rediker, *The Slave Ship: A Human History* (New York, NY: Penguin, 2008).

4 See also Peter Linebaugh and Marcus Rediker, *The Many-Headed Hydra: Sailors, Slaves, Commoners and the Hidden History of the Revolutionary Atlantic* (Boston, MA: Beacon, 2000).

5 Giorgio Agamben, *State of Exception*, trans. Kevin Attell (Chicago, IL: University of Chicago Press, 2005); Cesare Casarino, *Modernity at Sea: Melville, Marx, Conrad in Crisis* (Minneapolis, MN: University of Minnesota Press, 2002).

6 Linebaugh and Rediker, *The Many-Headed Hydra*.

7 Roxanne Dunbar-Ortiz, *An Indigenous Peoples' History of the United States* (Boston, MA: Beacon, 2015).

8 Slavoj Žižek, *The Plague of Fantasies* (London: Verso, 1997).

9 Michael Fuchs, "'What If Nature Were Trying to Get Back at Us?': Animals as Agents of Nature's Revenge in Horror Cinema," in *American Revenge Narratives: A Collection of Critical Essays*, ed. Kyle Wiggins (BerCham: 2018), 177–206, https://doi.org/10.1007/978-3-319-93746-5_8

10 Jennifer Schell, "Polluting and Perverting Nature: The Vengeful Animals of Frogs," in *Animal Horror Cinema: Genre, History and Criticism*, ed. Katarina Gregersdotter, Johan Höglund, and Nicklas Hållén (London: Palgrave Macmillan UK, 2015), 58–75, https://doi.org/10.1057/9781137496393_4; Nicole Matthews and Catherine Simpson, "Editorial: Nature Strikes Back! Genres of Revenge in the Anthropocene," *Australian Humanities Review* 57 (2014): 21–24.

11 See Jason W. Moore, *Capitalism in the Web of Life: Ecology and the Accumulation of Capital* (London and New York: Verso, 2015).

12 Richard Ellis, *The Great Sperm Whale: A Natural History of the Ocean's Most Magnificent and Mysterious Creature* (Lawrence, KS: University of Kansas Press, 2011).

13 Erich Fromm, *The Fear of Freedom* (London: Routledge, 2001); Herbert Marcuse, *Eros and Civilization: A Philosophical Inquiry into Freud with a New Preface by the Author* (Boston, MA: Beacon, 1974).
14 Mark Fisher, *Capitalist Realism: Is There No Alternative?* (London: Zero Books, 2009).

3. MONEY AS A MEDIUM OF VENGEANCE

1 Wang, Jackie. *Carceral Capitalism* (Los Angeles, CA: Semiotext(e), 2018).
2 Melinda Cooper, *Family Values: Between Neoliberalism and the New Social Conservatism,* (New York, NY: Zone Books, 2017).
3 See Max Haiven, "The Crypt of Art, the Decryption of Money, the Encrypted Common and the Problem of Cryptocurrencies," in *Moneylab Reader 2*, ed. Inte Gloerich, Geert Lovink, and Patricia De Vries (Amsterdam: Institute of Network Cultures, 2018), 121–37.
4 Charles C. Mann, *1491: New Revelations of the Americas Before Columbus,* (New York, NY: Vintage, 2006).
5 Roxanne Dunbar-Ortiz, *An Indigenous Peoples' History of the United States* (Boston, MA: Beacon, 2015).
6 Daniel Paul, *We Were Not the Savages: Collision Between European and Native American Civilization* (Blackpoint, NS: Fernwood, 2006); George S. Snyderman, "The Functions of Wampum," *Proceedings of the American Philosophical Society* 98, no. 6 (1954): 469–94.
7 Brenna Bhandar, *Colonial Lives of Property: Law, Land and Racial Regimes of Ownership* (Durham, NC and London: Duke University Press, 2018); Aileen Moreton-Robinson, *The White Possessive: Property, Power, and Indigenous Sovereignty,* (Minneapolis, MN: University of Minnesota Press, 2015).
8 See Nick Estes, *Our History Is the Future: Standing Rock Versus the Dakota Access Pipeline, and the Long Tradition of Indigenous Resistance* (London and New York, NY: Verso, 2019).
9 Lynn Gehl, *The Truth That Wampum Tells: My Debwewin on the Algonquin Land Claims Process* (Halifax: Fernwood Publishing, 2014); Lois Scozzari, "The Significance of Wampum to Seventeenth Century Indians in New England," *Hartford World History Archives*, 1997, http://www.hartford-hwp.com/archives/41/037.html
10 Louis Jordan, "Money Substitutes in New Netherland and Early New York," University of Notre Dame, Department of Special Collections, 2017, https://coins.nd.edu/colcoin/colcoinintros/NNWampum.html
11 Audra Simpson, *Mohawk Interruptus: Political Life Across the Borders of Settler States* (Durham, NC: Duke University Press, 2014); Bruce E. Johansen, *Forgotten Founders: Benjamin Franklin, the Iroquois and the Rationale for the American Revolution* (Ipswich, MA: Gambit, 1982), https://ratical.org/many_worlds/6Nations/FF.html
12 Kayanesenh Paul Williams, *Kayanerenkó:wa: The Great Law of Peace* (Winnipeg: University of Manitoba Press, 2018).

13 David Graeber, *Toward an Anthropological Theory of Value: The False Coin of Our Own Dreams* (New York, NY: Palgrave, 2001); George S. Snyderman, "The Functions of Wampum in Iroquois Religion," *Proceedings of the American Philosophical Society* 98, no. 6 (1954): 469–94.

14 Gehl, *The Truth That Wampum Tells*; Penelope Myrtle Kelsey, "Wampum and the Future of Hodinöhsö:ni' Narrative Epistemology," in *Reading the Wampum: Essays on Hodinöhsö:ni' Visual Code and Epistemological Recovery*, The Iroquois and Their Neighbors (Syracuse, NY: Syracuse University Press, 2014), 103–12; Richard Cullen Rath, "Hearing Wampum: The Senses, Mediation, and the Limits of Analogy," in *Colonial Mediascapes: Sensory Worlds of the Early Americas*, ed. Matt Cohen (Lincoln, NE: University of Nebraska Press, 2014), 290–321. On the many contemporary uses and resonances of wampum, I highly recommend Dutch-American artist Renée Ridgway's phenomenal, immersive work *Wampum World* on the subject: wampumworld.net

15 Margaret M. Bruchac, "Broken Chains of Custody: Possessing, Dispossessing, and Repossessing Lost Wampum Belts," *Proceedings of the American Philosophical Society* 162, no. 1 (2018): 56–105; David Murray, "Wampum," in *Indian Giving: Economies of Power in Indian-White Exchanges*, (Amherst, MA: University of Massachusetts Press, 2000), 116–40.

16 David Graeber, "Wampum and Social Creativity Among the Iroquois," in *Toward an Anthropological Theory of Value: The False Coin of Our Own Dreams* (New York, NY: Palgrave, 2001), 117–50.

17 Gehl, *The Truth That Wampum Tells*; Susan M. Hill, *The Clay We Are Made of: Haudenosaunee Land Tenure on the Grand River* (Winnipeg: University of Manitoba Press, 2017); Simpson, *Mohawk Interruptus*.

18 Paul Otto, "Henry Hudson, the Munsees, and the Wampum Revolution," in *The Worlds of the Seventeenth-Century Hudson Valley* (Albany, NY: SUNY Press, 2014).

19 K-Sue Park, "Money, Mortgages, and the Conquest of America: Money, Mortgages, and the Conquest of America," *Law & Social Inquiry* 41, 4 (2016): 1006–35.

20 Scozzari, "The Significance of Wampum."

21 See Jessica R. Cattelino, "From Locke to Slots: Money and the Politics of Indigeneity," *Comparative Studies in Society and History* 60, no. 2 (April 2018): 274–307.

22 Park, "Money, Mortgages, and the Conquest of America."

23 M. Schmidt, "Entangled Economies: New Netherland's Dual Currency System and Its Relation to Iroquois Monetary Practice," *Ethnohistory* 62, no. 2 (January 1, 2015): 195–216.

24 Paul, *We Were Not the Savages.*

25 Mary W. Herman, "Wampum as a Money in Northeast North America," *Ethnohistory* 3, 1 (1956): 21–33.

26 Elizabeth S. Peña, "Production in New Netherland and Colonial New York: The Historical and Archaeological Context" (PhD thesis, Boston University, 1990).

27 Paul Otto, "Wampum: The Transfer and Creation of Rituals on the Early American Frontier," in *Ritual Dynamics and the Science of Ritual*, ed. Axel Michaels (Wiesbaden: Harrassowitz Verlag, 2010), 177–88; Scozzari, "The Significance of Wampum to Seventeenth Century Indians in New England."

28 Murray, "Wampum."

29 Park, "Money, Mortgages, and the Conquest of America."

30 George Price, "Wampumpeag| The Impact of the 17th Century Wampum Trade on Native Culture in Southern New England and New Netherlands" (MA thesis, Department of History, University of Montana, 1996), https://scholarworks.umt.edu/etd/4042

31 Park, "Money, Mortgages, and the Conquest of America."

32 Bruchac, "Broken Chains of Custody"; Murray, "Wampum."

33 Cattelino, "From Locke to Slots."

34 Park, "Money, Mortgages, and the Conquest of America."

35 See also Bhandar, *Colonial Lives of Property*.

36 Marc Shell, *Wampum and the Origins of American Money* (Chicago, IL and London: University of Illinois Press, 2013).

37 On the vital importance of European (mis)readings of North American indigenous practices for the foundational thinking of modernity and the enlightenment, see Robbie Richardson, *The Savage and Modern Self: North American Indians in Eighteenth-Century British Literature and Culture* (Toronto: University of Toronto Press, 2019), https://doi.org/10.3138/9781487517946

38 Niall Ferguson, *The Ascent of Money: A Financial History of the World* (New York, NY: Penguin, 2008), 2.

39 Ferguson, *The Ascent of Money*, 13.

40 Ferguson, *The Ascent of Money*, 13.

41 See Michael Perelman, *The Invention of Capitalism: Classical Political Economy and the Secret History of Primitive Accumulation* (Durham, NC and London: Duke University Press, 2000).

42 Steven Pinker, *The Better Angels of Our Nature: Why Violence Has Declined* (New York, NY: Penguin, 2012).

43 Kunal Purohit, "As Debt Grows, More Indian Women Farmers Taking Their Lives," *Al-Jazeera English*, November 4, 2019, https://www.aljazeera.com/indepth/features/farm-debt-grows-indian-women-farmers-lives-191023193523782.html

44 For a range of such positions, see Gerald Schneider and Nils Petter Gleditsch, eds., *Assessing the Capitalist Peace* (London: Routledge, 2013).

45 Joseph Vogl, *The Ascendancy of Finance* (Cambridge and Malden, MA: Polity Press, 2017).

46 Michael Hardt and Antonio Negri, *Empire* (Cambridge, MA: Harvard University Press, 2000).

47 David Graeber, *Debt: The First 5000 Years* (New York, NY: Melville House, 2011).

48 Anita Nelson, *Marx's Concept of Money: The God of Commodities* (London and New York, NY: Routledge, 1999).

49 Costas Lapavitsas, *Political Economy of Money and Finance* (London and Basingstoke: Macmillan, 1999).

50 David Harvey, *The Limits to Capital*, 2nd ed. (London and New York, NY: Verso, 2006); See also Max Haiven, "Finance as Capital's Imagination?: Reimagining Value and Culture in an Age of Fictitious Capital and Crisis," *Social Text* 108 (2011): 93–124.

51 Bue Rübner Hansen, "Surplus Population, Social Reproduction, and the Problem of Class Formation," *Viewpoint* 5 (2015), https://viewpointmag.com/2015/10/31/surplus-population-social-reproduction-and-the-problem-of-class-formation/

52 Ruth Wilson Gilmore, *Golden Gulag: Prisons, Surplus, Crisis, and Opposition in Globalizing California*, (Berkeley, CA: University of California Press, 2007).

53 See Max Haiven, *Art after Money, Money after Art: Creative Strategies Against Financialization* (London and New York: Pluto, 2018), 50–63.

54 James C Scott, *Domination and the Arts of Resistance: Hidden Transcripts* (New Haven, CT: Yale University Press, 1990).

55 Jennine Hurl-Eamon, "Love Tokens: Objects as Memory for Plebeian Women in Early Modern England," *Early Modern Women* 6 (2011): 181–86; Eleanor Conlin Casella, "Enmeshed Inscriptions: Reading the Graffiti of Australia's Convict Past," *Australian Archaeology* 78 no. 1 (2014): 108–12; Michele Field and Timothy Millett, *Convict Love Tokens: The Leaden Hearts the Convicts Left Behind* (Adelaide: Wakefield, 1998).

56 Conlin Casella, "Enmeshed Inscriptions"; Field and Millett, *Convict Love Tokens*.

57 Peter Linebaugh, *The London Hanged: Crime and Civil Society in the Eighteenth Century* (Cambridge and New York, NY: Cambridge University Press, 1992).

58 Kirsty Reid ed., *Gender, Crime and Empire: Convicts, Settlers and the State in Early Colonial Australia* (Manchester: Manchester University Press, 2012).

59 Field and Millett, *Convict Love Tokens*.

60 Linebaugh, *The London Hanged*.

61 E. P. Thompson, *The Making of the English Working Class* (New York, NY: Pantheon Books, 1968).

62 Perelman, *The Invention of Capitalism*.

63 Linebaugh, *The London Hanged*.

64 George Caffentzis, *Clipped Coins, Abused Words and Civil Government: John Locke's Philosophy of Money* (New York, NY: Autonomedia, 1989).

65 Ian Haywood, *Romanticism and Caricature* (Cambridge: Cambridge University Press, 2013), 33–57; Paul Crosthwaite, Peter Knight, and Nicky Marsh eds., *Show me the Money: The Image of Finance, 1700 to the Present* (Manchester: Manchester University Press, 2014).

66 David Blaazer, "Reading the Notes: Thoughts on the Meaning of British Paper Money," *Humanities Research* 1 (1999): 39–54.

67 Reid, *Gender, Crime and Empire*.

68 Patel and Moore, *The History of the World in Seven Cheap Things* (Berkeley: University of California Press, 2018).

69 Andrea Smith, *Conquest: Sexual Violence and American Indian Genocide* (Cambridge, MA: South End Press, 2005).

70 See Patel and Moore, *The History of the World in Seven Cheap Things*; especially Chapter 2.

71 Field and Millett, *Convict Love Tokens*.

72 Nelson, *Marx's Concept of Money*.

73 Harry Cleaver, *Rupturing the Dialectic: The Struggle Against Work, Money, and Financialization* (Oakland, CA: AK Press, 2017).

74 Graeber, *Toward an Anthropological Theory of Value*.

75 Max Haiven, *Art After Money*.

76 David Ferris, "More Than A Nickel's Worth: A History of Hobo Nickels and Their Role In American Numismatics," *Professional Coin Grading Service (PCGS)*, November 7, 2000, https://www.pcgs.com/news/More-Than-A-Nickels-Worth-A-History-Of-Hobo-Nickels

77 *The Origin of Hobo Nickels and Early Nickel Carvers, The Original Hobo Nickel Society*, http://www.hobonickels.org/graphics/tri_fold.pdf

78 *Sister of the Road: The Autobiography of Boxcar Bertha as Told to Dr. Ben L. Reitman* (Oakland, CA: AK Press and Nabat, 2002).

79 Joyce Ann Romines, *The Hobo Nickel: An Exclusive Upgrade of Hobo Nickel Artistry* (Virginia Beach, VA: David Lawrence Rare Coins Press, 1996).

80 On the broader culture, politics, and practices of hobos, see Jim Tully, *Beggars of Life: A Hobo Autobiography* (Oakland, CA: AK Press, 2004).

81 *The Origin of Hobo Nickels and Early Nickel Carvers.* Pamphlet published by The Original Hobo Nickel Society, no date, http://www.hobonickels.org/graphics/tri_fold.pdf

82 Miranda Joseph, *Debt to Society: Accounting for Life under Capitalism* (Minneapolis, MN: University of Minnesota Press, 2014).

83 Walter Benjamin, "Theses on the Philosophy of History," in *Illuminations*, ed. Hannah Arendt (New York, NY: Schocken, 1969), 253–64.

84 LaFarge, "Eisbergfreistadt: The Fictive and the Sublime," *Visual Communication Quarterly* 16 (2009): 210–16; Carol Kaimowitz, "Notgeld: German Emergency Currency," *Financial History* (Summer 2013): 8–9; Richard E. Brown, "Meissen Notgeld: Ceramic Currency in a Time of Economic Catastrophe," *Mansfield Ceramics* (2017): 30–33.

85 Laura Phyllis Eccleston, "The Art of Money in the Weimar Republic: German Notgeld 1921–1923" (unpublished MA thesis, Art History, Bowling Green State University, 2011), http://rave.ohiolink.edu/etdc/view?acc_num=bgsu1308537043

86 Hakim Bey, *T.A.Z: The Temporary Autonomous Zone, Ontological Anarchy, Poetic Terrorism*, 2nd ed. (New York, NY: Autonomedia, 2003).

87 LaFarge, "Eisbergfreistadt."

88 See http://kahnselesnick.biz/eisbergfreistadt-installations/

89 Hakim Bey, *T.A.Z: The Temporary Autonomous Zone, Ontological Anarchy, Poetic Terrorism*, 2nd rev. ed. (New York, NY: Autonomedia, 2003).

90 On the radical joy alternative currencies can awaken, see Wendy V. Muñiz, "Public Thinker: Frances Negrón-Muntaner on Puerto Rico, Art, and Decolonial Joy," *Public Books*, December 12, 2019. https://www.publicbooks. org/public-thinker-frances-negron-muntaner-on-puerto-rico-art-and-decolonial-joy/

91 On the potential of such virtuosity in common, see Paolo Virno, *A Grammar of the Multitude: For an Analysis of Contemporary Forms of Life*, trans. Isabella Bertoletti, James Cascaito, and Andrea Casson (Los Angeles, CA: Semiotext (e), 2003).

92 Cornelius Castoriadis, "Radical Imagination and the Social Instituting Imaginary," in David Ames Curtis ed., *The Castoriadis Reader* (Cambridge and New York, NY: Blackwell, 1997, 319–37); Cornelius Castoriadis, "The Logic of Magmas and the Question of Autonomy," in David Ames Curtis, *The Castoriadis Reader* (Cambridge and New York, NY: Blackwell, 1997, 290–318).

93 Tom Hockenhull and Andrew Shore, "Defacing Coins like a Suffragette," *The British Museum Blog*, 2017, https://blog.britishmuseum.org/ defacing-coins-like-a-suffragette

94 Cildo Meireles, "Insertions into Ideological Circuits, 1970–75," in Will Bradley and Charles Esche eds., *Art and Social Change: A Critical Reader* (London: Tate Gallery, 2007, 181–86).

95 See http://www.delappe.net/intervene/rubber-stamp-currency-interventions/

96 Fred Moten and Stefano Harney, *The Undercommons: Fugitive Planning & Black Study* (Wivenhoe, New York, NY and Port Watson: Minor Compositions, 2013).

97 I have chosen here to pursue the even more evocative and powerful language that Moten and Harney draw on of fugitivity, indebted as it is to the struggles of the black diaspora. The reason is simply that it would (and must) require a whole other paper that complicates the notion of the proletarian presented here with a more robust account for race and colonialism.

KHLOÉ KARDASHIAN'S REVENGE BODY, OR THE ZAPATISA NOBODY?

1 On the misogynistic hyper-visibility of fat in the public sphere, and the hyper-invisibilization of the humanity of those deemed fat, see Jeannine A., Gailey *The Hyper(in)Visible Fat Woman: Weight and Gender Discourse in Contemporary Society* (New York, NY and Basingstoke: Palgrave Macmillan, 2014).

2 This is not uncommon in reality television. See for instance, Jérôme Bourdon, "Self-Despotism: Reality Television and the New Subject of Politics." *Framework: The Journal of Cinema and Media* 49, no. 1 (2008): 66–82. https://www.jstor.org/stable/41552512

3 Geert Lovink, *Sad by Design: On Platform Nihilism*, (London and New York: Pluto, 2019).

4   In this, *Revenge Body* is of a piece with a variety of other fat-focused and often highly exploitative and stigmatizing reality TV shows over the past two decades, notably *The Biggest Loser*. See Kate Holland, R. Warwick Blood, and Samantha Thomas, "Viewing *The Biggest Loser*: Modes of Reception and Reflexivity Among Obese People," *Social Semiotics* 25, no. 1 (January 2015): 16–32. https://doi.org/10.1080/10350330.2014.955980; Jina H. Yoo, "No Clear Winner: Effects of The Biggest Loser on the Stigmatization of Obese Persons," *Health Communication* 28, no. 3 (April 1, 2013): 294–303, https://doi.org/10.1080/10410236.2012.684143

5   For an overview, see Raj Patel, *Stuffed and Starved: Markets, Power and the Hidden Battle for the World's Food System* (Toronto: Harper Collins, 2007).

6   See Julie Guthman, *Weighing in: Obesity, Food Justice, and the Limits of Capitalism* (Berkeley, CA: University of California Press, 2011).

7   Gailey, *The Hyper(in)Visible Fat Woman.*

8   See, for instance, Londa L. Schiebinger, ed., *Feminism and the Body* (Oxford and New York, NY: Oxford University Press, 2000).

9   Michel Foucault, "Panopticism," in *Discipline and Punish*, ed. Alan Sheridan (New York, NY: Vintage, 1977, 195–228).

10 See Silvia Federici, *Beyond the Periphery of the Skin: Rethinking, Remaking, Reclaiming the Body in Contemporary Capitalism* (Oakland, CA: PM Press, 2019).

11 See for instance Ronald E. Purser, *McMindfulness: How Mindfulness Became the New Capitalist Spirituality* (London: Zero Books, 2019); Alexis Shotwell, *Against Purity: Living Ethically in Compromised Times* (Minneapolis, MN: University of Minnesota Press, 2016)

12 Kilombo Women's Delegation, "What Does It Mean to Live? Notes from the Zapatistas' First International Gathering of Politics, Art, Sport, and Culture for Women in Struggle," *Viewpoint Magazine*, June 7, 2018, https://www.viewpointmag.com/2018/06/07/what-does-it-mean-to-live-notes-from-the-zapatistas-first-international-gathering-of-politics-art-sport-and-culture-for-women-in-struggle/. The workshops to which the Delegation refers are listed as "gender violence, yoga for kids, stenciling, clay modeling, feminist manifestos, cooperative games, valorization and use of menstrual blood, gender, theater, dance and painting as a mode of healing, sensitivity training, agroecology, [the problem of what is referred to as] corrective rape, reusable menstrual pads, fabrication of personal hygiene tools, decolonizing our hips, a workshop about the body and creative resistances, a muralism workshop, women of color feminism, deconstructing genders, cyberfeminism, bodywork, self-massage workshop, reiki, abstract-figurative art, free writing, engraving, painting, book-making using personal experiences, abortion, bioconstruction, dance therapy, macrobiotic cooking, humor and gender, aroma touch, and reflexology" on the organizing website of the EZLN organizers (http://enlacezapatista. ezln.org.mx/2018/01/31/updates-on-the-first-international-gathering-of-politics-art-sport-and-culture-for-women-in-struggle/).

4. OUR OPIUM WARS

1 Aimé Césaire, *Discourse on Colonialism* (New York, NY: Monthly Review Press, 2000).

2 It is widely acknowledged that Coleridge wrote this poem as a tortured reflection on the experience of opium withdrawal. https://www.poetryfoundation.org/poems/43995/the-pains-of-sleep

3 Dieter Arnold and Adela Oppenheim, "The Temple of Dendur: Architecture and Ritual," *The Met*. https://www.metmuseum.org/about-the-met/curatorial-departments/egyptian-art/temple-of-dendur-50/architecture-and-ritual

4 Joanna Walters, "Artist Nan Goldin Stages Opioids Protest in Metropolitan Museum Sackler Wing," *The Guardian*, March 11, 2018, https://www.theguardian.com/us-news/2018/mar/10/opioids-nan-goldin-protest-metropolitan-museum-sackler-wing

5 Anna Serotta, "Conserving the Temple: A History," *The Met*. https://www.metmuseum.org/about-the-met/curatorial-departments/egyptian-art/temple-of-dendur-50/cleaning-and-conservation

6 David Armstrong, "The Family Trying to Escape Blame for the Opioid Crisis," *The Atlantic*, April 10, 2018. https://www.theatlantic.com/health/archive/2018/04/sacklers-oxycontin-opioids/557525/ Christopher Glazek, "The Secretive Family Making Billions From the Opioid Crisis," *Esquire*, October 16, 2017, https://www.esquire.com/news-politics/a12775932/sackler-family-oxycontin/

7 Joanna Walters, "'I Don't Know How They Live with Themselves' – Artist Nan Goldin Takes on the Billionaire Family behind OxyContin," *The Guardian*, January 22, 2018, http://www.theguardian.com/artanddesign/2018/jan/22/nan-goldin-interview-us-opioid-epidemic-heroin-addict-oxycontin-sackler-family

8 Beth Macy, *Dopesick: Dealers, Doctors, and the Drug Company That Addicted America* (New York, NY: Little, Brown and Co., 2018); Sam Quinones, *Dreamland: The True Tale of America's Opiate Epidemic* (New York, NY: Bloomsbury Press, 2016).

9 Quinones, *Dreamland*; Macy, *Dopesick*.

10 See Hito Steyerl, *Duty Free Art: Art in the Age of Planetary Civil War* (London and New York, NY: Verso, 2017).

11 Evans, Mel, *Artwash: Big Oil and the Arts* (London and New York: Pluto, 2015); Ginia Bellafante, "When Should Cultural Institutions Say No to Tainted Funding?," *The New York Times*, December 6, 2018, https://www.nytimes.com/2018/03/02/nyregion/when-should-cultural-institutions-say-no-to-tainted-funding.html

12 Joel Bakan, *The Corporation: The Pathological Pursuit of Profit and Power*, 2nd ed. (New York, NY: Free Press, 2005); David McNally, *Monsters of the Market: Zombies, Vampires, and Global Capitalism* (Chicago, IL: Haymarket, 2012)

13 David Todd, "John Bowring and the Global Dissemination of Free Trade," *The Historical Journal*, 51 (2008) https://doi.org/10.1017/S0018246X08006754

14 Ibid.
15 Frank Sanello and W. Travis Hanes III, *Opium Wars: The Addiction of One Empire and the Corruption of Another* (Naperville, IL: Sourcebooks, 2004).
16 Nick Robins, *The Corporation That Changed the World: How the East India Company Shaped the Modern Multinational*, 2nd ed. (London: Pluto Press, 2012).
17 For a brilliant, comprehensive and stimulating portrait of the full social, political and economic scope of the First Opium War, see Amitav Ghosh's trilogy of novels that begin with *Sea of Poppies*.
18 See Macy, *Dopesick*.
19 John Newsinger, *The Blood Never Dried: A People's History of the British Empire* (London: Bookmarks, 2006).
20 Lisa Lowe, *The Intimacies of Four Continents* (Durham, NC: Duke University Press, 2015); Sanello and Hanes III, *Opium Wars*.
21 ibid, 6.
22 ibid, 7.
23 Lowe, *The Intimacies of Four Continents*; Sanello and Hanes, *Opium Wars*.
24 Greg M. Thomas, "The Looting of Yuanming and the Translation of Chinese Art in Europe," *Nineteenth-Century Art Worldwide*, 7 (2008), http://www.19thc-artworldwide.org/autumn08/93-the-looting-of-yuanming-and-the-translation-of-chinese-art-in-europe
25 For a detailed account of this incident in the context of imperial racism, see Lily Cho, "Sweet and Sour: Historic Presence and Diasporic Agency," in *Asian Canadian Studies Reader*, ed. Roalnd Sintos Coloma and Gordon Pon (Toronto: University of Toronto Press, 2017), 279–98.
26 Joanna Walters, "Meet the Sacklers: The Family Feuding over Blame for the Opioid Crisis," *The Guardian*, February 13, 2018, http://www.theguardian.com/us-news/2018/feb/13/meet-the-sacklers-the-family-feuding-over-blame-for-the-opioid-crisis
27 "Elizabeth A. Sackler Supports Nan Goldin in Her Campaign Against OxyContin," *Hyperallergic*, 2018. https://hyperallergic.com/422738/elizabeth-sackler-nan-goldin-opioid-epidemic/
28 Quinones, *Dreamland*.
29 David Herzberg, 2006. "'The Pill You Love Can Turn on You' Feminism, Tranquilizers, and the Valium Panic of the 1970s," *American Quarterly* 58, no. 1: 79–103.
30 https://www.cdc.gov/drugoverdose/pdf/pubs/2017-cdc-drug-surveillance-report.pdf
31 Betsy McKay, "U.S. Life Expectancy Falls Further," *Wall Street Journal*, November 29, 2018, https://www.wsj.com/articles/u-s-life-expectancy-falls-further-1543467660
32 Macy, *Dopesick*.
33 Paul E. Knierim, *Tackling Fentanyl: The China Connection* (Washington, DC: US Department of Justice, September 6, 2018), https://www.dea.gov/documents/2018/09/06/paul-e-knierim-tackling-fentanyl-china-connection

34 Halpern, J. Blistein, D., 2019. *Opium: How an Ancient Flower Shaped and Poisoned Our World.* Hachette Books, New York.

35 Ahmad, D.L., 2014. *The Opium Debate and Chinese Exclusion Laws in the Nineteenth-Century American West*; Dominique Brégent-Heald, "Leaky Borders: Smuggling Opium and Chinese Labor in Progressive-Era Motion Pictures," *The Journal of American Culture* 37, 4 (2014): 393–403, https://doi.org/10.1111/jacc.12270; Gary Hoppenstand, "Yellow Devil Doctors and Opium Dens: A Survey of the Yellow Peril Stereotype in Mass Media Entertainment," in *The Popular Culture Reader*, ed. Christopher D. Geist and Jack Nachbar, 3rd ed. (Bowling Green, OH: Bowling Green University Popular Press, 1983), 171–85.

36 Hoppenstand, "Yellow Devil Doctors and Opium Dens.

37 See Christopher Diffee, "Sex and the City: The White Slavery Scare and Social Governance in the Progressive Era," *American Quarterly* 57, no. 2 (2005): 411–37, https://www.jstor.org/stable/40068272; Halpern and Blistein, *Opium.*

38 David T. Courtwright, "Opiate Addiction as a Consequence of the Civil War," *Civil War History* 24, no. 2 (1978): 101–11, https://doi.org/10.1353/cwh.1978.0039

39 Mary Lui, "Saving Young Girls from Chinatown: White Slavery and Woman Suffrage, 1910–1920," *Journal of the History of Sexuality* 18, no. 3 (n.d.), https://doi.org/10.5555/jhs.2009.18.3.393

40 Lowe, 97–98.

41 Barbara Goldberg, "Opioid Abuse Crisis Takes Heavy Toll on U.S. Veterans," *Reuters*, November 10, 2017, https://www.reuters.com/article/us-usa-veterans-opioids-idUSKBN1DA1B2 Vanda Felbab-Brown, "Afghanistan's Opium Production Is through the Roof – Why Washington Shouldn't Overreact," *Brookings Institute*, November 21, 2017, https://www.brookings.edu/blog/order-from-chaos/2017/11/21/afghanistans-opium-production-is-through-the-roof-why-washington-shouldnt-overreact/ Karen H. Seal, Ying Shi, Gregory Cohen, Beth E. Cohen, Shira Maguen, Erin E. Krebs, and others, "Association of Mental Health Disorders With Prescription Opioids and High-Risk Opioid Use in US Veterans of Iraq and Afghanistan," *JAMA*, 307 (2012), 940–47.

42 On opioids and masculinity more broadly, see Phyllis L. Baker, "Paranoids, Factoids, and Opioids: The Social Consequences of the Destruction of Cultural Scripts for Left-Behind Men," *The Sociological Quarterly* 60, no. 1 (January 2019): 1–25.

43 Bruce Einhorn, "America's Crackdown on The Opioid Crisis Hits Tasmania's Poppy Farmers," *Bloomberg*, October 24, 2017, https://www.bloomberg.com/news/articles/2017-10-24/the-u-s-opioid-crisis-hits-tasmania-s-poppy-farmers

44 Quinones, *Dreamland.*

45 Laurent De Sutter, *Narcocapitalism* (Cambridge: Polity Press, 2018).

46 Vivid descriptions of these dynamics can be found in Quinones, *Dreamland* (2016) and Macy, *Dopesick* (2018).

47 See Macy, *Dopesick* (2018); Peters, D.J., Monnat, S.M., Hochstetler, A.L., Berg, M.T., n.d. "The Opioid Hydra: Understanding Overdose Mortality Epidemics and Syndemics Across the Rural-Urban Continuum," *Rural Sociology* n/a. http://doi.org/10.1111/ruso.12307 See also CrimethInc Ex-Workers Collective, "The Opioid Crisis: White Despair and the Scapegoating of People of Color," *CrimethInc*, 2017, https://crimethinc.com/2017/10/09/the-opioid-crisis-how-white-despair-poses-a-threat-to-people-of-color

48 Johnston, G., 2019. "The Kids Are All White: Examining Race and Representation in News Media Coverage of Opioid Overdose Deaths in Canada", *Sociological Inquiry* https://doi.org/10.1111/sion.12269, Keller, Jared, "How America's War on Opioids Underscores the Racial Legacy of the Crack Epidemic," *Pacific Standard*, 2017. https://psmag.com/social-justice/a-tale-of-two-drug-wars, German Lopez, "The Deadliness of the Opioid Epidemic Has Roots in America's Failed Response to Crack," *Vox*, 2017, https://www.vox.com/identities/2017/10/2/16328342/opioid-epidemic-racism-addiction, Julie Netherland and Helena B. Hansen, "The War on Drugs That Wasn't: Wasted Whiteness, 'Dirty Doctors,' and Race in Media Coverage of Prescription Opioid Misuse," *Culture, Medicine, and Psychiatry*, 40 (2016), 664–86.

49 Daniel HoSang and Joseph E. Lowndes, *Producers, Parasites, Patriots: Race and the New Right-Wing Politics of Precarity* (Minneapolis: Univ Of Minnesota Press, 2019); Rebecca Tiger, "Race, Class, and the Framing of Drug Epidemics," *Contexts* 16, no. 4 (November 1, 2017): 46–51.

50 I have chosen not to cite the racist toxic bilge that churns about the internet on this topic.

51 Nadine Ehlers and Leslie R. Hinkson, eds., *Subprime Health: Debt and Race in U.S. Medicine* (Minneapolis, MN: University of Minnesota Press, 2017).

52 See Quinones, *Dreamland*; See also Jordan M. Harrison et al., "Trends in Prescription Pain Medication Use by Race/Ethnicity Among US Adults With Noncancer Pain, 2000–2015," *American Journal of Public Health* 108, 6 (April 19, 2018): 788–90; Kevin Jefferson, Tammie Quest, and Katherine A. Yeager, "Factors Associated with Black Cancer Patients' Ability to Obtain Their Opioid Prescriptions at the Pharmacy," *Journal of Palliative Medicine* 22, no. 9 (March 18, 2019): 1143–48.

53 Jason A. Ford, Melanie Sberna Hinojosa, and Harvey L. Nicholson, "Disability Status and Prescription Drug Misuse among U.S. Adults," *Addictive Behaviors* 85 (October 2018): 64–69; Netherland and Hansen, "White Opioids".

54 Nadia S. Ruta and Samir K. Ballas, "The Opioid Drug Epidemic and Sickle Cell Disease: Guilt by Association," *Pain Medicine*, 17, no. 10 (2016), 1793–98; German Lopez, "Why Are Black Americans Less Affected by the Opioid Epidemic? Racism, Probably," *Vox*, 2016, https://www.vox.com/2016/1/25/10826560/opioid-epidemic-race-black, Carlos, Ballesteros, "Racism Might Have Spared Black and Latino Communities from New Opioid Epidemic, Drug Abuse Expert Says," *Newsweek*, 2017, http://www.

newsweek.com/racism-opiod-epidemic-blacks-latinos-trump-704370
55 Christina Elizabeth Sharpe, *In the Wake: On Blackness and Being* (Durham, NC: Duke University Press, 2016, 10).
56 Sarah Zhang, "The Surgeon Who Experimented on Slaves," *The Atlantic*, 2018, https://www.theatlantic.com/health/archive/2018/04/j-marion-sims/558248/, Harriet A. Washington, *Medical Apartheid: The Dark History of Medical Experimentation on Black Americans from Colonial Times to the Present* (New York, NY: Anchor, 2006).
57 Elaine Denny, *Pain: A Sociological Introduction* (Cambridge: Polity Press, 2017).
58 Netherland and Hansen, "White Opioids"; Netherland and Hansen, "The War on Drugs That Wasn't".
59 See Shannon Monnat, cited in Harrison Jacobs, "The revenge of the 'Oxy electorate' helped fuel Trump's election upset," https://www.businessinsider.com/trump-vote-results-drug-overdose-deaths-2016-11?r=US&IR=T, Shannon M. Monnat, *Deaths of Despair and Support for Trump in the 2016 Presidential Election*, Department of Agriculture, Economics, Sociology and Education Research Briefs (State College, PA: The Pennsylvania State University, December 4, 2016) aese.psu.edu/directory/smm67/Election16.pdf
60 Sam Quinones, "Donald Trump & Opiates in America," *Personal Blog*, 2016, http://samquinones.com/reporters-blog/2016/11/21/donald-trump-opiates-america/ Jacobs, "The Revenge of the 'Oxy Electorate' Helped Fuel Trump's Election Upset".
61 Brianna Ehley, "Trump Campaigned on Defeating the Opioid Crisis. It's Hard to Tell If He's Winning," *Politico*, June 16, 2019, https://politi.co/2WJlPdo
62 Edward Helmore, "Opioids Emerge as Key Sticking Point for US-China Trade Deal," *The Guardian*, November 10, 2019, https://www.theguardian.com/us-news/2019/nov/10/opioids-us-china-trade-deal-trump; Steven Lee Myers, "China Cracks Down on Fentanyl. But Is It Enough to End the U.S. Epidemic?," *The New York Times*, December 1, 2019, sec. World, https://www.nytimes.com/2019/12/01/world/asia/china-fentanyl-crackdown.html
63 Quinones, *Dreamland*; Henry A. Giroux, "Trump and the Legacy of a Menacing Past," *Cultural Studies* 33, no. 4 (July 4, 2019): 711–39, https://doi.org/10.1080/09502386.2018.1557725
64 Jackie Wang, *Carceral Capitalism* (Los Angeles, CA: Semiotext(e), 2018); Naomi Klein, *The Shock Doctrine: The Rise and Fall of Disaster Capitalism* (Toronto, ON: Knopf, 2007).
65 Walter Benjamin, "The Work of Art in the Age of Mechanical Reproduction," in *Illuminations*, ed. by Hannah Arendt (New York, NY: Schocken, 1969), 217–51.
66 Susan Buck-Morss, "Aesthetics and Anaesthetics: Walter Benjamin's Artwork Essay Reconsidered," *October* 62, 1992, 3–41. It's worth noting that this observation was not particularly uncommon in Benjamin's day, when the medical condition of "nervous exhaustion" from the overstimulation of

modern life was a common explanation for mental illness, see De Sutter, *Narcocapitalism*.

67 Catherine Malabou, *What Should We Do with Our Brain?*, trans. by Sebastian Rand (New York, NY: Fordham University Press, 2008).

68 Paul Lewis, "'Our Minds Can Be Hijacked': The Tech Insiders Who Fear a Smartphone Dystopia," *The Guardian*, October 6, 2017, section Technology, http://www.theguardian.com/technology/2017/oct/05/smartphone-addiction-silicon-valley-dystopia

69 Franco Berardi, "Bifo," *The Soul at Work: From Alienation to Autonomy*, trans. by Giuseppina Mecchia and Francesca Cadel (Los Angeles, CA: Semiotext(e), 2009); Carl Cederström and Peter Fleming, *Dead Man Working* (Winchester: Zero Books, 2012); Geert Lovink, *Sad by Design: On Platform Nihilism*, 2019.

70 Sylvia Wynter and Katherine McKittrick, "Unparalleled Catastrophe for Our Species? Or, to Give Humanness a Different Future: Conversations," in *Sylvia Wynter: On Being Human as Praxis*, ed. Katherine McKittrick (Durham NC and London: Duke University Press, 2015), 9–89.

71 Wynter and McKittrick, "Unparalleled Catastrophe for Our Species."

72 For a thoughtful engagement, see Nikolas S. Rose, *Our Psychiatric Future: The Politics of Mental Health* (Cambridge: Polity, 2019), 116–33.

73 Zygmunt Bauman, *Wasted Lives: Modernity and Its Outcasts* (Oxford and Malden, MA: Polity, 2004).

74 Keeanga-Yamahtta Taylor, "No Time for Despair," *Jacobin*, January 28, 2017, https://jacobinmag.com/2017/01/trump-black-lives-racism-sexism-anti-inauguration

75 Robinson, William I. 2018. "The next Economic Crisis: Digital Capitalism and Global Police State." *Race & Class* 60 (1): 77–92.

V'S VENDETTA, OR JOKER'S RETRIBUTION?

1 "Global Study on Homicide: Gender-Related Killing of Women and Girls" (Vienna: United Nations Office on Drugs and Crime, 2019). https://www.unodc.org/documents/data-and-analysis/gsh/Booklet_5.pdf; "A National Epidemic: Fatal Anti-Transgender Violence in the United States" (Washington, DC: The Human Rights Campaign Foundation, 2019), https://assets2.hrc.org/files/assets/resources/AntiTransViolenceReport2019.pdf

2 Silvia Federici, *Caliban and the Witch: Women, Capitalism and Primitive Accumulation* (New York, NY: Autonomedia, 2005); Silvia Federici, *Witches, Witch-Hunting, and Women* (Oakland, CA: PM Press, 2018).

3 Alex Abad-Santos, "The Fight over Joker and the New Movie's 'Dangerous' Message, Explained," *Vox*, September 18, 2019, https://www.vox.com/culture/2019/9/18/20860890/joker-movie-controversy-incel-sjw.

4 Aaron Freedman, "It's Morning in Joker's America," *Jacobin*, October 1, 2019, https://jacobinmag.com/2019/10/joker-reagan-1981-martin-scorsese-king-comedy; Jeet Heer, "'Joker' Brings Class Warfare to the

Big Screen," *The Nation*, October 11, 2019, https://www.thenation.com/article/movie-joker-class/; Micah Uetricht, "Joker Isn't an Ode to the Far Right – It's a Warning against Austerity," *The Guardian*, October 11, 2019, https://www.theguardian.com/commentisfree/2019/oct/10/joker-far-right-warning-austerity

5   Chris Hoke, "Bad Guys with No Backstories Are Our National Addiction," *Medium*, December 4, 2019, https://medium.com/@chrishoke/bad-guys-with-no-backstories-are-our-national-addiction-5b244667b976

6   Franco Bifo Berardi, *Heroes: Mass Murder and Suicide* (London and New York, NY: Verso, 2015).

7   Quoted in Alex Khasnabish, *Zapatismo Beyond Borders: New Imaginations of Political Possibility* (Toronto: University of Toronto Press, 2008), 126–27.

8   For a full account, see E. Gabriella Coleman, *Hacker, Hoaxer, Whistleblower, Spy: The Many Faces of Anonymous* (London and New York, NY: Verso, 2015), especially Chapter 2.

9   On these histories, as well as the significance of masked protest more generally, see Andreas Beer, "Just(Ice) Smiling? Masks and Masking in the Occupy-Wall Street Protests," *European Journal of American Studies* 13, 4 (December, 2018); Paolo Gerbaudo, "Protest Avatars as Memetic Signifiers: Political Profile Pictures and the Construction of Collective Identity on Social Media in the 2011 Protest Wave," *Information, Communication & Society* 18, no. 8 (August 2015): 916–29.

10   Laurie Clarke, "Why Joker Masks Are the Perfect Political Protest Symbol," *Wired*, November 2, 2019, https://www.wired.co.uk/article/joker-masks-protests; Aidan McGarry, "The Joker to Guy Fawkes: Why Protesters around the World Are Wearing the Same Masks," *The Conversation*, November 13, 2019, http://theconversation.com/the-joker-to-guy-fawkes-why-protesters-around-the-world-are-wearing-the-same-masks-126458

11   "Alan Moore: The Last Angry Man (Interview)," MTV.com, September 1, 2006, https://web.archive.org/web/20060901005535/http://www.mtv.com/shared/movies/interviews/m/moore_alan_060315/

5. THE DEAD ZONE

1   This is the subject of Max Haiven, *Cultures of Financialization: Fictitious Capital in Popular Culture and Everyday Life* (London and New York, NY: Palgrave Macmillan, 2014).

2   Henry A. Giroux, "When Schools Become Dead Zones of the Imagination: A Critical Pedagogy Manifesto," *Policy Futures in Education* 12, no. 4 (2014): 491–99; David Graeber, "Dead Zones of the Imagination: On Violence, Bureaucracy, and Interpretive Labor. The 2006 Malinowski Memorial Lecture," *HAU: Journal of Ethnographic Theory* 2, no. 2 (December 19, 2012): 105–28.

3   Stephen King, *The Dead Zone* (London: Hodder, 2011), 177.

4   I have explored the significance of this period, especially the year 1973, in Max Haiven, *Art After Money, Money after Art: Creative Strategies Against Financialization* (London: Pluto, 2018), 64–110.

5 Fredric Jameson, "Cognitive Mapping," in *Marxism and the Interpretation of Culture*, ed. Cary Nelson and Lawrence Grossberg (Chicago, IL and London: University of Illinois Press, 1990), 347–60; See also Alberto Toscano and Jeff Kinkle, *Cartographies of the Absolute* (Winchester: Zero Books, 2015); Robert T. Tally, *Fredric Jameson: The Project of Dialectical Criticism*, Marxism and Culture (London: Pluto Press, 2014).

6 On the causes and consequences of this opacity, see Leigh Claire La Berge, *Scandals and Abstraction: Financial Fiction of the Long 1980s* (New York, NY: Oxford University Press, 2015).

7 Morgan Gstalter, "Stephen King Says Trump's Presidency Is 'scarier' than His Novels," Text, *The Hill*, July 12, 2019, https://thehill.com/blogs/blog-briefing-room/news/452794-stephen-king-says-trumps-presidency-is-scarier-than-one-of-his

8 Walter Benjamin, "Theses on the Philosophy of History," in *Illuminations*, ed. Hannah Arendt (New York, NY: Schocken, 1969), 253–64.

9 Mark Fisher, *Ghosts of My Life: Writings on Depression, Hauntology and Lost Futures* (Winchester: Zero books, 2014); Franco Bifo Berardi, *After the Future*, ed. Gary Genosko and Nicholas Thoburn (Oakland, CA: AK Press, 2011).

10 "NOAA Forecasts Very Large 'Dead Zone' for Gulf of Mexico," National Oceanic and Atmospheric Administration, June 10, 2019, https://www.noaa.gov/media-release/noaa-forecasts-very-large-dead-zone-for-gulf-of-mexico

11 Robert J. Diaz and Rutger Rosenberg, "Spreading Dead Zones and Consequences for Marine Ecosystems," *Science* 321, no. 5891 (August 15, 2008): 926–29, https://doi.org/10.1126/science.1156401

12 Donna Haraway, "Anthropocene, Capitalocene, Plantationocene, Chthulucene: Making Kin," *Environmental Humanities* 6 (2015): 162–63; See also Raj Patel and Jason W. Moore, *The History of the World in Seven Cheap Things* (Berkeley, CA: University of California Press, 2017).

13 Graeber, "Dead Zones of the Imagination."

14 Graeber, "Dead Zones of the Imagination,"112.

15 Giroux, "When Schools Become Dead Zones of the Imagination," 491–92.

16 Giroux, "When Schools Become Dead Zones of the Imagination," 497.

17 See, for instance, Keeanga-Yamahtta Taylor, *Race for Profit: How Banks and the Real Estate Industry Undermined Black Homeownership* (Chapel Hill, NC: University of North Carolina Press, 2019). Carol Anderson, *White Rage: The Unspoken Truth of Our Racial Divide* (New York, NY: Bloomsbury, 2017).

18 Michelle Alexander, *The New Jim Crow: Mass Incarceration in the Age of Colorblindness* (New York, NY: The New Press, 2010); Angela Y. Davis, *Are Prisons Obsolete?* (New York, NY: Seven Stories, 2011); Loïc Wacquant, "Class, Race and Hyperincarceration in Revanchist America," *Socialism and Democracy* 28, no. 3 (September 2014): 35–56.

19 Cam White, "Trading Active and Dead Zones with Binaries," *Benzinga*, May 18, 2016, https://www.benzinga.com/markets/binary-options/16/05/8004618/trading-active-and-dead-zones-with-binaries

20 Frank Pasquale, *The Black Box Society: The Secret Algorithms That Control Money and Information* (Cambridge, MA: Harvard University Press, 2015); Michael A. Peters, "Algorithmic Capitalism in the Epoch of Digital Reason," *Fast Capitalism* 14, 1 (2017), https://doi.org/10.32855/fcapital.201701.012.

21 César Albarrán-Torres, "Gambling with Markets: Stock Trading Apps and the Logic of Gamble-Play," in *Digital Gambling: Theorizing Gamble-Play Media* (London and New York, NY: Routledge, 2018).

22 Costas Lapavitsas, *Profiting Without Producing: How Finance Exploits Us All* (London and New York, NY: Verso, 2013).

23 Walden Bello, Nicola Bullard, and Kamal Malhotra, eds., *Global Finance: New Thinking on Regulating Speculative Capital Markets* (London: Zed, 2000).

24 Christopher Rude, "The Role of Financial Discipline in Imperial Strategy," ed. Leo Panich and Colin Leys, *The Empire Reloaded* 41 (2005): 82–107; Susanne Soederberg, *Debtfare States and the Poverty Industry: Money, Discipline and the Surplus Population* (London and New York, NY: Routledge, 2014).

25 Edward LiPuma and Benjamin Lee, *Financial Derivatives and the Globalization of Risk* (Durham, NC and London: Duke University Press, 2004).

26 Bullard, Bello and Malhotra, *Global Finance*.

27 Frances Thomson and Sahil Dutta, *Financialisation: A Primer*, Updated edition (Amsterdam: The Transnational Institute, 2018), https://www.tni.org/en/publication/financialisation-a-primer

28 Pasquale, *The Black Box Society*.

29 Max Haiven, "Finance as Capital's Imagination?: Reimagining Value and Culture in an Age of Fictitious Capital and Crisis," *Social Text* 108 (2011): 93–124; David Harvey, *The Limits to Capital*, 2nd ed. (London and New York, NY: Verso, 2006); Lapavitsas, *Profiting Without Producing*.

30 Ivan Ascher, *Portfolio Society: On the Capitalist Mode of Prediction* (New York, NY: Zone Books, 2016); Michel Feher, *Rated Agency: Investee Politics in a Speculative Age* (New York, NY: Zone Books, 2018); Annie McClanahan, *Dead Pledges: Debt, Crisis, and Twenty-First-Century Culture* (Stanford, CA and London: Stanford University Press, 2016).

31 Samuel Stein, *Capital City: Gentrification and the Real Estate State* (London and New York, NY: Verso, 2019); Peter Moskowitz, *How to Kill a City: Gentrification, Inequality, and the Fight for the Neighborhood* (New York, NY: Nation Books, 2017).

32 David Harvey, *Rebel Cities: From the Right to the City to the Urban Revolution* (London and New York, NY: Verso, 2012).

33 The Midnight Notes Collective, "New Enclosures," in *Subverting the Present, Imagining the Future: Insurrection, Movement, & Commons*, ed. Werner Bonefeld (New York, NY: Autonomedia, 2009), 13–26.

34 Moskowitz, *How to Kill a City*; Stein, *Capital City*.

35 Sarah Schulman, *The Gentrification of the Mind Witness to a Lost Imagination* (Berkeley, CA: University of California Press, 2012).

36 Manuel B Aalbers, ed., *Subprime Cities: The Political Economy of Mortgage Markets* (New York, NY: Wiley, 2012).
37 Manissa M. Maharawal, "San Francisco's Tech-Led Gentrification: Public Space, Protest, and the Urban Commons," in *City Unsilenced*, ed. Jeffrey Hou and Sabine Knierbein, (New York and London: Routledge 2017). https://doi.org/10.4324/9781315647241-3
38 Vinay Gidwani and Rajyashree N. Reddy, 2011. "The Afterlives of 'Waste': Notes from India for a Minor History of Capitalist Surplus," *Antipode* 43, 5: 1625–58; Traci Brynne Voyles, 2015. *Wastelanding: Legacies of Uranium Mining in Navajo Country* (Minneapolis, MN: University of Minnesota Press); Chris Hedges and Joe Sacco, *Days of Destruction, Days of Revolt* (New York, NY: Nation Books, 2014); Peter C. Little, "On the Micropolitics and Edges of Survival in a Technocapital Sacrifice Zone," *Capitalism Nature Socialism* 28, no. 4 (October 2017): 62–77.
39 "Out of Sight, Out of Mind: Gender, Indigenous Rights, and Energy Development in Northeast British Columbia, Canada" (Amnesty International, 2016), https://www.amnesty.ca/outofsight; "Resource Extraction Projects and Violence Against Indigenous Women," in *Reclaiming Power and Place: The Final Report of the National Inquiry into Missing and Murdered Indigenous Women and Girls* (Ottawa: National Inquiry into Missing and Murdered Indigenous Women and Girls, 2019), 584–94, https://www.mmiwg-ffada.ca/final-report/
40 Sarah Bradshaw, Brian Linneker, and Lisa Overton, "Extractive Industries as Sites of Supernormal Profits and Supernormal Patriarchy?," *Gender & Development* 25, no. 3 (September 2017): 439–54, https://doi.org/10.1080/1355 2074.2017.1379780
41 "Violence on the Land, Violence on Our Bodies: Building an Indigenous Response to Environmental Justice" (Berkeley, CA: Women's Earth Alliance and Native Youth Sexual Health Network, 2017), landbodydefense.org/uploads/files/VLVBReportToolkit_2017.pdf; Christina Hill, Chris Madden, and Nina Collins, "A Guide to Gender Impact Assessment for the Extractive Industries" (Melbourne: Oxfam Australia, 2017), oxfam.org.au/mining-gender; Jacqui True, *The Political Economy of Violence Against Women* (Oxford and New York, NY: Oxford University Press, 2012), 87–93.
42 See Ciaran O'Faircheallaigh and Saleem Ali, *Earth Matters: Indigenous Peoples, the Extractive Industries and Corporate Social Responsibility* (New York and London: Routledge, 2017).
43 Andrea Smith, *Conquest: Sexual Violence and American Indian Genocide* (Cambridge, MA: South End Press, 2005); "Violence on the Land, Violence on Our Bodies"; Joanne Barker, ed., *Critically Sovereign: Indigenous Gender, Sexuality, and Feminist Studies* (Durham, NC: Duke University Press, 2017); Leanne Betasamosake Simpson, *As We Have Always Done: Indigenous Freedom Through Radical Resistance* (Minneapolis, MN: University of Minnesota Press, 2017).
44 Sandro Mezzadra and Brett Neilson, "Extraction, Logistics, Finance: Global Crisis and the Politics of Operations," *Radical Philosophy* 178 (2013): 8–18;

For a fascinating account of the way this entanglement plays out in terms of "fracking" and unconventional oil extraction, see Bethany McLean, *Saudi America: The Truth About Fracking and How It's Changing the World* (New York, NY: Columbia Global Reports, 2018).

45 A. Stanley, "Resilient Settler Colonialism: 'Responsible Resource Development,' 'Flow-Through' Financing, and the Risk Management of Indigenous Sovereignty in Canada," *Environment and Planning A* 48, no. 12 (December 2016): 2422–42, https://doi.org/10.1177/0308518X16660352

46 Jean M. Twenge, "Have Smartphones Destroyed a Generation?," *The Atlantic*, September 2017, https://www.theatlantic.com/magazine/archive/2017/09/has-the-smartphone-destroyed-a-generation/534198/

47 Mark D. Griffiths, "Adolescent Social Media Use: How Do Social Media Operators Facilitate Habitual Use?," *Psychology Today*, January 11, 2019, https://www.psychologytoday.com/blog/in-excess/201901/adolescent-social-media-use-0

48 Geert Lovink, *Sad by Design: On Platform Nihilism*, (London and New York: Pluto 2019).

49 Max Haiven, "Can Pikachu Save Fannie Mae? Value, finance and imagination in the new Pokeconomy." *Cultural Studies* 26, (516–541).

50 Saleem Alhabash and Mengyan Ma, "A Tale of Four Platforms: Motivations and Uses of Facebook, Twitter, Instagram, and Snapchat Among College Students?," *Social Media + Society* 3, 1 (January 2017): https://doi.org/10.1177/2056305117691544

51 Maya Kosoff, "The Fall of Snapchat Shows Why Mark Zuckerberg Is Still King," *Vanity Fair*, August 8, 2018, https://www.vanityfair.com/news/2018/08/snap-social-media-user-growth-slowdown-facebook

52 Jakob Eckstein, "How Snapchat Makes Money," *Investopedia*, September 24, 2019, https://www.investopedia.com/articles/investing/061915/how-snapchat-makes-money.asp

53 Richard Seymour, *The Twittering Machine* (La Vergne, TN: The Indigo Press, 2019).

54 Siho Nam, 2018. "Cognitive Capitalism, Free Labor, and Financial Communication: A Critical Discourse Analysis of Social Media IPO Registration Statements," *Information, Communication & Society*, forthcoming; Shoshana Zuboff, *The Age of Surveillance Capitalism* (New York, NY: Public Affairs, 2019).

55 Seymour, *The Twittering Machine*; Zuboff, *The Age of Surveillance Capitalism.*

56 Paul Lewis, "'Our Minds Can Be Hijacked': The Tech Insiders Who Fear a Smartphone Dystopia," *The Guardian*, October 6, 2017, http://www.theguardian.com/technology/2017/oct/05/smartphone-addiction-silicon-valley-dystopia; Natasha Dow Schüll, *Addiction by Design: Machine Gambling in Las Vegas* (Princeton, NJ and Oxford: Princeton University Press, 2014).

57 Josh Constine, "Snapchat's Epic Strategy Flip-Flop," *TechCrunch*, November 13, 2017, http://social.techcrunch.com/2017/11/13/time-to-snap-into-action/

58 Lizette Chapman, "Inside the Mind of a Snapchat Streaker," *Bloomberg*, January 30, 2017, https://www.bloomberg.com/news/features/2017-01-30/inside-the-mind-of-a-snapchat-streaker; Twenge, "Have Smartphones Destroyed a Generation?"

59 Jaron Lanier, *Ten Arguments for Deleting Your Social Media Accounts Right Now* (New York, NY: Picador, 2019); Lovink, *Sad by Design*; Zuboff, *The Age of Surveillance Capitalism*.

60 James Bridle, *New Dark Age: Technology, Knowledge and the End of the Future* (London and Brooklyn, NY: Verso, 2018).

61 Lovink, *Sad by Design*, 1.

62 Lovink, *Sad by Design*, 27.

63 Lovink, *Sad by Design*, 18.

64 Melissa G. Hunt et al., "No More FOMO: Limiting Social Media Decreases Loneliness and Depression," *Journal of Social and Clinical Psychology* 37, no. 10 (November 8, 2018): 751–68; Simon Parkin, "Has Dopamine Got Us Hooked on Tech?," *The Observer*, March 4, 2018, https://www.theguardian.com/technology/2018/mar/04/has-dopamine-got-us-hooked-on-tech-facebook-apps-addiction; Susan Weinschenk, "Why We're All Addicted to Texts, Twitter and Google," *Psychology Today*, September 11, 2012, http://www.psychologytoday.com/blog/brain-wise/201209/why-were-all-addicted-texts-twitter-and-google. I would sound a note of skepticism here: while both psychologists and social media designers alike seem to find great explanatory power in dopamine, these analyses are highly premature. For one, the cocktail of neurochemistry that influences human behavior is almost unimaginably complex and still poorly understood, even by neuroscientists. For another, such explanations tend to fixate on totalizing biochemical explanations for what are, in fact, complex psychosocial and relational phenomena.

65 Franco Berardi, *Heroes: Mass Murder and Suicide* (London and New York, NY: Verso, 2015).

66 Yann Moulier Boutang, *Cognitive Capitalism*, trans. Ed Emery (Cambridge and Malden, MA: Polity, 2011).

67 Berardi, *Heroes*, 44.

68 Berardi, *Heroes*, 73–74.

69 Berardi, *Heroes*, 9.

70 Mother Jones magazine's publicly available database, which since 1982 has tracked the 118 "indiscriminate rampages in public places resulting in four or more victims killed by the attacker [excluding] shootings stemming from more conventionally motivated crimes such as armed robbery or gang violence" lists only four women as perpetrators. See Mark Follman, Gavin Aronsen, and Deanna Pan, "US Mass Shootings, 1982–2019: Data from Mother Jones' Investigation," *Mother Jones*, December 11, 2019, https://www.motherjones.com/politics/2012/12/mass-shootings-mother-jones-full-data/. Julie Bosman, Kate Taylor, and Tim Arango, "A Common Trait Among Mass Killers: Hatred Toward Women," *The New York Times*, August 10, 2019, https://www.nytimes.com/2019/08/10/us/

mass-shootings-misogyny-dayton.html; Helen Lewis, "To Learn About the Far Right, Start With the 'Manosphere,'" *The Atlantic*, August 7, 2019, https://www.theatlantic.com/international/archive/2019/08/anti-feminism-gateway-far-right/595642/

71 Francis Dupuis-Déri and Mélissa Blais, "The Montréal Massacre Is Finally Recognized as an Anti-Feminist Attack," *The Conversation*, December 6, 2019, http://theconversation.com/the-montreal-massacre-is-finally-recognized-as-an-anti-feminist-attack-128450; Roger I. Simon and Sharon Rosenberg, "Beyond the Logic of Emblemization: Remembering and Learning from the Montréal Massacre," in *The Touch of the Past: Remembrance, Learning, and Ethics* ed., Roger I. Simon (New York, NY: Palgrave Macmillan, 2005), 65–86.

72 See Judith Butler, "Performative Acts and Gender Constitution: An Essay in Phenomenology and Feminist Theory," *Theatre Journal* 40, no. 4 (1988): 519–31, https://doi.org/10.2307/3207893

73 bell hooks, *Feminist Theory: From Margin to Center*, 2nd ed. (Cambridge, MA: South End Press, 2000).

74 Simone de Beauvoir, *The Second Sex*, trans. H. M. Parshley, 1949, https://www.marxists.org/reference/subject/ethics/de-beauvoir/2nd-sex/

75 See Sylvia Wynter and Katherine McKittrick, "Unparalleled Catastrophe for Our Species? Or, to Give Humanness a Different Future: Conversations," in *Sylvia Wynter: On Being Human as Praxis*, ed. Katherine McKittrick (Durham, NC and London: Duke University Press, 2015), 9–89.

76 R. W. Connell and James W. Messerschmidt, "Hegemonic Masculinity: Rethinking the Concept," *Gender & Society* 19, 6 (December 2005): 829–59, https://doi.org/10.1177/0891243205278639

77 Shulamith Firestone, *The Dialectic of Sex: The Case for Feminist Revolution* (New York, NY: Farrar, Straus and Giroux, 2003).

78 hooks, *Feminist Theory*.

79 On the recent rise of, and debate over this term, see Bryant Sculos, "Who's Afraid of 'Toxic Masculinity'?," *Class, Race and Corporate Power* 5, no. 3 (November 2017), https://doi.org/10.25148/CRCP.5.3.006517

80 See, for instance, Steven P. Schacht and Doris W. Ewing, eds., *Feminism and Men: Reconstructing Gender Relations* (New York, NY: New York University Press, 1998).

81 George Ciccariello-Maher, *Decolonizing Dialectics* (Durham, NC: Duke University Press, 2016); Harry Cleaver, *Rupturing the Dialectic* (Chico, CA: AK Press, 2017).

82 David McNally, *Monsters of the Market: Zombies, Vampires, and Global Capitalism* (Chicago, IL: Haymarket, 2012).

83 Frantz Fanon, *Black Skin, White Masks*, trans. Richard Philcox, New ed. (New York, NY: Grove, 2008); See also Albert Memmi, *The Colonizer and the Colonized* (London: Earthscan, 2003).

84 Edward Said, *Orientalism*, 1st Vintage Books ed. (New York, NY: Vintage Books, 1979).

85 See Anne McClintock, *Imperial Leather: Race, Gender and Sexuality in the Colonial Context* (London and New York, NY: Routledge, 1995).

86   Aimé Césaire, *Discourse on Colonialism*, trans. Joan Pinkham (New York, NY and London: Monthly Review, 1972); Saidiya Hartman, *Scenes of Subjection: Terror, Slavery, and Self-Making in Nineteenth-Century America* (Oxford and New York, NY: Oxford University Press, 1997).
87   Theodore W. Allen, *The Invention of the White Race* (London: Verso, 1994); David R. Roediger, *Class, Race, and Marxism* (London; New York, NY: Verso, 2017).
88   Wynter and McKittrick, "Unparalleled Catastrophe for Our Species? Or, to Give Humanness a Different Future: Conversations."
89   See Chapter 1.
90   Annie McClanahan, "Serious Crises," *Boundary 2* 46, 1 (February 1, 2019): 103–32.
91   Soederberg, *Debtfare States and the Poverty Industry*; Jan Rehmann, "Hypercarceration: A Neoliberal Response to 'Surplus Population,'" *Rethinking Marxism* 27, 2 (April 3, 2015): 303–11, https://doi.org/10.1080/089 35696.2015.1007790
92   Sara R. Farris, "Social Reproduction, Surplus Populations and the Role of Migrant Women," *Viewpoint Magazine*, November 1, 2015, https://www.viewpointmag.com/2015/11/01/social-reproduction-and-surplus-populations/; Bue Rübner Hansen, "Surplus Population, Social Reproduction, and the Problem of Class Formation," *Viewpoint* 5 (2015), https://viewpointmag.com/2015/10/31/surplus-population-social-reproduction-and-the-problem-of-class-formation/; Tania Murray Li, "To Make Live or Let Die? Rural Dispossession and the Protection of Surplus Populations," *Antipode* 41 (January 2010): 66–93, https://doi.org/10.1111/j.1467-8330.2009.00717.x
93   Siyaves Azeri, "Surplus-Population and the Political Economy of Fear," *Critical Sociology*, November 10, 2017, https://doi.org/10.1177/0896920517737143; Zygmunt Bauman, *Wasted Lives: Modernity and Its Outcasts* (Oxford and Malden, MA: Polity, 2004); Rehmann, "Hypercarceration."
94   Daniel HoSang and Joseph E. Lowndes, *Producers, Parasites, Patriots: Race and the New Right-Wing Politics of Precarity* (Minneapolis, MN: University of Minnesota Press, 2019), 23–24.

CONCLUSION

1   I have found David Harvey's readings of Marx particularly helpful in charting the contradictions and overarching orientation of capital that emerge from intercapitalist competition. David Harvey, *Seventeen Contradictions and the End of Capitalism* (Oxford and New York, NY: Oxford University Press, 2014). I have also dwelled on it at some length in my attempts to understand financialization. See Max Haiven, *Cultures of Financialization: Fictitious Capital in Popular Culture and Everyday Life* (London and New York, NY: Palgrave Macmillan, 2014), especially

Chapter 1.

2 These dynamics are mapped in detail in Rosa Luxemburg, *The Accumulation of Capital*, Translated by Agnes Schwarzschild (London and New York, NY: Routledge, 2003). See also Raj Patel and Jason W. Moore, *The History of the World in Seven Cheap Things* (Berkeley, CA: University of California Press, 2017).

3 See Michael Hardt and Antonio Negri, *Empire* (Cambridge, MA: Harvard University Press, 2000); Michael Hardt and Antonio Negri, *Multitude: War and Democracy in the Age of Empire* (New York, NY: Penguin, 2004).

4 See Randy Martin, *Knowledge LTD: Towards a Social Logic of the Derivative* (Philadelphia, PA: Temple University Press, 2015).

5 Nick Srnicek, *Platform Capitalism* (Cambridge, Malden, MA: Polity, 2017); Randy Martin, *An Empire of Indifference: American War and the Financial Logic of Risk Management* (Durham, NC and London: Duke University Press, 2007).

6 For a summary of psychological findings on revenge fantasy, see Steven Pinker, *The Better Angels of Our Nature: Why Violence Has Declined* (New York, NY: Penguin, 2012), 529–46. See also Meredith Lillie and Peter Strelan, "Careful What You Wish For: Fantasizing about Revenge Increases Justice Dissatisfaction in the Chronically Powerless," *Personality and Individual Differences* 94 (May 1, 2016): 290–94; Brian Knutson, "Sweet Revenge?" *Science* 305, no. 5688 (2004): 1246–47.

7 L. H. Grobbink, J. J. L. Derksen, and H. J. C. van Marle, "Revenge: An Analysis of Its Psychological Underpinnings," *International Journal of Offender Therapy and Comparative Criminology* 59, no. 8 (July, 2015): 892–907.

8 Coby Gerlsma and Valerie Lugtmeyer, "Offense Type as Determinant of Revenge and Forgiveness After Victimization: Adolescents' Responses to Injustice and Aggression," *Journal of School Violence* 17, 1 (January, 2018): 16–27; Craig Haen and Anna Marie Weber, "Beyond Retribution: Working through Revenge Fantasies with Traumatized Young People," *The Arts in Psychotherapy*, The Creative Arts Therapies in the Treatment of Trauma, 36, 2 (April 1, 2009): 84–93.

9 This is, in one sense, a major theme in Freud's work, where an Oedipal vindictiveness must be processed and acculturated, both in the case of the individual as well as more broadly in civilization at large. See Sigmund Freud, *Civilization and Its Discontents*, Translated by James Strachey (New York, NY: W.W. Norton & Company, 2010); J. Steiner, "Revenge And Resentment In The 'Oedipus Situation,'" *International Journal of Psycho-Analysis* 77 (1996): 433–43.

10 Friedrich Wilhelm Nietzsche, *On the Genealogy of Morality*, Keith Ansell-Pearson, ed. Translated by Carol Diethe (Cambridge and New York, NY: Cambridge University Press, 2007).

11 George Orwell, "Revenge Is Sour," in *Fifty Essays* (Project Gutenberg, 1945), http://gutenberg.net.au/ebooks03/0300011h.html#part31

12 James Baldwin, *The Devil Finds Work: An Essay* (New York, NY: Vintage International, 2011), 44.

13 Slavoj Žižek, "The Seven Veils of Fantasy," in *The Plague of Fantasies* (London: Verso, 1997), 3–44.

14 On the "infrapolitical" possibilities of the revenge fantasy of the oppressed, and the way small, sometimes secret acts of petty vengeance can erupt into full scale revolt, see James C. Scott, *Weapons of the Weak: Everyday Forms of Peasant Resistance* (New Haven, CT: Yale University Press, 2000).

15 Ernst Bloch, *The Principle of Hope, Volume 1*, trans. Neville Plaice, Stephen Plaice, and Paul Knight (Cambridge, MA: MIT Press, 1995), 30–31.

16 Whether this is still best understood as the petit bourgeoisie or as the professional-managerial class or the middle class is a matter of heated debate. See, for instance, Erik Olin Wright, *Understanding Class* (London and New York, NY: Verso, 2015).

17 Slavoj Žižek, "The Seven Veils of Fantasy."

18 See Michel Foucault, *The History of Sexuality: An Introduction*, trans. Robert Hurley (New York, NY: Pantheon Books, 1978).

19 Daniel D'Adderio, "Game of Thrones: Inside the World's Most Popular Show," *Time*, 2017. https://time.com/game-of-thrones-2017/

20 See Ricahrd Seymour, *The Liberal Defence of Murder* (London and New York: Verso, 2012).

21 Camilla Fojas, "Border Absurd: The End-Times and the End of the Line," in *Zombies, Migrants, and Queers: Race and Crisis Capitalism in Pop Culture*, (Urbana, IL: University of Illinois Press, 2017).

22 Harsha Walia, *Undoing Border Imperialism* (Oakland, CA and Edinburgh: AK Press and the Institute for Anarchist Studies, 2013).

23 Barbara Ehrenreich and John Ehrenreich, "Death of a Yuppie Dream: The Rise and Fall of the Professional-Managerial Class" (New York, NY: Rosa Luxemburg Stiftung, 2013), http://www.rosalux-nyc.org/wp-content/files_mf/ehrenreich_death_of_a_yuppie_dream90.pdf; Nicholas Huber, "Secular Proletarianization," *Theory & Event* 22, 2 (April 26, 2019): 417–35, http://muse.jhu.edu/article/722832

24 David Harvey, *A Brief History of Neoliberalism* (Oxford: Oxford University Press, 2005).

25 Nick Srnicek, *Platform Capitalism* (Cambridge and Malden, MA: Polity, 2017).

26 Max Haiven, *Cultures of Financialization: Fictitious Capital in Popular Culture and Everyday Life* (London and New York, NY: Palgrave Macmillan, 2014), 43–73; Michel Feher, *Rated Agency: Investee Politics in a Speculative Age* (New York, NY: Zone Books, 2018). I would sound a note of caution here that the myth of entrepreneurship and investorhood functions in a largely disciplinary fashion but should not, necessarily, be seen as a fundamental shift in the structural processes of capitalist valorization. But such a question is beyond the scope of this project.

27 Joshua Clover, *Riot. Strike. Riot: The New Era of Uprisings* (London and New York, NY: Verso, 2016).

28 Lorenza Antonucci et al., "The Malaise of the Squeezed Middle: Challenging the Narrative of the 'Left behind' Brexiter," *Competition & Change* 21, 3 (June 2017): 211–29; Yıldız Atasoy, "The Islamic Ethic and the Spirit of Turkish Capitalism Today," in *Global Flashpoints: Reactions to Imperialism and Neoliberalism*, Socialist Register (New York, NY: Monthly Review Press, 2008), 121–40; Daniel Faber et al., "Trump's Electoral Triumph: Class, Race, Gender, and the Hegemony of the Polluter-Industrial Complex," *Capitalism Nature Socialism* 28, 1 (January 2, 2017): 1–15; Giacomo Gabbuti and David Broder, "Sowing the Seeds of Bolsonaro: An Interview with Ana Luiza Matos de Oliveira, Esther Dweck and Pedro Rossi," (18 May 2019), https://jacobinmag.com/2019/05/brazil-bolsonaro-workers-party-fiscal-policy; Arlie Russell Hochschild, "The Ecstatic Edge of Politics: Sociology and Donald Trump," *Contemporary Sociology* 45, 6 (November 1, 2016): 683–89; Mikkel Bolt Rasmussen, "Postfascism, or the Cultural Logic of Late Capitalism," *Third Text* 32, 5–6 (November 2, 2018): 682–88; Liv Sovik, "Brazil, Now," *Soundings* 71, 71 (April 1, 2019): 140–60.
29 Samuel Johnson, *Dictionary of the English Language*, Google ebook (London: John Williamson and Co., 1839), 800, https://play.google.com/store/books/details?id=1fMxAQAAMAAJ&rdid=book-1fMxAQAAMAAJ&rdot=1
30 bell hooks, *Killing Rage: Ending Racism* (New York, NY: Henry Holt, 1996).
31 Audre Lorde, "The Uses of Anger," *Women's Studies Quarterly* 25, 1–2 (1981–1997): 278–85.
32 Lorde, 283.
33 Quoted in Sara Ahmed, *The Cultural Politics of Emotion* (London and New York, NY: Routledge, 2004), 175.
34 Ahmed, *The Cultural Politics of Emotion*, 175.
35 Ahmed, *The Cultural Politics of Emotion*, 176.
36 Lorde, "The Uses of Anger," 285.
37 Glen Coulthard, *Red Skin, White Masks: Rejecting the Colonial Politics of Recognition* (Minneapolis, MN and London: University of Minnesota Press, 2014), 108–9.
38 Eve Tuck and K. Wayne Yang, "Decolonization Is Not a Metaphor," *Decolonization: Indigeneity, Education & Society* 1, 1 (September 8, 2012).
39 Eve Tuck and C. Ree, "A Glossary of Haunting," in *Handbook of Autoethnography*, ed. Stacy Holman Jones, Tony E. Adams, and Carolyn Ellis (London and New York, NY: Routledge, 2013), 642–43.
40 Tuck and Ree, "A Glossary of Haunting," 654.
41 *Abolition: Journal of Insurgent Politics*, "Manifesto for Abolition: A Journal of Insurgent Politics," 2017, https://abolitionjournal.org/frontpage/
42 Tuck and Ree, "A Glossary of Haunting," 644.
43 W. E. B. Du Bois, *Black Reconstruction in America, 1860–1880* (New York, NY: The Free Press, 1998).
44 Angela Y. Davis, *Abolition Democracy: Beyond Empire, Prisons, and Torture* (New York, NY: Seven Stories Press, 2005).
45 Ruth Wilson Gilmore, *Golden Gulag: Prisons, Surplus, Crisis, and Opposition in Globalizing California*, (Berkeley, CA: University of California Press, 2007).

46 Angela Y. Davis, *Freedom Is a Constant Struggle: Ferguson, Palestine, and the Foundations of a Movement*, ed. Frank Barat (Chicago, IL: Haymarket Books, 2016).

47 Max Haiven and Alex Khasnabish, *The Radical Imagination: Social Movement Research in the Age of Austerity* (London and New York, NY: Zed Books, 2014).

48 Alexis Shotwell, *Against Purity: Living Ethically in Compromised Times* (Minneapolis, MN: University of Minnesota Press, 2016).

49 Cornelius Castoriadis "Radical Imagination and the Social Instituting Imaginary," in *The Castoriadis Reader*, ed. David Ames Curtis (Cambridge and New York: Blackwell, 1997), 319–37.

50 Cornelius Castoriadis, "Power, Politics, Autonomy," in *Philosophy, Politics, Autonomy*, David Ames Curtis, ed. (Oxford and New York, NY: Oxford University Press, 1991).

51 Cornelius Castoriadis, "The Logic of Magmas and the Question of Autonomy," in *The Castoriadis Reader*, ed. David Ames Curtis (Cambridge and New York, NY: Blackwell, 1997), 290–318.

52 Max Haiven, *Crises of Imagination, Crises of Power: Capitalism, Creativity and the Commons* (London and New York, NY: Zed, 2014), especially Chapter 1. See also Max Haiven, "Finance as Capital's Imagination?: Reimagining Value and Culture in an Age of Fictitious Capital and Crisis," *Social Text* 108 (2011): 93–124.

53 Robin D. G. Kelley, *Freedom Dreams: The Black Radical Imagination* (Boston, MA: Beacon, 2002).

Index

Printed and bound by CPI Group (UK) Ltd, Croydon, CR0 4YY

23/04/2025

14661020-0003